MANAGEMENT MISTAKES

WILEY SERIES IN MANAGEMENT

MANAGEMENT MISTAKES

SECOND EDITION

Robert F. Hartley

Cleveland State University

JOHN WILEY & SONS

New York   Chichester   Brisbane   Toronto   Singapore

Library of Congress Cataloging in Publication Data:

Hartley, Robert F.
  Management mistakes

  (Wiley series in management, ISSN 0271-6046)
  1. Management—Case studies. I. Title. II. Series.
HD38.H3488 1986   658'.007'1173   85-22683
ISBN 0-471-81700-7

Printed in the United States of America

109876.

Contents

CHAPTER 1

Introduction

These cases represent classic management mistakes, some of which have been widely publicized. For example, the Edsel case is perhaps the most widely known mistake of all time. A variety of firms, industries, problems, and mistakes are presented. Most of the firms and enterprises are familiar to you—for example, Gillette, STP Corporation, the World Football League, Coors Beer, Adidas, Chrysler—although the details of their problems may not be. The time span ranges over several decades, although most of the cases involve fairly recent events. In cases where the mistakes occurred several decades ago—such as the Edsel, and Montgomery Ward's dictatorial and no-growth management—still the circumstances and what can be learned are far from dated.

ORGANIZATION OF CASES

These cases have been especially chosen to bring out certain points or caveats in the art of decision making. They have been selected to give a balanced view of the spectrum of business problems. Some of the mistakes are those of commission, in which wrong actions were taken; other cases involve mistakes of omission, in which no action was taken and the status quo was contentedly embraced amid a changing environment. We have sought to present examples that provide somewhat different learning experiences, where the mistake, or at least certain aspects of it, differs from the

1

other mistakes described in the book. We have endeavored to classify the mistakes under the important management functions of planning, organizing, leadership and strategy implementation, controlling, and, finally, ethical and social responsibility problems. Admittedly, however, some of the cases cannot be neatly compartmentalized into, for example, errors of planning or of controlling, because they involve broader and more pervasive mistakes.

Errors in Planning

We have included four examples of errors in planning. One, the World Football League, illustrates a travesty of overly optimistic and imprudent planning. It attempted to enter a relatively saturated market, against a powerful and established competitor, with an inferior product and inadequate financial and other resources. Rash and unsupported optimism has no place in the sober business environment.

At the other extreme, the J. C. Penney Company evinced a planning so conservative that no changes could be contemplated from what had been successful in the past, even though the environment for doing business represented a whole new ball game. Only the audacious action of a staff executive—who bypassed his superior in going to the board of directors, thereby violating one of the sacred dictums of organizational theory— opened the eyes of the company to the need for change.

Then there is Adidas. Here was a firm in the catbird seat, utterly dominating its industry at the beginning of the running boom. But somehow, incredibly, it let its advantage slip away. And hungry interlopers—Nike, among others—starting from scratch, carved up the burgeoning market for themselves, while Adidas in its planning continued to underestimate the strength and durability of running's popularity, as well as the growing strength and aggressiveness of its American competitors.

DuPont's Corfam—what seemed like a breakthrough with a substitute leather akin to the breakthrough with nylon a few decades before—depicts how even the most careful planning may be in error due to unforeseen contingencies and result in $100 million losses. How could such problems occur, and what can be learned that might prevent such multimillion dollar mistakes in the future?

Organizational Mishandling

We may not always realize the importance of an organization in paving the way for growth, but its failure can loom important and cause monumental mistakes. Part Two deals with three examples of organizational mishandling of major proportions. With Korvette we see how an organization must change, must adapt to increasing size, complexity, and distance. No matter how brilliant and innovative the founder, sober realities and sound management principles must be faced and adopted as the enterprise grows beyond the ability of one person to supervise directly.

The Edsel case could also have been placed under the planning section, because it provides us with the thoughtful realization that even the most detailed planning does not ensure success. We have placed this case in the organizational section, because it graphically illustrates the fallacy of creating an organization suited for the most ambitious plans and expectations without sufficient evidence that such expectations are likely to be realized.

One of the saddest cases in the book is that of the W. T. Grant Company, a large and mature firm founded in 1906. In the early 1970s it went on an expansion binge, far beyond the capabilities of its organization or its managerial and financial resources. The result was one of the worst business disasters in recent U.S. history.

Flawed Leadership and Strategy Execution

Part Three describes errors in leading and executing. One of the oldest cases in the book is that of Montgomery Ward: it completely shunned any expansion and hoarded its money after World War II in the mistaken belief that a severe depression would occur and that it could expand at much lower cost at that time. But more than this error in judgment, the Ward case evinces the dictatorial power and devastating consequences of one man, Sewell Avery, whose leadership style brooked no disagreements with his views. As a consequence, Ward lost ground to its major competitors, ground that has never been regained.

The Gillette Company's strategy permitted its dominance in the razor blade industry to be eroded by a stubborn reluctance to introduce its own stainless steel blade (because it thought this might cannibalize or take away sales from its highly profitable Super Blue Blade). Thereby, the door was opened for smaller, hungry competitors to gain an advantage they never could have otherwise.

The Coors case at first poses the question of whether a firm can be virtually invulnerable to competition. Coasting on a mystique that had somehow been built up for the product, Coors enjoyed great success, only to find it diminishing. With little advertising, no fear of competition, and aloof public and employee relations, the company's fortunes faltered badly in the face of more aggressive competition. The mystique that had been Coors' proved to be ephemeral.

As the decade of the 1980s began, U.S. industry found itself faced with a problem never before encountered in such severity. Foreign firms, especially those of Japan and West Germany, were producing better quality products for less cost than we were able to do. They were invading our domestic markets and placing many of our firms at a competitive disadvantage, resulting in hundreds of thousands of U. S. workers being laid off. In few industries was this invasion of foreign products more severe and disruptive than in the auto and steel industries.

Chrysler in the late 1970s and early 1980s epitomizes the dilemma facing many other U. S. firms, although the financial straits of Chrysler, brought on partly by bad management decisions in the past, made its position the more precarious. In this case we examine the background that made such foreign incursions possible and effective, and describe the situation facing the savior, Iacocca, when he took over.

The A. C. Gilbert Company is a case of a firm unable to handle a crisis. Although this toymaker should have recognized the environmental factors leading to its crisis long before it did, the greatest mistake was frenzied reactions that made matters worse. This case illustrates practically every mistake imaginable: successive rash decisions aimed at correcting the problem with no weighing of consequences or prudent evaluation of alternatives, along with a continual upheaval of the formerly stable organization. In the space of only 5 years, bad crisis leadership caused the 58-year-old company to fail.

Lack of Adequate Controls

Part Four deals with firms that were abysmally careless in their monitoring and controlling of certain aspects of their operations. The fast-food franchise operation, Burger Chef, showed unwise expansion even though it was under the auspices of a large and seasoned firm, General Foods. But the irresistible temptation to open hundreds of additional outlets over a few years' time, without proper operational fundamentals and without imposing strict controls over a far-flung organization, soon forced severe retrenchment. The Burger Chef division of General Foods never became a money maker, and was finally sold in 1982.

The Osborne Computer case represents perhaps the most extreme example of success and failure in the annals of American business. First on the scene with an inexpensive portable computer packaged with an abundance of software, sales rose to $100 million in only 18 months, only to come plummeting down as lack of systematic controls and feedback resulted in major miscalculations and huge and unexpected losses. And eager competitors quickly moved in to mitigate the initial Osborne product advantage.

The last case in this section concerns a conglomerate, Boise Cascade

Company, which for a while was the nation's biggest force in recreational land development. However, in following a policy of decentralization—but without imposing adequate controls—the company found that questionable selling tactics, coupled with a disregard for environmental constraints on the part of the recreational land subsidiary, were arousing great consumer and governmental resentments and pressures. The firm was forced to give up this part of its business altogether, incurring a loss of several hundred million dollars in the process.

Ethical and Social Responsibility Problems

No firm today can violate social and environmental constraints with impunity. The reputation or public image of a firm—how it is perceived by its various publics—can play a crucial role in success or failure.

Deceptive promotional claims made by the producers of STP were finally challenged by the media and eventually by the Federal Trade Commission. But this was after a useless product (as generally agreed upon by petroleum engineers and automotive experts) had achieved widespread success because of its macho association with racing and race drivers. In the case, we are confronted with the issue of whether an organization—and most appropriately, its board of directors—should exercise ethical controls over deceptive and otherwise misguided practices.

The Nestle case shows the impact of image problems coming from social irresponsibility and callousness. The firm marketed its infant formula in underdeveloped Third World countries that did not have the sanitation or educated public necessary to make the product safe. Nestle's stubborn persistence in doing so brought worldwide criticism and, eventually, boycotts and profit damage.

RISKS AND REACTIONS

Many decisions are made under conditions of uncertainty. We can seldom predict with any exactitude the reactions of customers or the countermoves and retaliations of competitors. Estimates of the success of new ventures become more "guesstimates" the further in the future we try to forecast. Business conditions, the environment of doing business, sometimes change slowly and predictably; they may change so subtly as to be practically unnoticed until a situation becomes critical, as with foreign import incursions; at other times, conditions change suddenly and with little warning. Yet firms can fail to predict and adjust to both gradual changes and the more sudden ones.

In looking at sick and failing companies, or even healthy ones that have experienced failures of certain aspects of their operations, the temptation is to be unduly critical. It is easy to be Monday-morning quarterbacks, to criticize decisions and actions with the benefit of hindsight. Mistakes are inevitable, given the present state of the art of business and the dynamic environment.

Granted that mistakes of omission or commission will occur, alert and aggressive management is characterized by certain actions or reactions:

1. There should be quick recognition of looming problems or present mistakes.
2. The causes of the problem(s) should be carefully determined.
3. Alternative corrective actions should be evaluated in view of the company's resources and constraints.
4. The chosen corrective action or response should be prompt. Sometimes this may require a ruthless axing of the product, the promotional approach, or whatever may be at fault.
5. There should be some learning experience coming from such mistakes; the same mistakes should not be repeated; the future operation should be improved as a result.

In reading these cases, you may want to judge them not only by how the problem or mistake could have been avoided, but also by how alert and aggressive management was in reacting.

Where possible in these cases, we have depicted the major personalities involved at the time. We invite you to imagine yourself in their positions, confronting the problems and decisions they faced at their points of crisis, or at the times when actions or lack of action led to a subsequent crisis. What would you have done differently, and why? We invite you to participate in the discussion questions and role-playing episodes appearing at the end of each case. We urge you to consider the pros and cons of alternative actions.

For Thought and Discussion

1. Do you agree that it is impossible for a firm to avoid mistakes? Why or why not?
2. How can a firm speed up its awareness of emerging problems so that it can take responsive action? Be as specific as you can.
3. Large firms tend to err more often on the side of conservatism and are slower to take corrective action than smaller firms. Would you speculate as to why this is so?
4. Which do you think is likely to be the more costly to a firm: errors of omission or errors of commission? Why?

PART ONE

PLANNING GONE AWRY

CHAPTER 2

World Football League—Reckless and Blindly Optimistic Planning

An operation—especially a new venture—can hardly succeed without detailed planning, that is, without specifically determining what is to be done over a wide range of decisions, from the clarification of goals and objectives, to establishing policies and procedures, to determining specific methods and schedules. Planning allows actions to be taken that are integrated, consistent, and purposeful. Mistakes can be avoided and problems can often be anticipated and overcome before crises develop. But even detailed planning must rest on prudent forecasts and reasonable premises. Planning cannot be done in an atmosphere of blind optimism and disregard for competitive and environmental realities. Yet, this was what the planners and organizers of the World Football League (WFL) were guilty of.

"The National Football League (NFL) has no strong rival," said the WFL's founding father and first commissioner, Gary L. Davidson. "It has grown arrogant and complacent. The doors are open to a rival. There are plenty of quality players available. A number of NFL players are discontent. The war is on!"[1]

[1] As quoted by Wells Twombly, "Super Flop I," *New York Times Magazine*, January 12, 1975, p. 10.

Conceptually, the idea seemed unassailable: another pro football league, only more colorful, more aggressive, more responsive to the fans and the players than the conservative NFL. All that would be needed for success was the organizational and promotional ability to secure the support of wealthy franchisees and then carry out the idea. And securing financial support ought not to be particularly difficult, because income tax laws regarding tax shelters were tailor-made to woo wealthy investors, as we shall see later. A bit of experience in developing new sports leagues would be an extra bonus, of course. And the man was available to provide all of these needed qualities: Gary Davidson.

HISTORY OF PRO FOOTBALL UP TO 1973

Over the years, football has gained in popularity to rival baseball as America's national pastime, despite a much shorter season and many fewer games played. Football first became popular at the college level, and in the early decades of this century many schools developed long-lasting rivalries. Emerging from the success of football at the collegiate level, the NFL was established in 1924, with six teams. But success was slow in coming and spectators were sparse. From time to time new professional football leagues were formed; they folded quickly, although some of the teams from these ill-fated leagues were added to the established NFL.

Eventually the NFL matured and gained in popularity. By 1959 it comprised the following teams:

Eastern Conference	Western Conference
New York	Baltimore
Cleveland	Chicago Bears
Philadelphia	Green Bay
Piittsburgh	San Francisco
Washington	Detroit
Chicago Cardinals	Los Angeles

In 1960, a major rival, the American Football League (AFL), was formed. It was to provide competition, not only for fan support but also for players and coaches. At the time of its establishment, the AFL had the following teams:

Eastern Division	Western Division
Houston	Los Angeles[a]
New York	Dallas
Buffalo	Oakland
Boston	Denver

[a] The Los Angeles franchise was soon moved to San Diego after incurring severe financial losses.

The AFL had the support of several influential and wealthy backers who helped "ensure" its success: for example, men like Barron Hilton and Lamar Hunt. The story is told of the newsman who remarked to Hunt's father, H. L. Hunt, that Lamar could lose $1 million a year on his Dallas Texans (now the Kansas City Chiefs). The senior Hunt is supposed to have replied after a thoughtful pause, "That means he has a hundred and twenty years to make it profitable."[2]

However, the new league lagged far behind the NFL in attendance in the early years. Table 2.1 gives a comparison of the attendance figures and number of games played for 1960–1969. For most of the 1960s the two leagues fought with each other for the top collegiate talent and also for recognition as the top league. Finally, in 1967, the two leagues met in a championship game, billed as the Super Bowl. Financial reward was the prime motivator for such a contest (61,946 spectators viewed the first Super Bowl), although the senior league undoubtedly thought the inferiority of the upstart AFL would be clearly proven. And it seemed to be: in 1967 it was Green Bay 35, Kansas City 10; in 1968, Green Bay 33, Oakland 14. The result of these Super Bowls was to help establish the credibility of the new league, even though it seemed below par to the senior NFL. This was to change dramatically and completely with the 1969 Super Bowl, when the AFL team, the New York Jets, with Joe Namath at the helm, won the Super Bowl 16 to 7 over Baltimore, in a tremendous upset. Now no one could say the AFL was inferior to the NFL.

During the 1960s, new teams had been added to each league and there was also some relocation of franchises to other cities. Then, in 1970, the AFL merged into the NFL, with the NFL now being divided into the National Conference and the American Conference. This merger of the two rival leagues at last ended the suicidal financial battle between the two leagues in recruiting talent.

[2]C. G. Burck, "Why Those WFL Owners Expect to Score Profits," *Fortune*, September 1974, p. 147.

Table 2.1 Comparison of Paid Attendance, Regular Season, AFL-NFL, 1960-1969

	AFL	NFL
1960	926,156 (56 games)	3,128,296 (78 games)
1961	1,002,657 (56 games)	3,986,159 (98 games)
1962	1,147,302 (56 games)	4,003,421 (98 games)
1963	1,208,697 (56 games)	4,163,643 (98 games)
1964	1,447,875 (56 games)	4,563,049 (98 games)
1965	1,782,384 (56 games)	4,634,021 (98 games)
1966	2,160,369 (63 games)	5,337,044 (105 games)
1967	2,295,697 (63 games)	5,938,924 (112 games)
1968	2,635,004 (70 games)	5,882,313 (112 games)
1969	2,843,373 (70 games)	6,096,127 (112 games)

Source: Robert L. Treat, *The Encyclopedia of Football* (New York: A. S. Bournes, 1977), p. 685.

The popularity of professional football continued to mushroom. At the end of 1970 the NFL, under its two new conferences, had a total attendance of 9,533,333, up from barely 4,000,000 for the two leagues only ten years before. By the end of 1973, the NFL had expanded its two conferences to a total of 26 teams, with a total attendance of 10,730,933. See Table 2.2 for attendance and number of games figures for 1970 through 1975.

The NFL had become a great growth industry, with football's gross revenues zooming by 210 percent—aided substantially by increased income from television—during the 10-year period ending in 1973. The Gross National Product during this time increased by only 88 percent. Between 90 and 100 million people—roughly half the population of the United States—were watching the Super Bowl telecast.

ESTABLISHING THE WORLD FOOTBALL LEAGUE

The burgeoning success of professional football was not lost on 38-year-old Gary Davidson. He was a typical Southern California "golden boy"—dimple-chinned, blond, tanned, addicted to exercise. He had passed his bar

Table 2.2 Paid Attendance, Regular Season, NFL, 1970-1975

1970	9,533,333	(182 games)
1971	10,076,035	(182 games)
1972	10,445,827	(182 games)
1973	10,730,933	(182 games)
1974	10,236,332	(182 games)
1975	10,213,193	(182 games)

Source: *Encyclopedia of Football*, p. 685.

exam in 1961 and joined a law firm specializing in the legal work involved in launching new businesses and dissolving sick ones. He soon came to realize the potential rewards to be made by the principals and promoters of such activities. (Within a decade, Davidson would be described by some of his former business colleagues as nothing more than "a slick rip-off artist," although he stoutly maintained that he was a major contributor to the American culture.)[3] As he saw it, he provided an important service to wealthy men who needed a means of nourishing their vanity—to be achieved by owning a professional sports team.

Besides being an idea man with the ability to sway others to his proposed ventures, Davidson had the experience of founding not one but two new leagues in other sports, both in the face of well-established and successful rival leagues: the World Hockey Association and the American Basketball Association. The fact that neither league had yet attained profitability was disregarded: each at least had achieved some measure of respectability, and there was always future promise.

Davidson had no undue difficulty in lining up franchisees for the new football venture. A WFL franchise could be had for $650,000 in 1974 (the decision was made in the summer of 1974 to put a $4.2 million price tag on any new franchises issued in 1975), far less than the $16 million it took to get an expansion team in the NFL. And with all teams starting from scratch in the WFL, there was at least an even chance of a franchise coming up with a league champion. In contrast, for $16 million for a new NFL expansion club, the owner could be virtually assured of being dead last for a long time.

The tax shelter consequences of an athletic franchise could be very attractive to a wealthy investor, because a depreciation allowance would permit a considerable amount of personal income from other sources to be written off and not be subject to income tax. Then, assuming that the new league was even moderately successful, the potential for significant appreciation of the investment—which would be taxable at lower capital gains rates—made this an especially attractive proposition. Furthermore, there was the example of the NFL to spur enthusiasm: the Philadelphia Eagles were bought in 1969 for $16 million and sold in 1973 for $21 million, thus resulting in $5 million in capital gains subject to the lowest income taxes— not bad for a 4-year commitment. Then, the "greater fool's philosophy" was also rampant: typically an owner says, "I may have been a fool to buy this, but there's a bigger fool who'll buy from me."[4]

---

[3] Twombly, p. 10.
[4] For more details on the tax savings consequences of investing in athletic teams, see Burck, p. 144.

Plans to Woo Customers

Davidson introduced to football some new gimmicks designed to enhance its spectator appeal. The league was organized into 12 teams, with a proposed 20-game season to start July 1974, weeks before the NFL commenced play. The new teams had such catchy and original names as the Chicago Fire, Philadelphia Bell, Southern California Sun, and Portland Storm. Changes in the rules of football designed to give it more action and entertainment were:

The ball will be kicked off from the 30-yard line to ensure more runbacks.

The goalpost will be moved back to the rear of the end zone.

Missed field goals will be returned to the line of scrimmage except when attempted inside the 20-yard line.

A two-point conversion attempt (passing or running) will be optional.

Receivers will need just one foot in bounds for a completion.

There will be a fifth quarter, split into two 7½-minute segments, to break ties.

Fair catches will not be permitted on punts.

An offensive back will be permitted to go into motion toward the line of scrimmage before the ball is snapped.

The hash marks will be moved in toward the center of the field.

An incompleted pass on fourth down will return the ball to the line of scrimmage. This replaces the rule that states that a fourth-down incomplete pass inside the 20-yard line shall be returned to the 20.

(Some of these rules changes were soon to be adopted by the NFL either in whole or with modifications). A multicolored football was to be used in contrast to the traditional drab brown. The season was to culminate with a championship World Bowl game between the top divisional leaders, which would determine the WFL equivalent to the NFL Super Bowl championship team.

The new league, no matter how innovative its playing rules might be, could hardly operate without a cadre of able players. The most attractive source for such players was obviously the ranks of the existing NFL teams. Drafting graduating collegians—in competition with the NFL—was more of a long-term supply source. The other recourse was to obtain pro castoffs—those unable to make it with an NFL team. Although this was hardly compatible with quality, it became a necessity if 12 teams were to be fielded.

Davidson and his organization recognized the obvious need to woo

NFL players—especially stars—over to the WFL camp. Consequently, it bid up salaries. It also undermined the cartel arrangements the NFL, as well as most other professional leagues, steadfastly maintained. Under the reserve clause or the slightly different option system, teams had been able to trade players at will, and even prevent them from playing anywhere else in a major league. But the WFL made itself a highly attractive alternative for NFL players willing to gamble on the league's future, because a player could fulfill his contract and then pick up and go to any team that wanted his services.

In its efforts to wrest major player talent from the NFL, a coup was achieved in the spring of 1974: three top-flight players of the Miami Dolphins, Warfield, Kiick, and Csonka, were signed for $3.5 million to begin playing for the WFL in 1975. This gained major credibility for the new league and led the way for other NFL stars to make the switch. On April 2, Ken Stabler, conference-leading quarterback of the NFL Oakland Raiders, signed a multi-year contract to play with the WFL Birmingham Americans, starting in 1975. One week later, Randy Johnson, number two quarterback of the New York Giants, and Calvin Hill, the Dallas Cowboys' 1000-yard rusher, signed multi-year contracts to play with the WFL Hawaiians in 1975. Other stars defecting for the 1975 season included Dallas Cowboy quarter-back Craig Morton; Claude Humphrey, Atlanta Falcon defensive end; Tom Mack, Los Angeles Ram guard; John Brockington, Green Bay Packer running back; and Daryl Lamonica, veteran quarterback teammate of Stabler.

Admittedly, however, the big names who were signed were not to join the WFL until 1975, because they were already under contract for the NFL 1974 season. The WFL was not as successful in signing collegiate players, with the exception of the Southern California team that did sign a number of UCLA and University of Southern California graduating seniors.

The effect of the new and aggressive competition for player talent was predictable. NFL salaries rose as much as 60 to 80 percent as a result of the Warfield, Kiick, and Csonka deal, and as frightened NFL owners acted to prevent the wholesale erosion of their talent. One player agent gleefully noted: "All it takes is one WFL owner to say, 'I don't care what it costs; I'm going to buy a winning team,' and that will blow the roof off, as far as money is concerned."[5]

[5] Herb Gluck, *While the Gettin's Good—Inside the World Football League* (New York: Bobbs-Merrill Company, 1975) p. 42.

Obtaining Places to Play

As the new league approached its July opening-game schedule, the future continued to look bright. The biggest problem for some teams was finding suitable stadiums, although it was generally conceded that older temporary stadiums could be used until new ones were built. The New York Stars finally had to settle for Downing Stadium on Randall's Island—". . . its turf was scarred, press box facilities were strictly high school level, the old stands were a splintered eyesore, the lighting system was totally inadequate for Wednesday-night football, and the locker rooms were built long before the age of present-day professional football squads."[6]

Two of the original franchises had to be moved before opening day. The Toronto Northmen were forced to vacate Toronto when the Canadian Parliament considered them too much of a threat to the sovereignty of the Canadian Football League in general, and the Toronto Argonauts in particular. The Washington Ambassadors also had to be moved, because the NFL Redskins had a tight lock on Washington's Robert F. Kennedy Stadium; they ended up in Orlando, Florida, with the use of the Tangerine Bowl, under the name Florida Blazers.

Now the 12 teams of the WFL were centered either in new uncharted cities for professional football, or in cities where rival NFL teams had persistently been a disappointment to their fans, like Houston, for example, which had won a total of only two games the previous two seasons. Similar chronic NFL losers deemed vulnerable were the Chicago Bears and the Philadelphia Eagles.

Davidson entertained future plans for expansion within five years to such cities as Tokyo, Madrid, London, Paris, Dusseldorf, Rome, Mexico City, and Stockholm. "There is absolutely no way this league can fail," he confidently proclaimed.[7]

Gaining TV Exposure

The new league needed a television contract to help establish its credibility and to provide some additional revenues beyond gate receipts. Although at this time a contract as lucrative as those of the NFL teams could hardly be expected—each NFL team was paid about $500,000 a year—still the importance of TV exposure could not be minimized and might indeed be vital to the new league. And Davidson came through, despite the already saturated TV network sports programming, with a TV contract that would

[6] Ibid., p. 91.
[7] Twombly, p. 10.

net each team about $100,000 for the year: "But this year's not for the money; it's for the exposure."[8]

Five of the six weekly WFL games were to be broadcast on Wednesday nights in the hometowns of the teams that were on the road. The sixth, the so-called "game of the week," was to be televised nationally on Thursday nights (football widows could well weep, with the starting of a full schedule of football programming in July). In these early days of the new league's operation, the ratings suggested that die-hard fans were hungry enough for their sport in July to disrupt customary summer evening activities once or twice a week.

THE FIRST SEASON—AN ADVENTURE IN ILL-FATED MISCALCULATIONS

The beginning of the season augured well. The league's first nationally televised game, on a hot July evening in Jacksonville, Florida's Gator Bowl, drew 60,000 spectators and captured a satisfactory 16 percent of the national TV audience. The game itself was exciting, with the home team Jacksonville Sharks beating the New York Stars on a blocked punt late in the fourth quarter.

In the July 11 *Jacksonville Journal,* an Associated Press story read:

> The World Football League was a box office success in its debut last night, with over 200,000 fans in attendance in five cities. Philadelphia announced 55,534 fans paid their way into John F. Kennedy Stadium, tops in the league, and only the Florida Blazers played before an announced crowd of fewer than 30,000.[9]

But the situation quickly deteriorated. In August, both the Philadelphia Bell team and the Jacksonville Sharks admitted that paid attendance figures for their first two home games had been greatly exaggerated. For example, Philadelphia had reported the sale of 121,000 tickets when actually only 20,000 were sold. Before IRS investigators, a Philadelphia Bell executive ruefully excused the release of the phony figures because "if the truth got out we would've been a joke."[10]

Attendance woes were now looming menacingly, with actual figures well below the estimated breakeven point needed of around 35,000 average paid attendance per game. In late August, 12,000 fans came to see the New York Stars maul the Houston Texans. In the rematch in Houston's vast

[8] Burck, p. 197.
[9] Gluck, p. 136–7.
[10] Ibid., p. 154.

Astrodome, 7000 Texans were in attendance. On Labor Day, on the Stars' home field, 6000 fans watched. The following week, less than 3500 customers watched the Stars against the Florida Blazers in the rain.

Things got no better for the league as September matured. On September 18, the debt-ridden Houston franchise was transferred to Shreveport, Louisiana. On September 21, the quarterback of the Detroit Wheels sent a distress message to Davidson: "The situation here is desperate. We haven't been paid in weeks. We've been calling off practice sessions because we can't afford the laundry service."[11] On September 24, the WFL took over the deeply in debt Jacksonville franchise. Gary Davidson gathered $65,000 in escrow funds to partially satisfy Jacksonville players who had gone without paychecks for 5 weeks and were threatening to strike.

The situation was not to improve, not now with the NFL in its full schedule. As the gloomy season progressed, newspapers began to give less coverage to WFL activities (except when there was something negative to report). One consequence of the Chicago newspapers' silence about an upcoming game between the Chicago Fire and the New York Stars was that fans were not informed about a rescheduling of the game, with 5000 trooping out to Soldier Field one evening too soon.

In October, the owner of the Chicago club threatened to take his team out of the league unless a new commissioner was installed and the league offices shifted from Davidson's Newport Beach, California, locale to New York City. Gary Davidson readily resigned as commissioner.

The final standings of the teams for the 1974 season are shown in Table 2.3. The average attendance per game for the 12 teams was 21,000, well below the breakeven point. Almost all the teams broke the record for the most money lost in a single season. The previous record, $1.3 million, was rung up in 1960 by the Los Angeles Chargers of the then newly formed AFL before the franchise was shifted to San Diego, where they were later to become the successful San Diego Chargers.

With such losses, all the teams were in serious financial trouble. Some of the financial woes bordered on ludicrous. For example, the New York Stars in midseason moved to Charlotte, North Carolina, and became the Charlotte Hornets. Less than three weeks after this move, officers arrived to attach their uniforms for nonpayment of bills owed in New York. The same fate was to befall the Birmingham Americans, who won the first (and only) World Bowl at the conclusion of the season before 32,000 spectators (still

---

[11]Ibid., p. 171.

Table 2.3 World Football League Final Standings, 1974

	Western Division		
	W	L	T
Southern California	13	7	
Hawaii	9	11	
Portland	7	12	1
Shreveport	7	12	1
	Central Division		
	W	L	T
Memphis	17	3	
Birmingham	15	5	
Chicago[a]	7	12	
Detroit[a]	1	13	
	Eastern Division		
	W	L	T
Florida	14	6	
Charlotte	10	10	
Philadelphia	8	11	
Jacksonville[a]	4	10	

below breakeven), only to have their uniforms confiscated by a creditor after the game.

The players found themselves in pitiable circumstances, as some went for weeks without pay. Some found themselves charity cases, being fed and clothed by sympathetic fans; players in Hawaii were left stranded without funds thousands of miles from home; players in Orlando were turned away from banks and stores while trying to cash personal checks. The coach of the Florida Blazers had to supply the clubhouse with toilet paper himself during the tail end of the season.

In the meantime, the football players who said they were jumping to the WFL in 1975 were trying to back off from such an ill-conceived idea. Ken Stabler, for example, had signed to play for Birmingham—for more money of course, but also because this was close to his home. However, the Birmingham club failed to pay him the agreed $30,000 on a specified date before the Oakland Raiders ended their season. Before reconsidering the contract, he wanted a guarantee the Birmingham Americans would still be playing in his home state the next year, but could gain no such assurance.

The only true winner was Gary Davidson. For 1974, he had a $100,000 guaranteed salary and was also paid 10 percent of the receipts from the television contracts.

THE SECOND SEASON—1975

After the fiscal disaster of 1974, many people expected the WFL to fold permanently at the end of its title game. However, Chris Hemmeter, a 35-year-old millionaire from Hawaii, devised a new plan for a revitalized attempt by the WFL in 1975. His credentials seemed most reassuring. In 1967, when he was only 28, he had made his first million in the restaurant business. Now he was chairman of the executive committee of the Bank of Honolulu. Hemmeter realized the problems of the previous year and felt that better organization and management were needed to promote a new image for the league, one where debts were paid on time. His plan involved the following:

1. Gate receipts and television income were to be broken down proportionately for the following:
    42% Players' and coaches' salaries
    10% Stadium rental
    10½% League assessments
    37½% Operating expenses and profit account
2. New owners were required to help pay past WFL debts as well as maintain a large working capital.
3. Travel expenses were to be prepaid before the start of the season.
4. Gate-sharing with visiting teams was to be reintroduced to provide a more equitable balance.

Hemmeter calculated that with fewer frills and overhead expenses, the breakeven point for a team would be 17,000 paid attendance per game. In referring to his plan, Hemmeter optimistically stated: "The plan is mathematically infallible."[12]

San Antonio was added for 1975, whereas Detroit and Florida were dropped. However, all clubs but Memphis and Philadelphia were under new management. The lineup of teams for 1975, and their win-loss record is shown in Table 2.4.

For the 1975 season, the league hoped to benefit from a number of name NFL players who were now free to join the new league. In addition, Hemmeter hoped to sign Joe Namath for the 1975 season, but this fell through. The lack of credibility suffered from the previous season still appeared to hamper operations. The final straw, however, was the inability of the league to obtain a national TV contract. The revenue became so sparse that some teams could not even afford to pay the cheerleaders $10 a

---

[12] As quoted in J. Marshall, "Once and Future League," *Sports Illustrated*, April 21, 1975, p. 29.

Table 2.4   WFL Standing, 1975[b]

	Western Division	
	W	L
Southern California	7	5
San Antonio	7	6
Shreveport	5	7
Hawaii	5	7
Portland	4	7
Chicago[a]	1	4

	Eastern Division	
	W	L
Birmingham	9	3
Memphis	7	4
Jacksonville	6	5
Charlotte	6	5
Philadelphia	4	7

[a] Team disbanded Sept. 2, 1975.
[b] League disbanded Oct. 22, 1975. The schedule originally called for 20 games.

game; other teams hired ambulance drivers as trainers for the team. The league went to a quiet death just past the halfway mark of the season. The great experiment was over. At the end, Hemmeter had this to say: ". . . Maybe pro sports is a little too swinging for me . . . most of us are bankers and we lacked charisma."[13]

What happened to the players of the doomed league? The NFL at first would not accept them, but pressure from court action by a number of players reversed the ruling; some began filtering back to either their former teams or to others that needed their specialty. For the time being, Csonka, Kiick, and Warfield remained with Memphis, which, along with Birmingham, attempted to join the NFL as complete teams for 1976. They were unsuccessful.

WHY THE FAILURE?

The rosy promise of the WFL faded so quickly. How could this be? The motives and abilities of Gary Davidson can be criticized, but this was no con job. Even though he emerged with his financial future secure, he could

[13] W. O. Johnson, "Day the Money Ran Out," *Sports Illustrated*, December 1, 1975, p. 85.

INFORMATION SIDELIGHT

THE BREAKEVEN POINT

A breakeven analysis is a vital tool in making go/no-go decisions about new ventures. This can be shown graphically as follows:

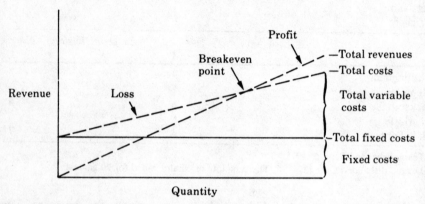

Below the breakeven point, the venture suffers losses (as the WFL did); above it, the venture becomes profitable.

Hypothetical Example for a WFL Team
For this example, let us assume that salaries, uniforms and supplies, stadium rent, promotional expenses, transportation and meals, league assessments, interest expenses, and miscellaneous operating expenses are estimated for the first year to be $4,600,000. These are fixed costs or overhead the team would incur regardless of attendance. Let us further assume that at an average ticket price of $7, about $0.60 would be variable costs, leaving $6.40 to cover the overhead and any profit. The attendance needed to break even is:

$$\frac{\text{Total fixed costs}}{\text{Contribution to overhead}} = \frac{\$4,600,000}{\$6.40} = \begin{array}{l}718,750 \text{ for a 20-} \\ \text{game season, or about} \\ 35,940 \text{ per game}\end{array}$$

An attendance of 21,000 would then be far below such a breakeven point.

These expenses can be estimated quite closely. What cannot be determined as surely are the attendance figures. Now, of course, an organization can do certain things to affect the breakeven point. Obviously, the breakeven point will be lower if the overhead can be reduced, say from $4,600,000 to $4,200,000; some expenses and frills might be eliminated. Higher ticket prices would also result in a lower breakeven (but would probably affect attendance adversely). Promotional expenses can be either increased or decreased and would affect the breakeven point; they would probably also have an impact on attendance. So there are a number of variables that can be controlled, although the range of discretion for an expensive operation such as a professional football team is not very great. The most practical way of reaching and surpassing the breakeven point to make a profit is to increase attendance. And this the WFL was not able to do. With hindsight, this should have been a "no-go" decision.

hardly have reveled in the attack by the press on his reputation; his wife filed for divorce, and his creation was collectively over $20 million in debt—he himself had been rather ignominiously pressured into resigning as commissioner. But bad business judgment was certainly present in quantity.

The direct causes of the failure are easily identifiable:

1. Fan support was lacking, and average attendance fell considerably short of the breakeven point.
2. Television coverage was lacking, especially in the second year of the WFL.
3. At least for the crucial first year, the league lacked big-name talent, even though some had been signed for the 1975 season. The caliber of play, therefore, had to be conceded as inferior to the NFL.
4. The owners were unwilling or unable to contribute additional capital to continue their teams and the league.

Although these were the surface causes, we must probe deeper to ascertain the factors or contributors to them.

If we calculate the percentage year-to-year increase in paid attendance for AFL-NFL football, we see that since 1966 attendance had been, for the most part, increasing at a decreasing rate. (See Table 2.5 for the percentage figures, based on the total attendance data given in Tables 2.1 and 2.2.) Especially since 1970, the percentage increase in attendance had steadily fallen, until in the recession year of 1974, when the WFL commenced operation, attendance actually decreased, the first such decrease in pro football since 1951. At the same time, more and more games were being played, rising from 154 combined AFL-NFL games in 1965 to 182 by 1968. This strongly suggests that saturation was occurring with pro football, with

Table 2.5   Percentage Increase in Paid Attendance Pro Football, 1960-1973 (Exclusive of Post-Season Games)

Year	Percent Increase over Previous Year
1961	23.05
1962	3.25
1963	4.30
1964	11.89
1965	6.75
1966	16.85
1967	9.83
1968	3.43
1969	4.96
1970	6.64
1971	5.69
1972	3.67
1973	2.72
1974	(4.61) decrease
1975	(.23) decrease

virtually every major city having one or more teams, with the season becoming longer and longer, and with more and more TV coverage.

At the time of the establishment of the WFL in 1973, there were 26 professional football teams in the NFL, covering all geographical areas of this country. The founders of the WFL considered their opportunity and potential market as similar to those at the formation of the AFL in 1960. But, at that time, there were only 12 professional football teams, and the popularity of pro football was just beginning to emerge. The environment was much different in 1973, but this went undetected.

The WFL made two flawed premises in regard to locating their franchises. First, teams were established in small cities, such as Charlotte, North Carolina, and Shreveport, Louisiana, without considering whether there was enough population to support a major football franchise. The other faulty premise was that major cities that had losing NFL teams were ripe candidates for a new league entry.

In addition to indications of a saturation of attendance, TV saturation of sporting events was becoming more and more evident by 1974, especially when the seasons for the different sports overlapped, as they increasingly did. Table 2.6 shows the sporting events on TV for New York City during one week in October 1974. This was fairly typical of prime TV markets, and it did not include ABC's "Wide World of Sports" or CBS's "Sports Spectacular", diversified Saturday and Sunday afternoon shows that pro-

Table 2.6 Example of Sporting events on TV Week of October 14 to 20, 1974, New York City[a]

Monday	Football
Tuesday	Baseball
Wednesday	Baseball
	Hockey
Thursday	Football
	Baseball
	Hockey
Friday	—
Saturday	Football
	Football
	Baseball
	Basketball
	Horseracing
Sunday	Football
	Football
	Football
	Football
	Baseball

[a] Not included is ABC's "Wide World of Sports" or CBS's "Sports Spectacular," which are diversified Saturday and Sunday afternoon shows.

vided still more sports exposure. Friday traditionally is a blank spot in professional sports broadcasting, partly because most high school athletic events are scheduled for Friday evening. This heavy TV lineup of established sports necessarily would put a substantial obstacle in the path of an upstart, unproven, and (in the absence of name players) presumed inferior newcomer professional league. Although the early start of the WFL season (in July) ensured some initial TV exposure, this was quickly lost when the regular NFL season commenced.

The product was inferior. Like it or not, in 1974 the WFL fielded teams composed of second- and third-rate players. This is a natural consequence for any expansion team, and much more so for an entire expansion league. For something as specialized and demanding as big-time pro sports, the pool of available talent is limited. There are only so many adequate and/or superior athletes. The introduction of a whole new league created a serious imbalance in the supply and demand situation for good football talent. The consequence could not be surprising, given a limited financial pool: inferior players—even mere bodies—had to be relied upon for many positions.

The best players are tied to their own teams with contracts. Eventually, if the newcomer can dangle enough money and can wait long enough, some of the big names—along with other less well-known, but capable players—will shift allegiance. In the case of the NFL, a surprising number of big names were induced to come over, but not for the 1974 season. Had the WFL remained strong and viable into 1975, it undoubtedly would have fielded much better players. The lack of money—especially the reluctance of the owners to sink more money into their enterprises—led to a serious all-around image of inferiority, not only of players, but also of facilities. A poor product placed in an environment of declining potential, trying to match strongly entrenched competition, hardly had a fighting chance.

Finally, the loss of credibility coming from the widespread exposure of greatly padded attendance figures undoubtedly cast a lasting negative pall over the entire league, particularly with influential sports writers, as well as with any prospective financial backers. As the season progressed, the sorry publicity of missed payrolls, franchise shifting and folding, and confiscated equipment and uniforms because of nonpayment of debts further destroyed any credibility and created an image—which was to carry on into the short-lived 1975 season—of a loser from the start. Furthermore, the negative press murdered the possibility of TV advertising, and with it the likelihood of TV coverage for 1975.

WHAT CAN BE LEARNED?

When an organization—be it a business firm with a tangible product, or an enterprise such as we have here that is providing some service, in this case entertainment—is a newcomer going up against strongly entrenched competition, the need for careful planning is the greater. Utmost care must be given to carefully assessing the business potential, the competitor's weaknesses, if any, as well as what unique strengths the newcomer might have. The risk/reward situation must be carefully assessed: are the possible rewards great enough to be worth the risks? Gary Davidson, in his intuitive feel that here was a tax write-off opportunity that would be attractive to wealthy team owners, adapted the planning to the opportunity—without considering the practicality of it all. The task of achieving a profitable niche for a new and unknown organization, especially one whose resources are limited vis-à-vis the established competition, must not be taken lightly. This presents some of the strongest challenges management can encounter with the need for careful planning the greatest.

The WFL based most of its efforts on the smooth talk and optimistic statements of an acknowledged promoter. The enticement of a tax shelter for rich investors, as well as the macho thrill of owning an athletic team, led investors to accept the idea with only scanty assessment of the potential and of the risks of heavy financial failure. Confidence and, admittedly, some innovative ideas in making pro football more entertaining are not substitutes for careful analysis and planning.

What can we generalize as a constructive learning experience from the WFL debacle?

First, plans for a new endeavor must give first priority to whether there is indeed sufficient business potential to support an interloper. In the case of the WFL, the evidence suggests there was not. Saturation with both attendance and TV coverage was becoming evident, as shown in Tables 2.5 and 2.6. The major WFL thrust was to smaller cities and to those supposedly disillusioned with poorly performing NFL teams. Unfortunately, no effort was made to determine what population was needed to support a pro football team and enable it to exceed the breakeven point. Furthermore, reckless planning did not consider that the poorly performing NFL cities would hardly be patsies for a newcomer that could not assure them of a higher quality of performance.

Second, if an organization is to make inroads against an entrenched competitor, it must plan for sufficient resources to tolerate several years of losses and heavy developmental expenses. In the case of the WFL, such resources were severely lacking, at least for 1974, so that there was no time available to build and improve the operation.

Third, public relations that have to do with the public image of an organization must be scrupulously protected, especially during the vulnerable formative period. There must be no insinuation of spurious dealings or lessening of product quality. Yet, the WFL erred in this area almost from the beginning.

Finally, the strategy of an interloper must offer customers something unique, something desirable enough to make them switch, or at least test it. The WFL had an innovative approach to making pro football more entertaining. But its ideas were easily copied. The next year, in fact, the NFL adopted some of the playing ideas proposed by the WFL. Consequently, the sole competitive advantage of the WFL in offering a more exciting brand of football was quickly nullified by NFL rule changes.

The result was that the WFL found itself with a static or even declining business potential, inferior resources in the way of player talent and stadium and other facilities, and with nothing unique that might have made it attractive to a sufficiently large body of customers. Its reckless planning took no account of the existing situation, the resources of the enterprise, the strength of competition, or the time required to build a successful operation. Gary Davidson built a castle on a paper foundation.

For Thought and Discussion

1. Do you think the WFL gave up too soon?
2. Do you think Joe Namath would have made the difference?
3. Would adequate financial resources have made the WFL viable?
4. Discuss the pros and cons of optimistic versus conservative planning.

Invitation to Role Play

1. Assume the role of Chris Hemmeter. It is the second season, after the disaster of 1974. What would you have done to give the WFL a better chance of achieving viability? Be as specific as you can.
2. Assume the role of business manager for a particular franchise of the WFL in 1974. You have carefully calculated that the present breakeven point in attendance is about 35,000 per home game, and your team is averaging only 20,000. Develop a plan to achieve breakeven for the remaining five home games. (Assume that your city has a population of 300,000, and 200,000 more people live within 50 miles).

CHAPTER 3

J. C. Penney Company—"The Old Ways Are Best"

In contrast to the rash planning for the World Football League are errors of ultraconservatism, of unbending relunctance to change the policies and practices that once had made an enterprise successful but are now out-moded. The J. C. Penney Company, for almost 2 decades, was an example of the latter. For reasons we will shortly explore, it could not bring itself to rise from its rut of being primarily a cash-and-carry operation in small rural towns—at a time when the general public was demanding credit, one-stop shopping, and when the shift of population was to larger cities and suburbs. Finally, with the company struggling in the dust raised by its more progressive competitors, only a critical memo by a staff executive—who, in bypassing his superior, was putting his own career on the line—brought a realization of the urgent need to reevaluate 40-year-old policies and ways of doing business. But first, let us look at the successful start and early growth of the Penney Company.

THE BEGINNING

At sunrise on a spring morning in 1902, a young man, Jim Penney, opened a tiny dry goods store in Kemmerer, a frontier town in the southwest corner of Wyoming. He called the store the Golden Rule, remembering his father's admonition to deal with people according to the Biblical injunction: "There-fore all things whatsoever ye would that men should do to ye, do ye ever so to them."[1] The opening day was advertised by handbills distributed through-out the town. Penney remained open that day until midnight, and his sales were $466.59. After that he opened at 7 A.M. on weekdays and 8 A.M. on Sundays, and remained open as long as there was a miner or sheepherder on the street. Sales for the first year were $28,898.11.[2]

Penney faced a tough competitor in Kemmerer. The town was dominated by a mining company, and a company-owned store had practically a local monopoly with most business done on credit or with the scrip issued by the mining company. Penney did not offer any credit, nor could he accept the scrip. What he did offer was values so much better that customers were willing to pay cash and carry home their purchases. He had no fancy fixtures—all the merchandise was piled on tables where customers could see and touch, and there was one price for all. Penney also had a returned-goods policy: if customers were not satisfied, they could return the purchase and get their money back.

Jim Penney had not always been successful in his business dealings. He was born on a farm in Missouri in 1875 into the big family of a poor Baptist minister. Upon graduating from high school, he worked as a clerk in a local dry goods store. His salary was $2.27 a month. But poor health forced him to resign and move West. Not wanting to work for someone else, he scraped up enough money to open a butcher shop in Longmont, Colorado. However, he soon lost this along with all his savings. His first venture into entrepreneurship had failed. The second venture was not to fail; the little store in the small mining town in Wyoming became the seed of the J. C. Penney Company.

THE SUCCESSFUL GROWTH YEARS

Penney was not content to run just one store. As the store in Kemmerer prospered, he thought of opening other stores. By 1905 he had two stores with total sales just under $100,000. In 1910, Penney changed his company's name from the Golden Rule to the J. C. Penney Company. By this time the chain had grown to 26 stores in six western states. He kept to the same strategy that had worked well in Kemmerer. He tried to give his customers honest values, which usually meant the lowest possible prices; he stayed with a cash-only policy, and he had no fancy fixtures or high overhead

[1] Tom Mahoney and Leonard Sloane, *The Great Merchants* (New York: Harper & Row, 1966), p. 259.
[2] Ibid., p. 259.

expenses. Thus, he could offer low prices and still make money. Not the least of the success factors at this time was the environment Penney had chosen for his business. He confined his stores to small towns where the Penney managers could be well-known, friendly, and respectable members of the community. The lack of strong competition that would have been encountered in larger cities helped the burgeoning growth, a growth from one store to almost 1500 in only 30 years.

Something else, another uniquely Penney policy, was also necessary for such a growth rate to be achieved. Where could Penney possibly find the trained, competent, and honest managers to run the hundreds of stores that were being opened? And almost as important, where could he find the financial resources to open so many stores in such a short period of time and stock them with sufficient merchandise?

Jim Penney both financed and created the managerial resources needed by taking in "partner associates." As each store manager was able to accumulate enough capital out of his store's earnings, he could buy a one-third partnership in a new store, *if* he had trained one of his employees to the point where he could go out and effectively manage such a new store. Here then we have the great incentive to provide the resources needed by such a growing company: motivation by each store manager to find the best qualified employees and give them the best possible training. And profits would often be plowed back into the company to pay off partnership interests or to back new outlets.

By 1924 there were 570 stores and partners. Now, to get the outside financial help needed to sustain further growth, the partnerships were formed into a corporation under which the stores became company owned. The days of managers getting one-third shares of stores were over. And the complexion of the company now underwent a major change.

Up to this time, store operations had been highly individualized, with each manager making his own decisions within rather general policies. Such looseness of organization now gave way to more centralized policies and activities, a trend that was to continue in the decades to come. Operations were made more uniform, with strict budgeting systems, improved operational methods, store arrangements, merchandise, and promotions planned by experts and followed by all stores. Central buyers had more authority over managers as to what goods and prices they would carry. And store managers were now evaluated against other store managers as to their performance; promotions to better stores or to the home office went to the better producers. Penney's was beginning to shape itself into a unified and efficient organization. Growth continued, despite the depression of the 1930s, as shown in Table 3.1.

Table 3.1 Growth of J. C. Penney Company by Stores and Sales

Year	Numer of Stores	Sales (Dollars)
1902	1	28,898
1905	2	97.653
1912	34	2,050,641
1919	197	28,783,965
1926	747	115,957,865
1933	1,466	178,773,965
1940	1,586	302,539,325

Source: Norman Beasley, Main Street Merchant (New York: McGraw-Hill, 1948). p. 222.

EMERGING PROBLEMS

Despite the substantial growth of the Penney Company and the firm entrenchment it had achieved in middle America, by the 1950s some questions were beginning to be raised about the theretofore successful policies. Did they need to be changed? Were they archaic for society at that time? Was the Penney Company vulnerable to competition as perhaps never before?

General merchandise firms were customarily compared with Sears. Sears was the benchmark, the model for efficient, progressive, large-scale enterprise. Montgomery Ward and Company found itself stacking up poorly against Sears due to a nonexpansion policy after World War II. And now the J. C. Penney Company, in looking at comparative sales statistics with Sears, found itself wanting.

Significant as Penney's achievement was in leading his company through difficult years of adolescence and rapid growth, the conservatism of his associates caused a long delay in the market adaptations needed for the 2 decades following World War II—credit, merchandise diversification, and catering to the urban market. Table 3.2 shows the growth of credit during this period, a period in which the Penney Company stuck resolutely with its cash-and-carry philosophy. Initially, such a policy had been compatible with the needs of a population dissatisfied with the lethargic inefficiencies of many independent stores and their high prices. But 4 decades later a reevaluation was sorely needed.

Diversification of merchandise lines was also long delayed. Penney's remained only a dry goods and clothing operation until the 1960s. Appliances, furniture and carpeting, sporting goods, auto supplies—merchandise categories long carried by other general-merchandise chains such as Sears and Ward's and by department stores—were ignored by Penney's. Finally, most of the Penney stores were in the more sparsely settled smaller

Table 3.2   Trend in Consumer Credit, 1940–1970 (Billions)

	1940	1950	1955	1960	1965	1970
Installment: Consumer goods, other than automobiles	$1.8	$4.8	$7.6	$11.5	$18.5	$31.5
Noninstallment charge accounts	1.5	3.4	4.8	5.3	6.4	8.0
Ratio of total consumer credit to disposable personal income	10.9%	10.4%	14.1%	16.0%	19.0%	18.4%

communities west of the Mississippi. The populous and growing East and burgeoning metropolitan areas were not Penney's domain.

A reassessment of policies was needed, indeed was long overdue. Although the viability of the firm was not yet in jeopardy, its stature as a competitive entity in the mainstream of American retailing was. But how difficult it seems to be to combat ingrained resistance to change.

The Batten Memo

In 1957, despairing of top management's willingness to change, the assistant to the president of Penney's, William M. Batten, wrote a memo to the board of directors that was to have far-reaching consequences.

It was probably one of the most influential and widely publicized memos in modern corporate history. Batten had started with the company as an extra salesman 26 years before, and had come a long way. Now he was ready to stake everything on what he saw was a desperate need to change. He sent a memo to the board of directors criticizing the conservatism of the company for not reacting to a changing America.

In the 1950s, population growth was centering in the metropolitan areas. Income per capita was rising, and consumer buying power was being attracted toward "want" rather then "need" type of merchandise. Fashion was consequently becoming more important, and Penney's was extremely weak here. The memo bluntly stated that the world in which the Penney Company had prospered was fast disappearing and that, if Penney's hoped to survive, it would have to change.

Batten suggested conducting a Merchandising Character Study to define the kinds of stores that should be operated. He suggested the study should concern three basic areas:

1.   To assess Penney's immediate position in merchandising compared with chief competitors such as Sears and Ward's

---

INFORMATION SIDELIGHT

RESISTANCE TO CHANGE

People as well as organizations have a natural reluctance to embrace change. Change is disruptive. It can destroy accepted ways of doing things and familiar authority-responsibility relationships. It makes people uneasy, because their routines will likely be disrupted; their interpersonal relationships with subordinates, co-workers, and superiors may well be modified. Positions that were deemed important before the change may be downgraded. And persons who view themselves as highly competent in a particular job may be forced to assume unfamiliar duties amid the fear that these cannot be handled as well.

Resistance to change can be combatted by good communication with participants about forthcoming changes. Without such communication, rumors and fears can assume monumental proportions. Acceptance of change can be facilitated if employees are involved as fully as possible in planning the changes, if their participation is solicited and welcomed, and if assurance can be given that positions will not be impaired, only changed. Gradual rather than abrupt changes also make a transition smoother as participants can be initially exposed to the changes without drastic upheavals.

In the final analysis, however, needed changes should not be delayed or cancelled because of their possible negative repercussions on the organization. If change is necessary, it should be initiated. Individuals and organizations can adapt to change—it just takes a bit of time.

---

2. To forecast market opportunities by examining changes in population and trends in shopping, work, and leisure
3. To spell out desired changes in goods and services and voids in the marketplace that required filling.

After 2 years, in 1959, the Merchandising Character Study was completed. The conclusions were that Penney's was selling only soft goods and limited home furnishings, and that most of the advertising appeals were to women. It was decided that Penney's needed to pull in the entire family in areas having the greatest population growth. As one vice–president commented in regard to the preponderance of apparel and home furnishings:

We had no browsing areas for men while their wives shopped, like paint and hardware departments. We had nothing to attract the kids, like a toy department. We realized we needed to tend more toward the one-stop shopping idea.[3]

The year following his audacious memo, Batten was made president of Penney's with the mandate to implement the changes necessary. The question was whether it was now too late to catch up with its competitors, to regain the ground lost during the years of conservative and unchanging policies. The problems were at last defined and known to all. But could they be overcome, and quickly?

AT LAST, CHANGE

In September 1958, Penney's began testing the feasibility of offering credit. At first, only 24 stores were the object of this experiment. More than 3 years were required for Penney's to establish its credit operation chainwide. But at least the necessity of credit to keep up with changing times, and to do well with the big-ticket items such as television and washing machines, was realized.

Coming late into the consumer credit field, however, afforded Penney's certain advantages. An almost completely computerized system was designed, in contrast to other retailers who had started with manual systems and then were forced to computerize at an enormous cost. In order to operate its credit system manually, 37 centers would be needed to serve all the stores. However, with the use of the advanced IBM computers, only 14 regional credit offices had to be set up. At the time of Penney's installation, Sears was the only other retailer who could allow customers to shop in any store across the country and receive one bill.

By 1962, all stores offered credit. By 1964, the results were notable: 28 percent of Penney's sales volume was done on credit. Revenues in 1964 amounted to $600 million from more than 5 million active accounts. By 1966, credit sales were responsible for 35 percent of all sales; by 1973, credit sales were over 38 percent of total sales. By 1967, Penney's had 12 million charge accounts, twice the number of Diners Club and American Express combined.

As intended, the establishment of credit led the way for Penney's to diversify its merchandise mix. It began to follow Sears into carrying hard goods (appliances, furniture, and the like) along with its soft goods. For many years Penney's had been the nation's largest seller of women's hosiery, sheets and blankets, coats and dresses, work clothes, and men's

[3] Alfred Law, "From Overalls to Fashion Wear," *Wall Street Journal*, October 22, 1964, p. 1.

INFORMATION SIDELIGHT

IMPORTANCE OF CREDIT

As an extreme example of the importance of credit in enhancing comsumer demand and consequent purchasing, consider the Superior, Wisconsin Penney store in 1959, one of the early stores experimenting with credit. Superior, an iron-ore shipping port at the far western end of Lake Superior, experienced wide fluctuations in business and income due to weather, strikes, and economic slowdowns. Sales at this Penney store had remained static for over 3 years. The first year that credit was offered, sales increased over 30 percent.

Admittedly, the Superior example is not a typical Penney store. The need for credit by people with irregular incomes is the greater. In place of credit, Penney's had always offered the "layaway plan." Here a store held the selected goods for a customer until they were completely paid for—often by small weekly or biweekly payments—and only then released them to the customer. This plan was heavily pushed by Penney's for expensive items and for merchandise sold in advance of the season. But increasingly, customers did not want deferred gratification of their wants. Not if some other store was giving credit, thereby permitting them to have the immediate pleasure of a desired product.

---

underwear. Prior to 1960, soft goods averaged 95 percent of total sales. Admittedly, soft goods, to some extent, had shielded Penney's from the ups and downs in the economy, because soft goods normally are the last thing people cut down on during hard times; appliances and furniture, on the other hand, can usually be postponed or deferred until times look better. But such soft goods typically afford a low markup, and profitability rests on high turnover and sales volume. There is also a limit to how much soft goods the market can absorb, and certainly sales and profit potential is ultimately limited without diversification beyond soft goods.

First attempts at merchandise diversification came as Penney's moved into higher-priced women's dresses, leather goods, and furniture. Merchandise assortment was widened by adding designer dresses and youth-minded sportswear for both men and women. By 1962, Penney's began to add hard goods, with the new merchandise appearing in new or enlarged stores, and to a lesser extent in other stores where space could be found. In 1963, Penney's opened it first full-line department store having such new departments for Penney's as appliances, televisions, sporting goods, paint, hardware, tires, batteries, and auto accessories. The new stores subsequently allocated about 25 to 30 percent of total floor space to these new lines of hard goods.

By 1965, Penney's had 173 stores with radio-TV departments, 103 with major appliances, 67 with sporting goods, 58 carrying paint and hardware, and 42 centers handling tires, batteries, and auto accessories. Diversification had begun in earnest.

Penney's also sought to offer hard goods in stores that were too small to stock such goods. General Merchandise Company, a small but highly automated mail-order company, was acquired in 1962. Catalog centers were then set up in many stores as a means of offering customers a much wider variety of goods. In 1971, catalog sales moved into the black, and Penney's at last had the means to compete on equal terms with the long-established businesses of Sears and Ward's.

Replacement of older, smaller soft-line stores averaging from 30,000 to 40,000 sq ft with new full-line units was also proceeding in earnest. These new stores ranged in size from 43,000 to 220,000 sq ft, averaging 165,000. Other diversifications into discount stores (Treasure Island stores), drug stores (Thrift Drug), and supermarkets proceeded. Overseas expansion was also occurring with a controlling interest in a major Belgian retailing firm, Sarma, S.A., obtained in 1968, while in 1971 Penney's entered the Italian market.

The conservative policies had been abandoned and replaced with a vigorous growth orientation. But could the sales and profits that were lost ever be completely retrieved? Perhaps the most important question was: could the ground lost to Sears in the decade and a half of outmoded policies ever be regained?

A MISTAKE RECTIFIED

By the late 1960s and into the 1970s, Penney's was at times almost matching the expansion effort of Sears, a firm more than twice as large. Table 3.3 shows the capital expenditures for Sears and Penney's during those years, as well as the percentage of these expenditures to sales. You can see from this table the much greater percentage of sales commitment of Penney's to expansion. But has Penney's been able to make up the lost ground?

Table 3.4 shows the sales volume since 1940 of Penney's compared with Sears. It also shows the market share of Penney's relative to Sears, that is, the percentage of Penney's sales to total Sears and Penney's sales. Figure 3.1 shows the market share of Penney's more graphically, as well as the trends during the long period of 1940 to 1974.

You can see from these charts that the sharp upward trend in market

Table 3.3   Capital Expenditures of Sears and Penney's, 1968–1973

	Sears		Penneys	
Year Ending January	Capital Expenditures (000,000)	Percentage of Sales	Capital Expenditures (000,000)	Percentage of Sales
1968	$186	2.5	$111	4.0
1969	139	1.8	127	3.8
1970	211	2.4	139	3.7
1971	259	2.8	204	4.9
1972	339	3.1	185	3.8
1973	392	3.2	210	3.4

Source: Adapted from Moody's Industrials, and respective annual reports.

Table 3-4   Relative Sales Volumes, Penney's and Sears, 1940–1974

			Market Share (Sales as a Percentage of Total Penney's and Sears Sales)	
Year	Penney's (000)	Sears (000)	Penney's	Sears
1942	$ 490,295	$ 915,058	35	65
1944	535,363	851,535	38	62
1946	676,570	1,045,259	39	61
1948	885,195	1,981,536	32	68
1950	949,712	2,168,928	31	69
1952	1,079,257	2,932,338	28	72
1954	1,107,157	2,981,925	27	73
1956	1,290,867	3,306,826	28	72
1958	1,409,973	3,600,882	28	72
1960	1,437,489	4,036,153	26	74
1962	1,553,503	4,267,678	27	73
1964	1,834,318	5,115,767	26	74
1966	2,289,209	6,390,000	26	74
1968	2,745,998	7,330,090	27	73
1970	3,756,092	8,862,971	30	70
1972	4,812,239	10,006,146	32	68
1974	6,243,677	12,306,229	33	67

Source: Adapted from respective annual reports.

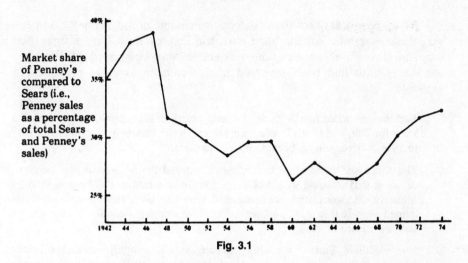

Market share of Penney's compared to Sears (i.e., Penney sales as a percentage of total Sears and Penney's sales)

Fig. 3.1

share (or sales relative to those of Sears) in the early and mid-1940s was reversed in the late 1940s. Penney's market share then eroded badly, reflecting the outmoded policies of Penney's. Not until 1970 was Penney's able to improve its market share and begin a new favorable upward trend. Even though the actions in the 1960s improved the situation, the results are still far below the trend established earlier and the market share previously attained.

The recent growth efforts of Penney's can hardly be faulted or even improved upon. The fact remains, however, that unless major competitors also stumble, a substantial lead built up by one firm due to less aggressive or more error-prone efforts of another firm, is not likely to be caught. (A later case describes the ultraconservative efforts of Ward's, also during about this same period of time and also involving Sears as the major competitor.)

HOW COME THE LAPSE OF 1945-1958?

It is one of the anomalies of human endeavor that individuals of great accomplishment and innovativeness can be both visionary and short-sighted, inspired and blind. Henry Ford is perhaps the foremost example of such strengths and weaknesses: originating mass production of the automobile, but steadfastly refusing to budge from his original idea of a black Model T.

Jim Penney and his company fell into a similar myopia of resistance to changing times. The policies that worked so well in the early years of the Penney Company became outmoded. But still, the temptation is to stick with the historically successful and proven. There is difficulty in breaking from accepted ways of doing things.

Partly accounting for the resistance to change of the Penney Company was the leadership. For the most part, top Penney executives fought their way up through the ranks; the leadership was composed of Penney's associates who had been involved in the company's early growth. For example:

Earl Sams worked first as James Penney's clerk in Kemmerer, then managed a store for him, and in 1917 became president of the company, serving from 1917 to 1946, whereupon he became board chairman.

The successor of Sams, Albert Hughes, tutored Penney's sons in Latin but, deciding that retailing would be more exciting, started in the Penney store in Moberly, Missouri, and later managed stores in Utah and Georgia. He was named president in 1946 and served until he stepped aside for Batten (of the famous memo) in 1958.

Even William Batten, the changemaker, was thoroughly imbued with the traditional Penney philosophy. He first worked for Penney in 1926 while attending high school, and joined the company full time in 1935 as shoe salesman.

After Batten moved up to chairman in 1964, Ray Jordan became president, culminating a Penney career which began in the small town of Picher, Oklahoma, in 1930.

The Penney Company can boast of its firm policy of promotion from within, and proudly point out examples of this in the ranks of its top executives. But we might ponder whether such a policy can be carried too far. The absence of new blood can be a negative influence. Although trainees may be inspired as to their opportunities and potential attainment, policies tend to become self-perpetuating and innovation stymied without the presence of fresh ideas or even disruptive influences from outsiders.

Of course, if a firm is to gird itself for change, it must first recognize and evaluate exogenous trends. A research department or a long-range planning staff may help here in sensing the environment and supplying information about changes to those executives who need to know. But most major changes in the environment should be obvious to all, simply by being alert to what is taking place in the industry and the economy. For example, data about the burgeoning popularity of credit were readily available from government statistics and industry data for many years before the Penney Company hesitantly began to act. Similarly, the movement of people from rural areas to cities and the ever-increasing stores in suburban shopping centers were nothing arcane or mysterious, but evident to all. Persons in responsible positions can see, but not perceive: they are blinded by their accustomed ways of doing things—until perhaps something shocks them, as

Batten's memo did, or as severely deteriorating operating results finally may. Alertness to the environment, a willingness to change, and, occasionally, even a willingness to initiate changes where the situation seems ripe—these are the attitudes of the successful and aggressive firm.

The Penney's example suggests the need for fresh blood in an organization. Total reliance on inbreeding and promotion from within tends to foster a narrow and parochial perspective. The traditional way of doing things often prevails in such an environment. (The fact that Batten, in moving up through the ranks, was able to point his finger at the flaws and emerging dangers in such an eminent tradition reflects all the more on his strengths. But he was the exception.) We are not suggesting here that the opposite course of action—heavy commitment to filling important executive positions with outsiders—is to be advocated. Such action plays havoc with morale of trainees and lower-level executives. Rather, a middle ground usually is more desirable—filling many executive positions from within the organization, promoting this idea so as to encourage both the achievement of present executives and the recruiting of trainees, and at the same time bringing strong outsiders into the organization where their strengths and particular experiences can be most valuable. Moderation then may be more desirable than major reliance either on promotion from within or from without.

The lack of innovativeness of the Penney Company in the 1940s and 1950s reflects a need in many organizations to foster innovative thinking among employees and executives. Top management support and encouragement of this is usually required. More than this, a receptivity to change and a willingness to change are important, because, if ideas are never acted upon, the creative instincts of an organization are soon atrophied.

Fostering innovation can take many forms. One way is to expose personnel to fresh thinking, either through some mix of sharp new people, or through seminars and institutes where there is exposure to people from other organizations and experiences. Stimulating creativity can also come from quickly recognizing and rewarding creative individuals.

Update

By 1984, Penney's had 1597 departments stores, 359 Thrift Drug stores, 1805 catalog sales centers, and a Brussels-based chain of 58 food and general-merchandise stores under the Sarma label, as well as six catalog distribution centers. It had phased out 37 discount units under the Treasury name at the end of 1980. In 1977, it had disposed of several other operations that were

---

INFORMATION SIDELIGHT

A RECOGNIZED MANAGEMENT PRINCIPLE: AVOID BYPASSING AND FOLLOW THE CHAIN OF COMMAND

Bypassing occurs when a subordinate goes over the head of his or her immediate supervisor to appeal a decision or request a directive from a higher authority. Sometimes the bypassing occurs in the other direction as, for example, if the vice–president of sales deals directly with a sales representative instead of going through the field supervisor. Invariably, the employee will give preference to the instructions of the senior executive, and the authority and influence of the immediate supervisor will be undermined.

While bypassing in general should be condemned and the chain of command (or line of authority) adhered to in communications and directives, this does not mean that all direct contacts between higher executives and employees in the lower ranks should be condemned. But, except for emergencies, they should usually be limited only to occasional contacts aimed at building morale or obtaining first-hand information. The other exception is in a grievance procedure in which the employee has a complaint that cannot satisfactorily be resolved with the supervisor. Industrial psychologists here would condone a free and open right of appeal, even though this smacks of bypassing.

The action of Batten in going over the head of his boss violated the integrity of the chain of command relationship, although he might claim the situation was an emergency and warranted such action.

---

not performing satisfactorily profitwise, including its Italian retail stores and the supermarket operation. By the early 1980s, major emphasis was being given to upgrading the fashion image of the company. The auto-care business was seen as incompatible with this and was dropped.

Sales and profits for 1984 for the five largest nonfood retailers were:

	Sales ($mil)	Profits ($mil)
Sears	38,828	1323.4
K mart	21,096	499.0
Penney	13,451	435.0
Federated	9,672	329.3
Dayton-Hudson	8,009	259.3

As can be seen, Penney's had gained ground relative to Sears, with its sales as a percentage of total Sears and Penney's sales being 38.7 percent, whereas, in 1974, they were 33 percent (see Table 3.4). But during the decade of the 1970s, K mart was the big success story, moving up to the number two retailer, behind only Sears.

For Thought And Discussion

1. Can you think of other less drastic incentives for store managers to develop trainees than that practiced by the Penney Company in its early years of growth?
2. Do you think the growth of the Penney Company in the last decade and a half could have been accomplished any quicker? If so, how?
3. What procedures might you have advised the Penney Company to undertake to keep plans and objectives up-to-date and responsive to environmental changes?

Invitation To Role Play

1. Place yourself in the position of Batten in 1957. Would you have taken the risk of sending a highly critical memo to the board of directors? What do you think would be the consequences of such a memo in some firms?
2. Assume the role of chief assistant to Batten after he has taken over the presidency in 1958. You have been assigned the responsibility of setting up the diversification into appliances, furniture, sporting goods, hardware, and other hard-line departments never before carried by Penney's. Be as specific as you can as to how you would go about doing this.

4

Adidas—Opening The Door For Competitors

In the early 1970s, Adidas dominated the running-shoe industry. It had done so for decades. Now it stood on the threshold of one of the biggest surges of popularity that any recreational pursuit had ever known. Tens of millions of people were to take up running or jogging in the next few years; other millions of nonrunners would be buying running shoes because they were comfortable, and because they conveyed an aura of fitness and youth—an image most people were not adverse to emulating.

Did Adidas cash in on this recreational boom of the century? In one of the classic errors of miscalculation and conservative planning, it underestimated the U. S. market. Even worse, it underestimated the aggressiveness of U. S. competitors. Most of these competitors were upstart firms that had not even been around at the beginning of the decade. In just a few years, Adidas was to be pushed aside by one of the fastest–growing firms outside the computer industry: Nike.

HISTORICAL BACKGROUND

Rudolf and Adolf Dassler began making shoes in Herzogenaurach, in what is now West Germany, shortly after World War I. Adolf, known as Adi to his family, was the innovator, and Rudolf was the seller of his brother's creations. The brothers achieved only moderate success at first, but then, in 1936, a big breakthrough came. Jesse Owens agreed to wear their shoes in the Olympics and won his medals in front of Hitler, the German nation, and the world. The lucrative association of shoes with a famous athlete was to trigger a marketing strategy that Adidas—and other athletic shoe manufacturers—was to practice from that point on.

In 1949, the brothers had a falling out and, indeed, never again spoke to each other outside of court. Rudolf took half the equipment and left his brother to go to the other side of town and set up the Puma Company. Adolf established the Adidas Company from the existing firm ("Adidas" was derived from his nickname and the first three letters of his surname). Rudolf and his Pumas never quite caught up with Adolf's Adidas, but they did become number two in the world.

Adolf was constantly experimenting with new materials and techniques to develop stronger, yet lighter shoes. He tested thorny sharkskin in attempts to develop abrasive leather for indoor flats. He tried kangaroo leather to toughen the sides of shoes.

The first samples of Adidas footwear were shown at the Helsinki Olympic Games of 1952. Then, in 1954, the German soccer team, equipped with Adidas footwear, won the World Cup over Hungary. The shoes were definitely a factor in the win, as Dassler had developed a special stud to screw into the shoes that allowed good footing on the muddy playing field that day; Hungary's shoes did not give the same traction.

Dassler's many innovations in the running-shoe industry included four-spiked running shoes, track shoes with a nylon sole, and injected spikes. He developed a shoe that allowed an athlete to choose from 30 different variations of interchangeable spike elements that could be adapted to an indoor or outdoor track as well as to natural or artificial surfaces.

With its great variety of superior products, Adidas dominated in the widely–publicized international showcase events. For example, at the Montreal games, Adidas-equipped athletes accounted for 82.8 percent of all individual medal winners.[1] This was tremendous publicity for the company, and sales rose to $1 billion worldwide.

But competitors were emerging. Prior to 1972, Adidas and Puma had practically the entire athletic shoe market to themselves. Although this was changing, Adidas seemingly had built up an insurmountable lead, providing footwear for virtually every type of sporting activity as well as diversifying into other sports-related product lines: shorts, jerseys, leisure suits, and track suits; tennis and swimwear; balls for every kind of sport; tennis racquets and cross-country skis; and the popular sports bag that carried the Adidas name as a prominently displayed status symbol.

[1] Norris Willett, "How Adidas Ran Faster," *Management Today*, December 1979, p. 58.

STRATEGIC PLANNING

The strategic planning originated by the Dassler brothers became the guiding influence for the entire industry. The Dasslers had long used international athletic competition as a testing ground for their products. Many years of feedback from these athletes led to continual design changes and improvements. Agreements were entered into with professional athletes to use their products. However, Adidas' strength was in international and Olympic events in which the participants were amateurs, and such endorsement contracts were more often made with national sports associations rather than with individuals.

Following the lead of Adidas and Puma, endorsement contracts with athletes have become commonplace. For example, every player in the National Basketball Association is under contract to at least one manufacturer. The going rate for an endorsement contract today ranges from $500 to $150,000. The athlete must wear a certain brand and appear in various promotional activities. It has become an industry practice to spend about 80 percent of the advertising budget for endorsements and 20 percent for media advertising. The distinctive logos that all manufacturers have developed are key to the effectiveness of these endorsement contracts. Such logos permit immediate identification of product; fans and potential customers can see the product actually in use by the famous athlete. These logos also permit effective product diversification into apparel, bags, and so on.

To increase volume quickly, production facilities were sought where shoes could be made cheaply and in great quantities, in areas such as Yugoslavia and the Far East. Medium-sized firms in such countries were therefore signed up as licensees and goods were produced to specifications. Great outlays for plants and equipment were thus avoided and costs could be kept low.

Finally, Adidas led the running-shoe industry into offering a very wide variety of shoe styles—shoes to fit all kinds of running activities, from various kinds of races to training shoes. Shoes were also offered for every type of runner and running style. The great variety of offerings, more than a hundred different styles and models for Adidas, was to be exceeded only by Nike as it charged to capture the U. S. market.

THE 1970s RUNNING MARKET

During the late 1960s and early 1970s, the environment affecting the running-shoe industry changed dramatically and positively. Americans were increasingly concerned with physical fitness. Millions of previously unathletic people were searching for ways to exercise. The spark that ignited the booming interest may have been the 1972 Munich Olympics. Millions of television viewers watched Dave Wottle defeat Russian Evgeni Arzanov in the 800-meters and Frank Shorter win the prestigious marathon. But the groundwork for the running boom had been laid before. The idea of fitness perhaps first came to the attention of the general public in a trailblazing book by Dr. Kenneth Cooper, *Aerobics,* which sold millions of copies and gave scientific evidence of the physical benefits of a running (or jogging) regimen. A little less than 10 years later, another book with monumental impact, *The Complete Book of Running* by James Fixx, also sold millions of copies and was on the best–seller list for months.

Through the decade of the 1970s, the number of joggers increased. Estimates by the end of the decade were that 25 to 30 million Americans were joggers, while another 10 million wore running shoes around home and town.[2] The number of shoe manufacturers also increased. The original three of Adidas, Puma, and Tiger were joined by new U. S. brands: Nike, Brooks, New Balance, Etonic, and even J. C. Penney, Sears, and Converse. To sell and distribute these new shoes, specialty shoe stores such as Athlete's Foot, Athletic Attic, and Kinney's Foot Lockers sprouted up nationwide. New magazines catering to this market were starting up and showing big increases in circulation: for example, *Runner's World, The Runner,* and *Running Times.* These provided the advertising media to reach runners with no wasted coverage.

COMPETITION

The Beginning of Nike

Phil Knight was a miler of modest accomplishments. His best time was a 4:13, hardly in the same class as the below 4:00 world-class runners. But he had trained under the renowned coach, Bill Bowerman, at the University of Oregon in the late 1950s. Bowerman had put Eugene, Oregon on the map in the 1950s when year after year he turned out world-record-setting long-distance runners. He was constantly experimenting with shoes, because of his theory that an ounce off a running shoe might make enough difference to win a race.

In the process of completing his MBA at Stanford University, Phil wrote a research paper that was based on the theory that the Japanese could do for athletic shoes what they were doing for cameras. After receiving his degree in 1960, Knight went to Japan to seek an American distributorship

[2] "The Jogging-Shoe Race Heats Up" *Business Week,* April 9, 1979, p. 125.

from the Onitsuka Company for Tiger shoes. Returning home, he took samples of the shoes to Bowerman.

In 1964, Knight and Bowerman went into business. They each put up $500 and formed the Blue Ribbon Shoe Company, sole distributor in the United States for Tiger running shoes. They put the inventory in Knight's father-in-law's basement, and they sold $8000 worth of these imported shoes that first year. Knight worked by days as a Cooper & Lybrand accountant, while at night and on weekends he peddled these shoes mostly to high school athletic teams.

Knight and Bowerman finally developed their own shoe in 1972 and decided to manufacture it themselves. They contracted the work out to Asian factories where labor was cheap. They named the shoe, Nike, after the Greek goddess of victory. At that time they also developed the "swoosh" logo, which was highly distinctive and subsequently was placed on every Nike product. The Nike shoes' first appearance in competition came during the 1972 Olympic trials in Eugene, Oregon. Marathon runners persuaded to wear the new shoes placed fourth through seventh, whereas Adidas wearers finished first, second, and third in these trials.

On a Sunday morning in 1975, Bowerman began tinkering with a waffle iron and some urethane rubber, and he fashioned a new type of sole—a "waffle" sole, whose tiny rubber studs made it more springy than those of other shoes currently on the market. This product improvement—seemingly so simple—gave Knight and Bowerman an initial impetus. The marketing strategy that propelled Nike to tops in the U. S. market was more imitative than innovative, however. It was patterned after that of Adidas. But the result was that the imitator outdid the originator.

Nike's Charge

The new "waffle sole" developed by Bowerman proved popular with runners, and this, along with the favorable market, brought 1976 sales to $14 million, up from $8.3 million the year before and only $2 million in 1972.

Nike stayed in the forefront of the industry with its careful research and development of new models. By the end of the decade, Nike was employing almost 100 people in the research and development section of the company. Over 140 different models were offered in the product line, some of these the most innovative and technologically advanced on the market. This diversity came from models designed for different foot types, body weights, running speeds, training schedules, and levels of skill for both sexes.

By the late 1970s and early 1980s, demand for Nikes was so great that 60 percent of its 8000 department store, sporting goods, and shoe store dealers gave advanced orders, often waiting 6 months for delivery. This gave

Table 4.1 Nike Sales Growth, 1976–1981

Year	Sales (millions of dollars)	Percentage Change from Previous Year
1976	$14	
1977	29	107%
1978	71	145
1979	200	182
1980	270	35
1981	458	70
1982	694	34

Source: Company annual reports.

Nike a big advantage in production scheduling and inventory costs. Table 4.1 shows the phenomenal growth of Nike, with sales rising from $14 million in 1976 to $694 million only 6 years later. Table 4.2 shows the competitive positions in the United States for the beginning of 1979. By then, Nike was the leader with 33 percent of the market; within 2 years it had taken an even more commanding lead, with approximately 50 percent of the total market.[3] Adidas' share was falling, well below that of Nike, and it also had U. S. firms such as Brooks and New Balance to worry about.

In 1980, Nike went public, and Knight became an instant multimillionaire, reaching the coveted *Forbes'* Richest Four Hundred Americans, with a net worth estimated at just under $300 million.[4] Bowerman, age 70, had sold most of his stock earlier, and owned only two percent of the company, worth a mere $9.5 million.

In the January 4, 1982 edition of *Forbes*, in the "Annual Report on American Industry," Nike was rated number one in profitability over the previous 5 years, ahead of all other firms in all other industries.[5]

Ingredients of Nike's Success

Unquestionably, Nike faced an extraordinarily favorable demand in the decade of the 1970s. Nike was in a position to take advantage of this, but so were other running-shoe manufacturers, most of whom had impressive gains during these years. But Nike's success went far beyond simply coasting with a favorable demand. Nike outstripped all its competitors, including the

---

[3] "Jogging's Fade Fails to Push Nike Off Track," *Wall Street Journal*, March 5, 1981, p. 25.

[4] "The Richest People in America—The *Forbes* Four Hundred," *Forbes*, Fall 1983, p. 104.

[5] *Forbes*, January 4, 1982, p. 246.

Table 4.2   U. S. Running-Shoe Competitive Positions, 1978

	Percentage of Total U. S. Market
Nike	33%
Adidas	20
Brooks	11
New Balance	10
Converse	5
Puma	5

Sources: Compiled from various published material, including "The Jogging-Shoe Race Heats Up," *Business Week*, April 9, 1979, p. 125.

theretofore dominant Adidas. Nike was able to overcome whatever aura or mystique such foreign producers as Adidas, Puma, and Tiger had. Its strategic planning was fully geared not only to tapping a burgeoning demand, but also to capturing the lion's share of such boom conditions.

Fundamental to Nike's strategic planning goals was a heavy commitment to a broad product line. It soon was to offer an even broader product line than Adidas, which had pioneered with a great variety of shoe styles. A broad product line can pose problems, however. It can be overdone and hurt efficiency, and it greatly adds to production and handling costs. Most firms are better advised to pare their product line and prune their weak products so that adequate attention and resources can be directed to the winners. Here we see the disavowal of such a policy, and yet Nike was one of the great successes of the decade, largely at the expense of Adidas.

Although Nike may have violated some product planning concepts, let us recognize what they accomplished and at what cost. By offering a great variety of styles, prices, and uses, Nike was able to appeal to all kinds of runners; it was able to convey the image of the most complete running-shoe manufacturer of them all. In a rapidly evolving industry in which millions of runners of all kinds and abilities were embracing the idea, such an image became very attractive. Furthermore, Nike found that it could tap the widest possible distribution with its breadth of products. It could sell its shoes to conventional retailers, such as department stores and shoe stores; it could continue to do business with the specialized running-shoe stores. It could even be not too concerned about discounters getting some Nike shoes, because there were certainly enough styles and models to go around— different models for different types of retail outlets—and everyone could be happy.

Short production runs and many styles generally add to production costs, but perhaps, in Nike's case, this was less of a factor. Most of the shoe production was contracted out—some 85 percent to foreign, mostly Far

Eastern, factories. Short production runs were less of an economic deterrent when many foreign plants were contracting for part of the production.

Early on, Nike placed heavy emphasis on research and technological improvement. It sought ever more flexible and lighter–weight running shoes that would be protective but also give the athlete, world-class or slowest amateur, the utmost advantage that running-shoe technology could provide. Nike's commitment to research and development was evident in the approximately 100 employees working in this area, many holding degrees in biomechanics, exercise physiology, engineering, industrial design, chemistry, and related fields. The firm also engaged research committees and advisory boards, including coaches, athletes, athletic trainers and equipment managers, podiatrists, and orthopedists, who met periodically with the firm to review designs, materials, and concepts for improved athletic shoes. Activities included high-speed photographic analyses of the human body in motion, the use of athletes on force plates and treadmills, wear-testing with over 300 athletes in an organized program, and continual testing and study of new and modified shoes and materials. Some $2.5 million was spent in 1980 on product research, development, and evaluation, and the 1981 budget was approximately $4 million. For such an apparently simple thing as a shoe, this was a major commitment to research and development.

Nike attempted no major deviation from the accepted and successful strategy norm of the industry. This norm had been established several decades before by Adidas. In summary, it primarily involved testing and development of better running shoes, a broad product line to appeal to all sectors of the market, a readily identifiable trademark or motif prominently displayed on all products, and the use of well-known athletes and prestigious athletic events to show off the products in use. Even the contracting out of much of the production to low-cost foreign factories was not unique to Nike. But Nike used these proven techniques better than any of its competitors, even Adidas, the pioneer. It geared all its resources to a single-minded commitment to aggressively grab a potential of almost limitless scope—for as long as this boom, fad, or changed life style would last.

ADIDAS' MISTAKES—WHAT WENT WRONG?

Adolph Dassler died in 1978. Perhaps this was a factor in Adidas' waning aggressiveness, although the management transition after his death appeared to have gone very smoothly. And actually, Nike had made its big inroads by this time. No, perhaps we have to seek further to find a suitable explanation for a front–runner stumbling to give the lead to someone coming from far back in the pack.

Undoubtedly, Adidas underestimated the growth of the market for running shoes. For a firm that had been four decades in this business and had always seen the stability of slow growth during these years, a skepticism about the extent and duration of the "boom" would seem most reasonable. And Adidas was not alone in misjudging the potential and the opportunity. Some of the U. S. firms that were traditionally strong in the lower-priced athletic shoe industry, notably Converse and Uniroyal's Keds, were caught flatfooted in the race to bring new and technologically improved models to the market. These major producers of tennis shoes and sneakers (Converse made two-thirds of U. S. basketball shoes) also vastly underestimated the potential and did not direct strong efforts until they were completely outclassed by Nike and several other U. S. manufacturers.

In gearing an operation for rapid growth, sales forecasting becomes a vital element of the planning and preparation for dealing with the opportunity at hand. All aspects of a firm's operation are necessarily based on the sales estimates for the coming period(s): for example, production planning and facilities, inventories, and sales staff and advertising efforts. But when sales are reaching uncharted territory, the firm faces the dilemma of optimistic versus conservative sales projections, as the following "Information Sidelight" discusses.

It seems evident that Adidas, in addition to underestimating the market, also underestimated the aggressiveness of Nike and the other U. S. manufacturers. Perhaps, being the leader with seemingly an unassailable position, this was a natural consequence. After all, foreign brands in many product lines commanded a mystique and attraction that no domestic brands could. And then, how could small U. S. manufacturers, starting practically from scratch, pose any serious threat to the more than 3 decades of seasoned experience of Adidas? So, the perception that U. S. firms were mere weak opportunists seemed not unreasonable.

But we know that U. S. manufacturers were not weak opportunists striving for a stray bone. Nike, among others, saw an opportunity, seized it, and charged. Perhaps this happening is less a reflection of Adidas' deficiencies than a credit to Nike. But we can still raise doubts about Adidas' role in the Nike inroads. Should not Adidas have been more alert in such an easy-to-enter industry? After all, neither the technology nor the plant investment requirements were such as to preclude other firms from entering the arena. Should not the front–runner have recognized this ease of competitive entry and acted aggressively to discourage it—especially when demand was increasing geometrically? Strong promotional efforts, new product introductions, a step–up in research and development, sharper pricing practices, expanding the network of dealers—these actions might not have prevented competition, but, given the resources of the market leader,

---

INFORMATION SIDELIGHT

**OPTIMISTIC VERSUS CONSERVATIVE SALES PLANNING—
CONSEQUENCES OF INACCURATE SALES FORECASTS**

The sales forecast—the estimate of sales for the period(s) ahead—
serves a crucial role, because it is the starting point for all planning and
budgeting. When the situation is volatile and rapidly growing, this
presents some high risk alternatives: should we be optimistic or conservative?

If the planning is conservative, the danger that the firm faces when its
market begins to boom is that it cannot keep up with demand and cannot
expand its resources sufficiently to handle the potential. It simply does
not have enough manufacturing capability and sales staff. The result
invariably is to abdicate perhaps a good share of this growing business to
competitors who are willing and able to match their capability and
strategic planning efforts to the demands of the market.

On the other hand, for a firm facing burgeoning demand, the judgment
should be made whether this is likely to be a short-term fad or a more
permanent situation. You can see how easily a firm can permit itself to
become overextended in the buoyancy of booming business, only to see
the collapse of such business actually jeopardizing its viability.

When a firm is operating under extreme conditions of uncertainty,
forecasted and actual results should be carefully monitored and the
forecast adjusted upward or downward as indicated by empirical sales
data.

---

they should have lessened the inroads. But Adidas did not take aggressive
counteractions until its dominance had been severely breached.

WHAT CAN BE LEARNED?

This case provides learning experiences both from the success of Nike and
from the mistakes of Adidas.

The success did not come primarily from innovative strategic planning,
from recognizing opportunities that no one else had, or from plowing more
resources into the effort than hapless competitors were able to muster. The
key ingredient of Nike's success was *effective imitation*.

Of course, imitation must be judicious. A strategy to be imitated should
be the most effective approach; it should be historically successful. In the

case of the running-shoe industry, the long-time strategy of Adidas in offering many models, in associating its brand with major athletic events and athletes themselves, in constantly seeking product improvement—these could hardly have been improved on, and all running-shoe manufacturers followed the same strategy—only Nike did it better.

In the effort to be imitative, a firm, of course, still needs to develop its own identity. By imitation we do not mean a slavish effort to be identical. Only the successful policies, standards, and actions are imitated. There is still room to develop the distinctive image, the trademark or logo, and an organization and management ever alert to new opportunities.

Finally, we see in this case how fragile dominance and being first in the industry can be. No firm, leader or otherwise, can afford to rest on its laurels, to disregard a changing business clime and aggressive but smaller competitors. Adidas had as commanding a lead in this industry as IBM had in computers. But Adidas let its guard down, and its aggressiveness lagged at a critical point.

A front–runner tends more toward complacency in the situation we have seen here. A sharply rising industry demand is reassuring and lulling. Sales will be increasing sharply for the industry leader during such a time, and this is conducive to complacency. But such increasing sales may mask a declining market position, in which competitors are making major gains at the expense of the dominant firm. Eventually, the momentum shifts to one or more of the now significant competitors. The once dominant firm may not be able to regain its position. Success for one firm can come from the mistakes of another—not so much mistakes of commission as of omission— in which needed actions were not taken or, at least, not until too late.

The critical lapse of Adidas, faced with the growing strength of Nike and its American contemporaries, as well as the greatly increasing industry potential, suggests a need for environmental scanning, and a closer attuning to the industry environment and better sensors for demand and competitive factors. Alert executives should be able to detect nascent changes by encouraging systematic feedback from those closest to the market—sales representatives, dealers, and suppliers—by keeping abreast of latest trade journal statistics and commentaries, and by working with a management information system that provides competitive analyses and trend data of early changes in market position. But there must be a willingness to act on significant changes in industry conditions, and this is something that veteran firms have difficulty in doing: that is, in disassociating themselves from perspectives and practices of a different past.

Update

The jogging boom peaked around 1982. Although the popularity of fitness continued unabated, many people turned to other pursuits as either a substitute for running or a supplement to a reduced running regimen. With the decreased potential, competitors found themselves contesting furiously for a somewhat smaller pie. Adidas turned to more aggressive efforts with new models and heavier promotion, but competitors were also more aggressive.

The front-runner, Nike, also began to experience some difficulties by 1984. To keep its growth record intact, it had diversified into apparel and pushed its overseas efforts. And, by 1984, apparel accounted for 21 percent of U. S. revenues, whereas foreign sales were 18 percent of all sales. But profits were disappointing. Despite sales of $920 million, profits plummeted some 65 percent from 1983, partly due to $27 million in write-offs, mostly for running shoes dumped below cost. Furthermore, Nike had made the same mistake as Adidas a decade earlier: underestimating an opportunity. Nike was late into the fast-growing market for shoes worn for the aerobic dancing that was sweeping the country, fueled by best-selling books by Jane Fonda and others.

The moral seems to be: no one is immune to mistakes, and success gives no assurance of continued success.

For Thought and Discussion

1. Do you think Adidas could have successfully blunted the charge of Nike? Why or why not?
2. In what ways does the age and experience of a firm tend to induce myopia and resistance to change?
3. "The success of Nike was strictly fortuitous and had little to do with powerful strategic planning." Evaluate this statement.
4. Discuss the pros and cons of optimistic versus conservative sales forecasts for a hot new product.

Invitation to Role Play

1. As an Adidas executive, how would you propose to counter the inital thrusts at your industry dominance by Nike and other U. S. running-shoe manufacturers?
2. As an executive for a medium-size U. S. running-shoe manufacturer, you recognize that the long–overdue lessening of the popularity of running is beginning to take place. What strategic planning recommendations would you make now?

5

Du Pont's Corfam— Miscalculations Defeat Careful Planning

Technological breakthroughs rarely occur. But when one does, it can translate into heady sales and profits for the fortunate firm. Sometimes an innovation seems so destined for success that it can hardly be stymied—such was the fate of nylon. In the spring of 1963, researchers and executives of E. I. du Pont de Nemours & Company were excited that they had developed a product destined to be another nylon in success: Corfam.

Twenty-five years of technological research had gone into Corfam; this was to be bolstered by detailed production and marketing planning. Nothing was to be left to chance. And the unqualified earlier success of nylon had convinced the du Pont executives that Corfam deserved a full commitment— no half-way measures for this "breakthrough."

Corfam was developed to replace leather for shoe uppers. It had some happy advantages over leather, although one characteristic was of some concern: it would not stretch or conform to the foot as leather did. To determine public acceptance of this new material, du Pont had consumers test 15,000 pairs of shoes made from Corfam under typical wearing conditions. Interestingly, many were not even aware that they were not wearing leather shoes. About 8 percent did admit that the Corfam shoes were uncomfortable, but this compared with 3 percent who complained about the comfort of leather shoes and a sizable 24 percent who found fault with the comfort of another leather substitute, vinyl-coated plastic shoes. The researchers at du Pont accordingly breathed a sigh of relief. The comfort attributes of Corfam were deemed to be not serious.

Further grounds for optimism came from long-range economic studies that predicted a major leather shortage by 1982 with 30 percent of all shoes to be made from alternative materials by that time. Because most leather substitutes, primarily the vinyl-coated fabrics, had a serious flaw of impermeability (inability to "breathe"), the opportunity for Corfam seemed clear. And 30 of the 36 shoe manufacturers approached by Du Pont representatives prior to Corfam's introduction indicated they wanted Corfam.[1]

THE PROMISE

In October 1963, Corfam was officially unveiled at the Chicago National Shoe Fair. The first national consumer advertising appeared in newspapers of 20 target market cities on January 26, 1964.

Corfam as a leather substitute offered certain advantages over real leather, which the advertising was able to stress. It breathed and flexed easily, yet did not lose its shape. It weighed only one-third as much as leather and could be advertised as more comfortable. It was highly resistant to abrasion and was water repellant. Unlike leather, it did not have to be polished; merely wiping with a damp cloth renewed the shine.

The uniformity of Corfam as a synthetic material offered definite advantages to shoe manufacturers over natural leather. While it cost somewhat more ($1.05 to $1.35 per square foot at that time, versus $0.50 to $1.00 per square foot for leather), these costs could be partially offset by other savings. For example, there was less waste; the material could be used more efficiently than leather pieces, which are often uneven and oddly shaped. Being of uniform thickness meant that the material could be machine cut, thus doing away with the expensive hand cutting of leather.

Du Pont was unstinting in its introductory promotional efforts. On February 23, 1964, the "Du Pont Show of the Week" on NBC TV featured Corfam. The company went on to spend $2 million advertising Corfam that year.

Du Pont's marketing strategy centered on getting Corfam accepted as high fashion, high quality. *Sports Illustrated, The New Yorker, Harpers Bazaar, Vogue,* and *Esquire* were the media selected to convey this image. Tight control was maintained over distributors, and du Pont sold direct only to manufacturers of high-priced men's and women's shoes. With a promising

---

[1] "Another Nylon?" *Forbes,* October 15, 1964.

future forecast for Corfam, there was little difficulty in attracting such manufacturers.

Retail distribution was limited to selected prestige retailers who were required to promote Corfam shoes heavily. In return, the retailers benefited from the extensive national advertising campaign. Du Pont also sent merchandising representatives to these retail outlets to help with displays and in the training of salespeople to sell Corfam shoes. This training emphasis concerned better fitting of customers. This was of vital importance to Corfam-made shoes, because the material did not stretch as leather did; the person fitted incorrectly would always find Corfam shoes uncomfortable.

With a high-style image, massive promotional efforts, and initial manufacturer and dealer enthusiasm, it appeared that Corfam was on its way. In August 1964, du Pont opened a new plant in Old Hickory, Tennessee, solely for the purpose of marketing Corfam material. Then, in 1966, the synthetic shoe market received a strong shot in the arm. Because of booming leather exports in 1965, the United States was experiencing a leather shortage and higher leather prices. Demand for Corfam outstripped the ability of du Pont's production to meet it. Corfam and nylon continued to be talked about in the same breath by du Pont researchers and executives.

BACKGROUND

The growth of du Pont occurred in two stages. Prior to 1930, the company grew by acquisitions that moved it into a number of different markets. After that, growth was primarily by internal innovation; technological research was used to find highly saleable new products protected by patents that would give du Pont an entrenchment in new markets to enjoy a return on investment far superior to that of less creative companies. With such a policy, du Pont increased its sales from $649 million in 1946 to $3 billion in 1965. About $4 billion was invested in plant and equipment, and more than $3 billion was paid in dividends to shareholders during this period without incurring long-term debt.

Such products as neoprene, the first synthetic rubber, and nylon, the first and still most important of all its synthetic fibers, were innovations coming from du Pont's research. While the cost of such research—over $100 million per year—was high, with much of it offering no immediate payoff or even leading to a commercially acceptable product, the few outstanding successes were certainly sufficient justification for such research efforts.

In the late 1930s, du Pont's first fundamental research on porous polymeric film took place. Nothing was done to exploit this work until the 1950s, when the fabrics and finishes department began to look seriously at the market for shoe uppers. A special poromeric—a two-layered material made up of a web base and a porous coating on top—was developed for this purpose and named Corfam.

In appraising the market potential of Corfam, a relatively new mathematical modeling technique known as venture analysis was used. Inputs for the model came from historical data of the shoe and leather industry, experimental data on costs of the pilot plant's operating capability, market testing for serviceability and perceived value on the part of distributors and consumers, and the judgments of experts in the shoe and chemical industries. The mathematical model predicted that a strong demand would result from a quality product unlike anything the public had ever known. Furthermore, the model predicted there would be an inadequate supply of leather for up to 20 years ahead. Provided that the assumptions put into the model were reasonably correct, the future appeared bright.

To solve cracking, softening, and hardening problems, du Pont tested Corfam shoes within the company. Under close du Pont supervision, top shoe manufacturers were contracted to produce small lots of shoes. These were then distributed to du Pont employees for the purpose of spotting any flaws in the material. After correcting problems resulting from wear (cracking, softening, and hardening), more than 15,000 pairs were given consumers use-testing. Corfam was now ready for the market.

PROBLEMS

The leather industry, of course, could be expected to try to counter the incursions of Corfam. After all, it was a direct substitute for leather. The trade association of the industry, Leather Industries of American (LIA), increased its advertising twofold after Corfam hit the market. Such slogans were used as, "Naturally you prefer leather; that's why they're trying to imitate it." The connotation was clear: the leather industry wanted to portray Corfam as a cheap substitute. LIA went as far as adding this little message at the end of every advertisement: "Important! Make sure you get what you pay for."

During 1965, the Old Hickory plant struggled with the process, and technical procedures resulted in the product being changed to improve it. Sales reached 10 million sq ft. But start-up difficulties, because of the complexity of the process, were resulting in low yields and high costs. Still, the quality control program was adhered to rigidly, and substandard material was destroyed rather than sold. Toward the end of the year, production problems began to ease.

In 1966, some 20 million sq ft were produced, and there was considerable optimism as losses decreased substantially from those of 1965. Production costs were being decreased and market demand remained high.

However, the market began demanding more attractive finishes in greater variety, so the cost of finishing increased significantly over forecasts. Furthermore, the leather market was experiencing fluctuating prices, so shoe manufacturers were alternately hot and cold toward substitute materials.

Corfam was also being plagued by several other problems regarding consumer acceptability of the material. The comfort question was being raised more often than earlier surveys had indicated. Despite the insistence of du Pont technicians that Corfam was more porous than leather and breathed easier, many wearers complained that the shoes felt hot. And, because this material would not acquire a permanent stretch as leather did, wearers complained of the tight fit despite prolonged wear. Du Pont suggested as a solution that consumers purchase a slightly larger size. But this idea met the irrational psychological fact that few people wanted to admit having bigger feet.

Other influences were also at work. An increasing number of shoes was being imported to the United States. European shoes, especially women's, became popular as a result of their elegant materials and workmanship and their high style. Because of lower material and production costs, these foreign-made leather shoes were priced below those made of Corfam.

Vinyl-coated fabrics were also finding spectacular growth as shoe upper materials. These plastic materials, widely used for automotive and office upholstery because of a leather-like appearance, had sales of about 30 million pairs per year prior to the introduction of Corfam. Producers of vinyl-coated fabrics could offer a wide variety of colors, embossments, and other finishes at about half the retail price of Corfam. By the beginning of 1967, such shoes were selling at the rate of more than 100 million pairs a year and still increasing. In 1967, Georgia-Bonded Fibers, General Tire and Rubber Company, B.F. Goodrich, Union Carbide, Armstrong Cork, Celanese, and 3M all entered the synthetic market to provide Corfam with additional competition.

Despite the initial success of Corfam in the United States, efforts to market Corfam in Europe were not successful. At first, production was so limited that the strong U.S. demand necessitated limiting sales to domestic consumption. At last, in December 1967, du Pont announced a concerted effort to tap the European market. In Europe, however, high-priced shoes made up a much lower percentage of the total market. And du Pont was not able to persuade foreign shoe manufacturers to offer Corfam shoes in any but the highest price lines, thus greatly limiting volume potential. By the time Corfam was ready for the European market, two competitive materials, clarino and ortix, were already available in lower-priced shoe lines. Furthermore, Corfam, in going overseas, had to absorb various tariffs (22.2 percent for example, in the United Kingdom).[2] European consumers steadfastly showed preference for softer materials and not for the firmness characteristic of Corfam.

STILL, PROMISE

Throughout 1966 and 1967, efforts were made to increase production efficiency, enlarge the capability of the original plant, and generate sufficient production economies to reduce prices. Leather prices began firming, and, although no big price reductions were made for Corfam, orders began accelerating. But the plant, in trying to keep up with demand, experienced production difficulties and fell behind the planned production level until late in 1967. About 24 million sq ft were shipped in 1967, and at the end of the year the backlog of unshipped business totaled over 10 million square feet. However, excessive expenses involved in adapting the plant to higher production levels resulted in losses that exceeded those of 1966.

For 1968, the outlook appeared brighter. Demand continued strong and production problems had been solved so that the backlog of orders could be handled without serious delay. Operating costs were improving also, raising expectations that the corner had been turned. Sales reached 35 million sq ft in 1968, and prices were dropped to an average of a little under $0.80/sq ft. Although the operation was still not realizing profits, losses had fallen significantly.

However, instead of an indication of better things to come, 1968 turned out to be the year of highest production and sales, and demand thereafter faltered. Several adverse factors were becoming apparent. First, the leather industry had responded to the Corfam threat to their business and was producing and heavily promoting very soft, glovelike leather particularly appropriate for the casual dress becoming popular at the time. Leather prices were softening, and the price disadvantage of Corfam was becoming greater. Imports continued to increase, and vinyl shoes were gaining larger market shares. The result was that Corfam's sales declined almost 25 percent in 1969.

In October 1970, du Pont introduced Corfam II as a lower-cost porometric, as well as one having certain improved characteristics. Expectations were that the more competitive prices, which could now be offered, would rejuvenate demand for Corfam. But such was not to be.

The synthetic market had ceased to grow. In addition, Japan had entered the market with a good quality, inexpensive material to provide still more competition for American manufacturers. Still worse, vinyls were

---

[2] "Du Pont Stubs Its Toe," *Dun's Review*, June 1967, p. 61.

becoming available at one-third to one-fifth less than synthetics, and vinyls were considered high style, making them the ideal choice of many customers.

ABANDONMENT

On April 14, 1971, after 7 years of heavy losses estimated to range from $80 to $100 million, President Charles B. McCoy announced to shareholders that du Pont was abandoning Corfam. A key problem with Corfam had been its inflexible production process that could respond to neither leather price cuts nor style changes. With sales not living up to expectations, indeed, with the sales trend sharply downward and with foreign imports pinching the U. S. market, this decision was made.

The company ceased Corfam production and order-taking in June of 1971. Du Pont sold its remaining Corfam supplies for $6 million to a Boston leather brokerage firm, George Newman & Company, and later sold its technology and production equipment for the Old Hickory, Tennessee, plant to Polimex-Sekop, a Polish government-owned manufacturing operation. This sale included selling rights under du Pont patents throughout the world, excluding North America and Japan. Polimex-Sekop expected to continue production of Corfam for the Polish market. Most of the people involved with the poromeric venture, totaling about 1000 at the peak, were reassigned within du Pont.

WHAT WENT WRONG?

The predictions of the venture analysis model described earlier at the preintroductory stage of Corfam can be compared with the actual situation that existed in 1968, 5 years after Corfam was introduced. The comparisons of actual with predicted results showed that:

The volume of material sold was approximately that originally predicted (35 versus 37 million sq ft).

The average price obtained for the material was approximately as predicted.

Costs of making the impregnated fibrous web and of coating it were approximately as predicted.

A more expensive woven interlayer had to be used in some of the production, which added between 10 and 15 percent to total mill cost.

Costs of finishing due to the variety of effects needed (to meet fashion needs) added 15 to 25 percent to mill cost.

Technical expenses were about double the forecasted figure for the fifth year.

INFORMATION SIDELIGHT

CONTINGENCY PLANS

Planning involves resource deployment through the use of budgets. Resources to be deployed include both manpower and facilities: the number of people to be involved in the particular aspect of the operation and the amount of money and kind of facilities to be required to meet planned goals and expectations. Such resource deployment depends on certain assumptions made about both the external and internal environment. When plans are made for major projects, such as Corfam, and resources committed according to long-range predictions of as much as 5 years and more, the success of the commitment depends greatly on the accuracy of the assumptions that are made. When, as events unfold, it can be seen that certain assumptions were either overly optimistic or overly pessimistic, then plans and resource deployments need to be revised—otherwise breakeven points (see Chapter 2) may be unrealistic or unattainable.

Contingency plans are well used when dealing with a new product or project and an uncertain future. Different plans may thereby be developed for the different contingencies or sets of conditions that may occur. For example, Plan A may assume a certain level of acceptance, and a particular volume and cost of production; Plan B may be developed for better-than-expected circumstances; Plan C may be ready to put to use if early results are discouraging. When such plans are drawn up in advance, a firm is better able to cope with varied outcomes and can either marshall additional resources or cut back to more realistic expectations.

Du Pont could have made better use of contingency planning for different levels of foreign competition, reactions of leather manufacturers, and production quantity and cost levels. Somewhat lesser expectations, more competitive prices, perhaps a lower breakeven point because of reduced resource deployment—these might have brought Corfam to profitability, albeit with a potential far less than originally dreamed.

Marketing expense was about twice the forecasted figure, partly reflecting heavy competitive conditions and the inability to establish Corfam strongly in the market.[3]

---

[3] W.D. Lawson, "History and Analysis of Corfam," unpublished in-house report for du Pont Company, November 1972.

Certainly one of the reasons for the demise of Corfam was the inability to lower production costs enough to penetrate a wider market. Eighty percent of the total shoe market at the time of Corfam's inception was in the $11.00 and below price. Corfam was aimed at the $15.00 to $20.00 and up market, which comprised only 10 percent of the total shoe market.

WHAT CAN BE LEARNED?

Du Pont's experience with Corfam illustrates the difficulty of correctly forecasting sales and profits in the distant future. Such forecasting is especially tenuous when the product is significantly different. Despite the use of sophisticated mathematical models, there were enough misjudged and unexpected factors to ruin the predictions. Does this not suggest that the prudent firm should keep itself flexible with contingency plans and prompt budgetary revisions so that it can roll with the punches, gear its operations up or down, shift strategies to adapt to current conditions perhaps unforeseen several years before? We must recognize the near-impossibility of correctly predicting all the factors that may affect sales and profit performance.

Complicating the forecasting problems of du Pont were the vigorous reactions of the leather industry. Its advertising budget was greatly increased, and denigrating innuendos portrayed Corfam as a cheap substitute. The leather industry introduced new, softer, and less expensive leathers well geared to the emerging popularity for casual dress. Still, the reactions of the leather industry should not have been unexpected. Generally, industries of low growth—and this described the shoe industry—tend to react very aggressively to the threat of competitive inroads. With the total pie or market not expanding much, a powerful newcomer will have to take business from existing firms, which can be expected to fight the intrusion desperately.

Production and engineering problems—and their concomitant, quality control problems—are likely to persist with a radically new technology. It takes time to correct problems and smooth out inefficiencies in the production process, although, certainly, one could have hardly expected such problems to continue for years as they did with Corfam. But the situation is not unlike that faced by automobile manufacturers when they bring out a new and significantly different model: many defects have to be corrected, and this can take months and even several years before customers have reasonable assurance of a trouble-free car (some would say that such an achievement is even beyond the reach of U.S. car makers).

Sometimes a firm finds that a long-planned and practiced strategy is just not working out; it must be repudiated and a different strategy imposed, or else the product must be dropped. Du Pont, of course, opted for the latter—after years of losses. But different markets and different strategies might have been attempted and perhaps success could have come. For example, Corfam might have been withdrawn from most of the shoe market, especially high-fashion women's shoes, and instead been directed to work shoes, where the particular product features might have been more advantageous. It might have been introduced to the luggage market, to handbags, to furniture covering. We certainly have no assurance that one or more of these strategies would have been successful, given the information available long after the fact, but at least there are possibilities that might have been considered and might have made Corfam viable. No firm should be so rigid in its planned strategy that alternatives that could prove far more profitable than original plans and polices cannot be explored.

UPDATE

In 1981, Corfam was far from dead. Poland, which bought the process from du Pont, was not only selling Corfam, or PolCorfam as they call it, in its own country, but was exporting it to the U.S. for such shoe makers as Edison Brothers and Brown Shoe (whose shoes are stamped "manmade material"). The price of leather, $0.50 to $0.60 a foot when Corfam was first introduced, was $1.50 a foot and rising, thereby making Corfam a more attractive alternative. The 1980-1981 selling season was particularly strong for Corfam: alligator and lizardlike products were fashionable, with real alligator skin selling for $1.38 a foot. Corfam provided a realistic and much less expensive imitation. Although total production figures for PolCorfam are impossible to obtain, its versatility was such that it was even being sold to U.S. semiconductor firms who use it to make silicon wafers.[4] Could du Pont have made an even bigger mistake in selling Corfam?

For Thought And Discussion

1. With the benefit of hindsight, do you think du Pont should have ever introduced Corfam? Why or why not?
2. Discuss the pros and cons of conservative versus optimistic planning forecasts.
3. The advantages of Corfam over leather were that Corfam was more scuff-resistant, water-repellant, and durable. However, many people did not see the advantages as worth the additional cost in dress shoes. Do you think du Pont should have aimed its efforts at another market? How successful would you estimate this would have been?

[4] Maurice Barnfather, "Polish Joke," *Forbes*, March 2, 1981, p. 46.

4. In view of the success of Poland with Corfam, do you think du Pont should have sold the process to Poland? Evaluate as many facets of this decision as you can.

Invitation To Role Play

Assume the role of the du Pont executive responsible for recommending to the executive committee the long-range planning strategy for Corfam in the spring of 1963. What would you propose? Be specific and defend your rationale using the facts known about Corfam up to that time.

PART Two

ORGANIZATIONAL MISHANDLING

6

Korvette—An Organization Must Change With Growth

An often sad commentary of small ventures becoming successful and growing into large enterprises is that the founder is unable to cope with the changes that size makes. The talents for successfully founding a business and shepherding its early growth to beyond the ranks of small firms unfortunately are not the same as required for coping with the complexities of a now large organization. Some such founders—perhaps with the help of their friendly bankers—recognize their limitations and bring new blood into their operation—persons who are skilled at understanding and administering large organizations. But this does not always happen. Sometimes founders and their immediate associates are unable to recognize this perversity of their talents and try to run the increasingly complex organization with the same management styles as when it was much smaller. The results are often disastrous, and the rosy dreams, the golden future, become badly tainted. Alas, this was the fate of the once-acclaimed Korvette's.

The Korvette chain of discount department stores represented the classic American success story. Its rise was the story of one man, Eugene Ferkauf, who started in 1948 with a tiny luggage shop one flight up on East 46th Street in Manhattan. With a simple strategy of undercutting department stores 10 to 40 percent on hard goods, his corporation grew to over $700 million in sales by 1965. In the process, he revolutionized merchandising and profoundly altered the policies of conventional retailers. Malcolm McNair, Harvard's famous professor of retailing, rated Ferkauf as one of the

six greatest merchants in the United States, alongside men like Frank
Woolworth, John Wanamaker, and J. C. Penney. But, somehow, the heady
success story began to change, dramatically, drastically, and irrevocably.
And a few years later, McNair was to retract his assessment of Ferkauf.

THE DREAM THAT WAS KORVETTE

Gene Ferkauf began his retail career in his father's luggage store. However,
he was visionary and eager to grasp opportunities as he saw them. He
disagreed with his father's traditional philosophy of merchandising, which
was to sell goods at list or manufacturers' suggested prices and reap the
rewards of good profit per unit sale. He dreamed that maybe only a small
profit per unit sale might yield the greater total profit, *if sales volume could
be increased greatly by so doing*. Accordingly, Ferkauf struck out on his
own, opening a luggage shop in a second-floor loft on an offstreet of
Manhattan.

The name for the business he chose rather arbitrarily: E. J. Korvette.
(The E stands for Eugene, his first name; the J for Joseph Blumenberg, his
friend who became treasurer of the company; and "Korvette" was the name
of a Canadian submarine chaser in the first world war that was spelled with
a C but was changed to a K.) Although the base stock was luggage, as an
accommodation to his customers Ferkauf began selling appliances at just
about cost. Soon he branched out into fountain pens and photography
equipment. In the early days, Ferkauf sold all his appliances for $10 over the
wholesale cost: "If a guy came in to buy stereo equipment that cost the firm
$1000, we would just mark it up ten bucks and he took it home."[1]

And people began lining up on the sidewalk outside and down the block
to get into the store to purchase such bargains. Ferkauf found he was making
money with the appliances and was operating at a million–dollar–a–year
rate. By the end of 1951, he had moved his store to street level and opened
a branch in Westchester. Sales climbed to $9,700,000 in 1953.

Gene Ferkauf was a quiet man; he shunned the public limelight. At
stockholder meetings he liked to sit mute. He even absented himself from a
reception celebrating the new quarters for Yeshiva University's Ferkauf
School of Social Work. He believed in casual clothes, had a contempt for
formality, and spurned an office and other executive amenities. But he
believed in friends.

In the early 1950s, a group of 38 men, almost all Brooklyn high school
pals of Ferkauf, ran the company. They were called the "open-shirt crowd"
or "the boys." Korvette's management operated from a dingy old building

[1] "Korvettes Tries for a Little Chic," *Business Week*, May 12, 1973, p. 124.

with Ferkauf presiding at a beat-up desk in one corner. And the company grew, incredibly, from $55 million to $750 million in sales within 10 years, thereby becoming one of the fastest growing companies in the history of retailing. In the early 1960s, the company was opening huge new stores on the average of one every 7 weeks.

In the 1950s and early 1960s, Korvette led the discount revolution that was sweeping the country. The American consumer relished the idea of low prices, of items priced up to 40 percent less than department stores' prices. Korvette profits and stock seemed headed for the stratosphere. And the business philosophy was so simple: if you have sales volume, even with a low markup, you are going to make a profit. To do so, however, Korvette and the other discounters operated with austere surroundings. Stores and fixtures were simple; even pipe racks were used for hanging garments; no services such as credit or delivery were offered at first; and self-service was the rule to cut down on salary expense. Just as important as paring costs, lean stocks of merchandise were offered—a narrow selection of best-selling sizes and styles—to maximize merchandise turnover and thereby increase the return on investment.

As the company persisted in its discounting policies, it came up against state fair-trade laws, which permitted manufacturers to set the minimum prices for which their goods could be sold by retailers. Some of the major manufacturers, including General Electric, wanted to maintain an image of quality and to protect their regular dealers from price cutting. Korvette, by selling below the fair-traded prices, was vulnerable to lawsuits by such manufacturers. At the time the company went public in 1965, 34 fair-trade lawsuits were pending against it. This was not as bad as might seem, however. Enforcement of fair trade rested with the manufacturer who wanted it for his products. And in 1956, Korvette received a legal boost when a New York court threw out a suit brought by the Parker Pen Company on the grounds that Parker was not sufficiently enforcing its fair-trade program. Many manufacturers were finding enforcement difficult amid the spate of discount stores. In addition, the lack of severe penalties prescribed by the courts for violating fair trade (in many cases, only court costs were levied against the offending discounter) further limited its effectiveness as a deterrent to price cutting by Korvette and others. Actually, fair trade and list prices aided discount stores, because customers could readily see the base price from which the item was discounted.

In his growth policies, Ferkauf had the theory that it was better to open a cluster of stores in a metropolitan area, to saturate an area, rather than spread out more thinly nationwide. Where 3 or 4 or more stores were located in one metropolitan area, advertising costs could be shared, as could warehousing, servicing, and certain other expenses. Customer acceptance could be gained more quickly from the massive presentation of stores and promotional efforts. Following this strategy, by 1966 Korvette had 10 stores in the New York metropolitan area, 5 in Philadelphia, 4 in Baltimore-Washington. Between 1963 and 1965, 5 large stores had been opened in metropolitan Chicago, 3 in Detroit, and 2 in St. Louis.

But, by 1966, the company was in trouble, and could not handle its growth nor digest its accumulated size.

TROUBLE !

In the 4 years between 1962 and 1966, store space and sales volume more than tripled. But "genius though Ferkauf might be at minding the store, he had neither the temperament nor the desire to mind the office."[2] When Korvette had no more than a dozen outlets, Ferkauf, on "foot patrol," could give on-the-scene guidance. But his organization failed to provide any serious substitute for the diminishing face-to-face supervision of Ferkauf and his home-office executives. The constant addition of stores placed enormous pressures on management. There were enough work and problems in running existing operations without bringing on additional operations at the same time. Buyers who were busy filling the needs of the old stores somehow had to provide for the new stores as well. Advancement, of course, was fast. Section and department managers moved quickly into jobs as store managers and less-experienced people took their places. But there was little time either to develop top-notch management people or to be selective in screening for the best.

Along with the sheer number of stores opening, the doubling and tripling of floor space, and merchandise and management problems, several other factors were destined to create trouble for Korvette by the mid-1960s. One was the geographical aspect of the expansion. As long as new stores were added in the East, and particularly around metropolitan New York City, the close contact of stores with Ferkauf and the home office could still be maintained. However, expansion to Detroit, Chicago, and St. Louis practically negated this close personal guidance and control.

There were difficulties in lining up enough good management people to run these distant operations, and profits outside New York generally ran behind. But Ferkauf had the dream of becoming a national company, and his cluster philosophy seemed well-geared to tapping other metropolitan markets. However sound it was in theory, there were drawbacks. Invading a

[2] Lawrence A. Mayer, "How Confusion Caught Up with Korvette," *Fortune*, February 1966, p. 154.

market area with not just one, but several stores, induced the strongest kind of competitive reaction from established merchants. In Chicago, for example, Sears and other retailers reacted vigorously to Korvette's entry with heavy price reductions and promotional efforts. This blunted the efforts of Korvette to gain solid market position.

Further strains were caused by a switch to soft goods and fashion merchandise. Ferkauf, as most discounters, started out discounting so-called hard goods: refrigerators, washing machines, TV and stereo equipment, small appliances such as irons, toasters, blenders, etc., and photo equipment. But the route to a general-merchandising operation brought Korvette into clothing and other soft goods, which offered higher profit margins. However, the risks of markdowns and unsalable inventories resulting from fashion and seasonal obsolescence were high, and the demands on management were more than for the more staple hard goods. Eventually, Korvette's inability to handle the soft goods and fashion end of the business profitably led to Korvette merging with Spartans Industries, an apparel conglomerate that specialized both in manufacturing and retailing low-end fashion goods.

Food merchandising also harassed Ferkauf. In 1961, Korvette had 2 supermarkets. Then the firm started adding supermarkets, winding up with 22, 6 of them in Detroit and Chicago, unfamiliar territory to an Eastern retailer inexperienced in the local purchase of meat and produce in these areas. There was good rationale for expanding with supermarkets: consumers generally stock up with groceries weekly; by building supermarkets adjacent to discount stores, heavier and more constant customer traffic can be realized.

Unfortunately, the basic tenet of discount merchandising, high turnover, was disregarded with the food operation. These food stores were opened without warehousing, which meant they had to stock more goods if out-of-stocks were to be minimized. But a heavy inventory was not compatible with lean fast-moving stocks and high turnover. Furthermore, competition in the supermarket industry was increasing about this time, and losses from this operation reached $12 million by 1964. Ferkauf was forced to turn to the outside for help.

Hill Supermarkets, a 42-store chain on Long Island, seemed the answer. Hilliard J. Coan, Hill's chief executive, ran a profitable operation with net of $1,036,000 from sales of $119 million in 1964. He also had a warehouse on Long Island big enough to supply both Hill's needs and Korvette's in the East. Ferkauf persuaded Hill to merge with Korvette, and Coan became the executive in charge of the $200 million food division. Meanwhile, the food stores in Chicago and Detroit were leased to a local operator.

But the merger with Hill was not to solve the food problems. Shop-Rite,

SPAN OF CONTROL

One of the major principles of organizational theory is that the span of control—the number of subordinates reporting to an executive—should be small enough so that they can be properly supervised. A number of factors can affect this optimum span. Obviously, the more experienced and able the executive is, as well as the subordinates, and the more stable and similar the operations are, the wider the span that can be adequately handled. But there is a limit to how many subordinates one person can supervise effectively. Many experts have studied organizations and concluded that higher management can supervise from 4 to 8 subordinates, whereas the span can reach 8 to 15 or occasionally more at the lower management levels.

Intimately related to span of control is another aspect of organizational theory: levels of supervision. A span that is too wide can be narrowed by adding one or more supervisory levels, as shown below:

Wide span, one supervisory level:

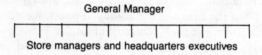

General Manager

Store managers and headquarters executives

Moderate span, two supervisory levels:

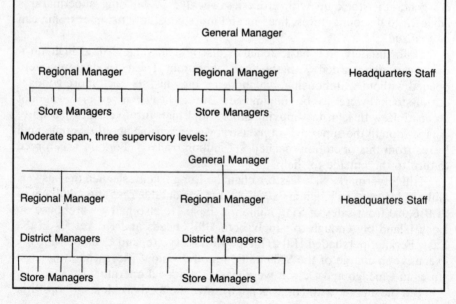

General Manager

Regional Manager   Regional Manager   Headquarters Staff

Store Managers   Store Managers

Moderate span, three supervisory levels:

General Manager

Regional Manager   Regional Manager   Headquarters Staff

District Managers   District Managers

Store Managers   Store Managers

> As you can see, the narrower the span—that is, the fewer subordinates supervised by or reporting to one executive—the more supervisory levels and the more executives (and their secretaries and staffs) are required.
>
> Although a span can be unmanageably wide, as Ferkauf's was, there are some drawbacks to establishing additional levels of supervision. The wide span is advantageous in terms of cost, because fewer executives and their staffs must be paid. Also, the more executive levels involved, the more difficult and the less accurate becomes communication up and down the levels. Decision-making will be less flexible and slower because more executives will be involved. Morale may also be adversely affected in an organization with many levels, simply because the senior executives are further removed and have less direct personal influence with rank and file employees and lower-level executives. Therefore, span of control decisions need to be balanced with the desirability of keeping supervisory levels to a minimum.

an efficient supermarket chain, began aggressively promoting with low prices on Long Island. This drastically affected Hill's profits at the very time it was trying to assume operation of the Korvette food division. In 1968, after several years of frustration, quits was finally called on the food operation, and Hill-Korvette Supermarket Division was sold for cash.

The final problem plaguing Korvette was its furniture department. This was a leased operation by the H. L. Klion Company. However, the lessee was undercapitalized, and serious management and inventory problems were emerging by 1963, the time when Korvette was undertaking its greatest expansion efforts. Inventory controls, accounting, and deliveries broke down, and the furniture departments in the newer stores never made it into the black. To add to the problems, two strikes hit Klion in 1964, and nondeliveries caused customers to cancel $2 million worth of orders. With the strikes finally settled, much of this merchandise in specially ordered colors and fabrics—odds and ends for which little demand existed—jammed stores and had to be heavily marked down.

Although the furniture operation was leased, customers were unaware of this. So Korvette bore the brunt of complaints about service and delivery, and its reputation was being badly affected. In 1964-1965, Klion lost $2,667,000 and was approaching bankruptcy. Supplying some financial help was not enough, and Korvette was forced to take over the Klion Company and underwrite its heavy losses to try to preserve the Korvette reputation. Along with Klion, Korvette acquired the Federal Carpet Company, a lessee that had a profit of $700,000 in 1964 and that shared space with Klion in the furniture department. Federal Carpet executives were given responsibility for running the combined carpet-and-furniture division. But it continued to be a profit drain, and the confidence of customers was slow to be rebuilt.

There was another, smaller, ill-fated venture about this time. The success of Avon in selling cosmetics door-to-door prompted Korvette to try something similar. However, losses were so heavy that this operation was soon discontinued.

1966, THE YEAR OF DECISION

The strains in the Korvette operation were beginning to show clearly by 1966. Although net sales for the last 6 months of fiscal 1965 were more than 10 percent ahead of the same period the year before, earnings declined from $16,634,000 to $13,877,000. Then, for the generally unprofitable first quarter of the year, Korvette saw the deficit grow from $1,124,000 in 1965 to $4,452,000 in 1966. There were other indications of trouble as well. Inventory turnover was down by one-third from 1961. Sales per square foot had also fallen by one-third. And Korvette stock had dropped from a peak of 50½ in May 1965 to 13 by the beginning of 1966.

The substantial losses experienced in the furniture division contributed to this worsening picture; food still was not doing well. And now, even the main-store departments of the older stores were experiencing declining sales. In 1966, Hilliard Coan, the former president of Hill Supermarkets, became president of Korvette. He tried to tighten the loose organization by clarifying executive duties and making work loads more equitable. Additional experienced merchandising executives were hired, and the company moved to install its own data processing. A new warehouse to serve as the first distribution center was built in northern New Jersey, thereby being rather centrally located for the Eastern stores. This permitted the company to buy more expeditiously, supply store needs for certain items more quickly, and also eliminate some wholesalers.

At last the expansion policies were being toned down. Only three new stores were opened in 1966; attention was turned to the existing stores and efforts made to increase their customer traffic.

Rather unexpectedly, on September 25, 1966, Korvette merged with Spartans Industries. Charles Bassine, the chairman of Spartans, had his own chain of Spartans discount stores and had also acquired the Atlantic Thrift chain of 46 discount stores. Spartans had only $375 million in sales compared with $719 million for Korvette in 1965. However, Ferkauf was eased out of active management, left Spartans in 1968 to develop his own boutique chain, and faded from the limelight. Bassine turned his attention to developing tighter controls for the Korvette operations: controls over merchandise, costs, markups, markdowns, shrinkage, and expense—the aim, a much tighter ship.

AFTER 1966

Despite the stronger management that Spartans provided, the Korvette operation could not regain its previous strength. An attempt was made to raise Korvette's profit margins by upgrading the merchandise with higher-priced lines, but this served to drive away many of the old bargain-hunting customers. Although sales of Spartans Industries were now over $1 billion, there was a continual fight to generate profits. Bassine tried to unload the unprofitable parts of his operation, such as the supermarkets, but profits were little improved. Then, in 1970, the apparel business was hit by a flood of cheaper foreign imports, and a recession hurt retail sales. In 1970, the Korvette division lost $3.7 million.

In 1971, a "third rebirth"[3] took place, as Spartans merged with Arlen Realty & Development Corporation, a big real estate developer. Arlen was run by Bassine's son-in-law and had participated in the building of some of the Korvette stores in the late 1950s and 1960s. Besides bringing younger blood into the top management, the merger enabled Korvettes (an "s" was added at this time, and the "E. J." dropped) to cut its tax bill with the help of Arlen's big tax shelter, property depreciation.[4]

POSTMORTEM

Both internal and external factors contributed to the faltering of Korvette. Competition was changing, becoming keener than it had been. Not only Korvette, but many other early discounters were also faltering or had succumbed. Internal factors undermined the firm and made it less able to cope effectively with the strong competition.

Internal Factors

Vigorous expansion creates problems and stresses for any organization. In Korvette's case, the expansion came from a rather small base of 9 stores; suddenly there were 25. Supervision and control, which formerly could be handled on a face-to-face basis, moved away from this possibility. The span of control widened beyond what one person could adequately handle.

Until the middle 1960s, Korvette did not have the kind of controls

[3] "Will the Store Be Minded?" *Forbes*, August 15, 1971, p. 44.
[4] "Korvettes Tries for a Little Chic," *Business Week*, May 12, 1973, p. 124, 125.

INFORMATION SIDELIGHT

THE DEADLY PARALLEL

As an enterprise becomes larger and, if a retail enterprise, opens more and more stores, a particularly effective organizational arrangement is one in which operating units of comparable characteristics can be established. Sales, expenses, and profits can then be readily compared; strong as well as weak performances can be identified, and action taken accordingly. Besides providing control and performance evaluation, the deadly parallel fosters intrafirm competition, and this can stimulate best efforts. For the deadly parallel to be used effectively, the operating units must be as equal as possible in sales potential. But this is not difficult to achieve with retail units, as departments and stores can be divided into various sales volume categories—often designated as A, B, and C stores—and operating results of stores within the same volume category can then be compared. Although the deadly parallel is particularly effective for chain-store organizations, it can also be used with sales territories and certain other operating units where sales and applicable expenses can be allocated so that profit contributions can be directly measured and compared with similar units.

---

needed for the size of operation it was attaining—controls coming from well-defined policies, objectives, and plans for the various aspects of the operation, such as for markups, markdowns, merchandise turnover, and the various categories of expenses. The business was run rather informally, with little advance planning and coordination at a time when size precluded the effectiveness of such informality. The growth was too fast; there was not sufficient time for digestion and for developing sound policies for coping with such growth.

Trained executives were lacking at all levels, from home-office buyers and store managers to department and section managers. Because promotion was necessarily fast, ill-trained and marginal people were thrust into responsible positions; bodies had to be found to fill certain spots. There was no management development, and no organized executive training. Korvette could have gone outside the organization to fill important slots, and began doing so in the 1960s for some of the top home-office positions. But at middle– and lower–management levels, discount stores often lacked the prestige to attract top-notch people. And then, cronyism was traditional and rampant in the organization, and this poses some serious flaws as the following "Information Sidelight" discusses.

Part of the problem in recruiting top-notch people stemmed from the organizational policies of Ferkauf. Management was highly centralized; the home office dictated all merchandising and other policies, and store managers and other store executives were given little authority. But, if rapid growth was to be achieved in an absence of tight controls, decentralization giving more authority and responsibility to store executives would have helped. This would have meant both higher-paid and more carefully selected store executives.

There is contagion in expanding rapidly, in opening massive new stores every 6 or 7 weeks—everyone from top management on down becomes preoccupied with the new units coming on the scene. Older, established stores tended to be overlooked until they were faltering badly, at which point effective solutions were sometimes no longer possible. Furthermore, while communications poured from the home office, good communications upward from the stores were lacking, because store executives carried little authority; no procedures had been established for systematically providing such feedback. Consequently, worsening situations went unnoticed.

The cluster strategy of entering metropolitan areas with a number of stores as simultaneously as possible was splendid in theory as a means of creating massive promotional impact while apportioning advertising expenditures among a number of stores. However, as we noted earlier, this sometimes aroused severe competitive reactions, and at some point the cluster concept could be carried too far: new Korvette stores began to hurt older Korvette stores in the same metropolitan area.

A final internal troublesome factor was the image of Korvette. At first, in the golden days of the chain, the discount image—bare-bones prices—had great customer appeal. However, as Korvette expanded with more stores and into apparel and fashion items, Ferkauf's conception of the company changed. He no longer saw it as a discount store, but rather as a promotional department store. In line with this, he opened a store on Fifth Avenue in Manhattan, only a few blocks from some of the most fashionable stores in the world, such as Bonwit Teller and Lord & Taylor. A massive chandelier was placed in the lobby, indicative of the disavowal with the "sordid discount" image. "We have Cadillacs that pull up to the store, and women get out and enjoy, as everybody enjoys, being able to buy something a little bit cheaper than they normally would. We have some of the most famous people come in to our stores."[5]

But, as this upgrading of merchandise proceeded, markups rose from

[5] Per an interview with Murray Beilenson, secretary and general merchandise manager, as reported in Robert Drew-Bear, *Mass Merchandise: Revolution and Evolution* (New York: Fairchild Publications, 1970), p. 124.

INFORMATION SIDELIGHT

PROS AND CONS OF CRONYISM AND NEPOTISM

Cronyism is the selection of friends for high executive positions. In general, cronyism offers these advantages to an organization:

1. The loyalty of these executives is fairly ensured, because they are already close friends and presumed confidants of the chief executive.
2. Communication and a close working relationship is enhanced.
3. Strengths and weaknesses of each individual should be known factors and not come as unpleasant surprises, as they can when outsiders are brought into the organization.

The major drawbacks of selecting most or all of the top cadre of executives from close personal friends are:

1. Such a small body of executive candidates may bring very limited expertise and abilities to the organization.
2. A narrow organizational perspective is promulgated, because most of these people will have come from similar backgrounds and probably have similar views on most matters.
3. Morale and motivation of the rest of the organization may be atrophied because of the perceived lack of advancement opportunities.
4. Because people have been selected more on a basis of friendship than ability, there may be a real reluctance to pressure them for performance and to discipline or discharge those who are performing poorly.
5. As a result of the above factors, such organizations tend toward complacency and conservatism.

On balance, the drawbacks and dangers of cronyism far outweigh the benefits.

Related to cronyism, and a phenomenon of many small and medium-sized family-owned business, is the reserving of important managerial positions for family members and relatives: this, of course, is nepotism. The pros and cons are similar to those of cronyism.

less than 8 percent in 1950 to some 33 percent in 1965. The problem was, if Korvette was to escape their discount image, how could they do so and yet keep their old customers? Korvette was becoming similar to the basement operations of department stores—that is, carrying standard markup items supplemented by loss leaders used for promotional purposes. As merchandise was upgraded, as new stores were more elaborate, as services such as credit began to be offered, higher overhead was the result. The uniqueness, the particular customer segment that had been so effectively appealed to, began to be lost. Gradually, Korvette was moving toward the expense structure of traditional retailers, but without quite the same level of expertise that department and specialty stores possessed in the way of quality and fashion merchandising.

External Factors

With Korvette leading the way, the onslaught of discounters onto the conventional retail scene in the 1950s and early 1960s was traumatic; some called it the revolution in retailing. However, by the mid-1960s, other retailers had been exposed to discount competition for some 10 years. Many were beginning to counter it, and even to act aggressively against discounters. Department stores and appliance retailers had blunted the initial competitive advantage of discounters either by matching them price for price on identical goods, or else by stocking their own private branded appliances and other items that prevented price comparisons. Many retailers had shifted parts of their operations to self-service and had eliminated some of the frills that made their operations high in cost. And the major advantage that discounters had of relying on high merchandise turnover to yield a good return on investment despite low markups was being copied to some extent by other retailers. Meantime, average costs and markups were rising for all discounters. The result, predictably, was that customers no longer streamed to just any discount store. Discount firms such as Tower Marts International, Grayson-Robinson Stores, Marrud, John's Bargain Stores, and smaller firms that expanded too rapidly were in financial jeopardy.

As the discount-store industry began maturing in the 1960s, other kinds of discounters came on the scene—well-financed, well-managed—and swept away marginal competitors. K mart, the discount subsidiary of S.S. Kresge Company, began what was to become the world's largest discount operation, tightly run, having highly paid store management, a carefully supervised training program (recruiting college graduates), and with solid financial resources behind it. Major department-store corporations, such as Dayton-Hudson, L.S. Ayres, and Allied Stores, opened discount subsidiaries, again carefully run with well-trained, high-caliber personnel, and definitive policies. These latter discount stores had the advantage of years of experience with fashion merchandising because of their mother firms. They grew slowly, carefully, testing the water, experimenting to find the best way. The future belonged to them.

WHAT CAN BE LEARNED?

The dilemma that confronted Korvette was by no means unique among the discounters of the day. Rising on a wave of consumer enchantment with lower prices and the self-service and parking conveniences of the discount stores, many small chain owners found themselves with a few successful stores and developed grandiose plans for expansion. Many thus overextended themselves, financially and organizationally, and were in trouble. The difference with Korvette was that the attained size was much greater than most of its contemporaries before problems began to overwhelm it. Largely, this is a credit to the work load of a peripatetic Ferkauf, who was able to supervise directly a rather large number of stores before it became too much for him.

But the experience of Korvette and the smaller discount-store casualties points to the need for *controlled growth*. Usually, this means a slower, more planned growth. In so doing, the importance of carefully building and structuring an organization cannot be too strongly stressed. Objectives, policies, and management and financial controls should be well defined. In particular, lines of authority and performance measures should be specified—who is responsible for what, and how is performance to be measured? Along with this, attention should be given to the spans of control of the various executives. As spans become too wide with growth, provision must be made for making them more manageable, probably by establishing more executive levels.

Only when there is controlled growth is it likely that a seasoned and strong management team can be available so that experienced merchandising, buying, shipping, and accounting departments can function smoothly. In developing the most effective operation, some testing usually is necessary so that adjustments and modifications can be made where needed. Without time to sit back and analyze past successes and failures, a firm really is proceeding with a blind expansion. Faults are not detected in time and are uncorrected; strengths or areas of potential opportunity are not pinpointed and acted upon. For example, a well-run discount operation needs strong and well-thought-out policies regarding store security (because, with self-service and fewer employees per customer than traditional stores, shoplifting and employee theft are more tempting) and the control of waste and shrinkage.

For an organization desiring the most rapid expansion, there are strong arguments for a decentralized management. Most discounters, such as Zayre, Spartans, and Korvette, were centralized with home-office executives having major authority for most policies and decisions regarding store operation and merchandise. In the most extreme cases, store managers only "carry the keys"; that is, they are responsible for opening and closing the store, seeing that adequate workers are on hand, store maintenance, and displays and other dictates of the home office. They have little opportunity to exert initiative and accordingly are neither well paid nor very high caliber.

One of the most successful examples of rapid growth in retailing was that of the J.C. Penney Company. As described in Chapter 3, Penney's achieved this fantastic growth without sacrificing either operational effectiveness or strong managerial resources through one of the strongest uses of decentralized management in the history of retailing.

A few discount firms, notably K mart, decentralized and gave their store managers much more authority over operations and merchandising. These managers were well trained (7 to 10 years before becoming K mart managers, versus 1 to 2 years for some discount chains) and well paid.

Korvette's experience points out another caveat: *difficulty in upgrading image*. Ferkauf made his initial entry into the market by gaining a reputation as an aggressive discounter of appliances. But, as he expanded, he tried to upgrade. These attempts to redefine Korvette as a promotional department store aimed at higher-income clientele continued for years with no conspicuous success. To attempt to upgrade a company's image is difficult and can cost a firm its old bargain-conscious customers without gaining significantly from other customers.

Update

Did Arlen's acquisition of Korvette from Spartans bring the discount chain back to the marketplace as an aggressive and progressive factor? Sadly, not at all. Its momentum had been lost, never to be regained. Under Arlen, Korvette continued trying to convince customers that it was no longer a discount chain but rather a "quality promotional department store." It succeeded only in confusing customers about its identity.[6] In the years after the Arlen acquisition, Korvette either lost money or barely broke even. Eventually, Arlen had to pick up a $7.7 million tab for the Korvette loss sustained in closing its furniture and carpet departments.

[6] For more detail, see "Arlen's Dream Versus Korvettes' Reality," *Forbes*, April 15, 1977, p. 85–93.

In early 1979, Korvette experienced its third transfer of control. Arlen was able to sell a majority 51 percent interest in the Korvette 50-unit chain to a French retail and manufacturing group, Agache-Willot, for $30 million. The new ownership expressed its approval of a policy of changing the image of the Korvette operation from just low prices to fashion quality at reasonable prices.[7]

The approval and satisfaction of Agache-Willot with their acquisition was not long-lasting. Continued losses and cash crises plagued the retailer, and bankruptcy was threatened in 1980 before the French parent agreed to restructure $55 million of debt to institutional lenders. The decision was made to liquidate the company gradually, and by the middle of 1981, only 12 stores were still owned—and they were in the process of being sold. Korvette, the pioneer discounter, is little more than a memory.

In contrast, K mart, which had caught the discount ball repudiated by Korvette and was running with it, had climbed to become the number two nonfood retailer in the United States, behind only Sears, with sales of over $21 billion in 1984 and profits of almost $500 million.

For Thought And Discussion

1. Why did Korvette have such difficulty competing with fashion goods when it was so successful with appliances and other hard goods?
2. We have noted that one of the serious problems Korvette faced during its rapid growth was a lack of adequate systems and procedures, particularly regarding feedback and controls from the stores. What controls or performance measures would you want to have established in this situation?
3. Personal supervision by Ferkauf was possible when he had only a small number of stores in a limited area. With steady expansion, such personal supervision was no longer possible. What might have been done at this point to ensure adequate supervision of stores?
4. What image do you think Korvette should have tried to develop, and what was the best way to do this? Critically evaluate the various alternatives.

Invitation To Role Play

1. Place yourself in the role of Eugene Ferkauf, a tremendous innovator and leader of the discount movement. You have just been proclaimed by famed educator Malcolm McNair as one of the six greatest merchants in U.S. history. You are humble, yet ecstatic at this honor. Now to prove it. How? Be as specific as possible.
2. You have been hired as a staff assistant to Ferkauf. He has given you particular

[7] "Arlen Realty Says It Agrees to Sell 51% of Korvettes," *Wall Street Journal*, October 26, 1978, p. 18.

responsibility for planning the organizational changes needed to handle the increased size and expected growth of the company. Draw up detailed plans for changing the present highly centralized and almost unstructured organization, for attracting high-caliber people, and for establishing executive development programs and performance evaluations. If you need to make assumptions, then state them.

CHAPTER 7

The Edsel—
Organizational
Incompatibility with
Potential

The factors behind the Edsel demise were more than strictly organizational, although an expensive and separate dealer organization was a major factor. The Edsel case could also have been placed in the section on Planning, since the product itself, the name, how it was introduced, quality control problems—all these contributed to the demise. But, without the separate and expensive dealer organization, might there still be an Edsel today? Who can say?

This is perhaps the classic business mistake of the modern era, the one most widely publicized and commented upon. Interestingly enough, the same firm, the Ford Motor Company, was also responsible for another monumental blunder, this one before the era of modern business.

AN EARLIER BLUNDER

Henry Ford introduced the Model T in 1909. It sold initially for $850 and was available in only one color, black. The Model T quickly became a way of life. Ford conducted mass production on a scale never before seen, introducing and perfecting the moving assembly line so that the work moved to the worker. Ford sold half the new cars made in this country up to 1926 and had more than double the output of his nearest competitor, General Motors (GM). Prices by 1926 had fallen to as low as $263. For 17 years, the Model T had neither model changes nor significant improvements, except for a lowering selling price as more production economies were realized.

But, by the mid-1920s, millions of Americans wanted something fancier, and GM brought out Chevrolet, featuring color, comfort, styling, safety, modernity, and—most of all—a showy appearance. And the Model T was doomed.

In desperation, Henry Ford had the Model T painted attractive colors; fenders were rounded, the body lengthened and lowered, the windshield slanted. But still sales declined. Finally, in May 1927, Ford stopped production altogether for nearly a year while 60,000 workers in Detroit were laid off, and a new car, the Model A, slowly took shape, with a changeover estimated to have cost Ford $100 million. Although the Model A was successful, the lead lost to GM was never to be regained.[1]

In the 1920s, a failure in market assessment was devastating. To some extent, the failure of the Edsel was also due to bad market assessment. This led to overly ambitious expectations and organizational planning.

THE EDSEL

The Edsel, Ford's entry into the medium-price field, was introduced for the 1958 model year in early September of 1957. This gave it a jump on competitors, who traditionally introduce new models in October and November of the previous year. Ernest Breech, the board chairman of the Ford Motor Company, set the 1958 goal for the Edsel Division at 3.3 to 3.5 percent of the total auto market. In a 6-million-car year, this would be about 200,000 cars. However, the company executives considered this a very conservative estimate and expected to do much better. Ten years of planning, preparation, and research had gone into the Edsel. The need for such a car in the Ford product line appeared conclusive. Approximately $50 million was spent for advertising and promotion in the pre-introduction and introduction of the car. And, in the late summer of 1957, the success of the massive venture seemed assured. The company did not expect to recover the $250 million of development costs until the third year, but the car was expected to be operationally profitable in 1958.

Rationale

The rationale for the Edsel seemed inescapable. For some years, there had been a growing trend toward medium-priced cars. Such cars as Pontiac, Oldsmobile, Buick, Dodge, DeSoto, and Mercury were accounting for

---

[1] Adapted from Jonathan Hughes, *The Vital Few* (Boston: Houghton Mifflin, 1966), pp. 274–358.

one-third of all car sales by the middle 1950s, whereas they had formerly contributed only one-fifth.

Economic projections confirmed this shift in emphasis from low-priced cars and suggested a continuing demand for higher-priced models in the decade of the 1960s. Disposable personal income (expressed in 1956 dollars) had increased from about $138 billion in 1939 to $287 billion in 1956, with forecasts of $400 billion by 1965. Furthermore, the percentage of this income spent for automobiles had increased from around 3.5 percent in 1939 to 5.5 or 6.0 percent in the middle 1950s. Clearly, the economic climate seemed to favor a medium-priced car such as the Edsel.

The Ford Motor Company had been weakest in this very sector, where all economic forecasts indicated the greatest opportunity lay. GM had three makes, Pontiac, Oldsmobile, and Buick, in the medium-price class; Chrysler had Dodge and DeSoto appealing to this market; but Ford had only Mercury to compete for this business, and Mercury accounted for a puny 20 percent of the company's business.

Studies had revealed that every year one out of five people who bought a new car traded up to a medium-priced model from a low-priced car. As Chevrolet owners traded up, 87 percent stayed with GM and one of its three makes of medium-priced cars. As Plymouth owners traded up, 47 percent bought a Dodge or DeSoto. But as Ford owners traded up, only 26 percent stayed with the Ford Motor Company and the Mercury, its one entry in this price line. Ford executives were describing this phenomenon as "one of the greatest philanthropies of modern business," the fact that Ford uptraders contributed almost as much to GM's medium-price penetration as Chevrolet had been able to generate for GM.[2]

So the entry of the Edsel seemed necessary, if not overdue.

Research Efforts

Marketing research studies on the Edsel covered a period of almost 10 years. The conclusions were that the personality of the new car (called the "E-car" initially, before the Edsel name had been selected) should be one that would be regarded as the smart car for the young executive or professional family on its way up. Advertising and promotion, accordingly, would stress this theme. And the appointments of the car would offer status to the owner.

The name for the E-car should also fit the car's image and personality. Accordingly, some 2000 names were gathered, and several research firms

---

[2] Henry G. Baker, "Sales and Marketing Planning of the Edsel," in *Marketing's Role in Scientific Management*, Proceedings of the 39th National Conference of the American Marketing Association, June 1957, pp. 128–9.

sent interviewers with the list to canvass sidewalk crowds in New York City, Chicago, Willow Run, and Ann Arbor, Michigan. The interviewers asked what free associations each name brought to mind. But the results were inconclusive.

Edsel, the name of Henry Ford's only son, had been suggested for the E-car. However, the three Ford brothers in active management of the company, Henry II, Benson, and William Clay, were lukewarm to this idea of their father's name spinning "on a million hubcaps." And the free associations with the name Edsel were on the negative side, being "pretzel," "diesel," and "hard sell."

At last, 10 names were sent to the executive committee, but none of them aroused any enthusiasm. The name Edsel was finally selected, although it was not one of the recommended names. Four of the ten names submitted were selected for the different series of Edsel: Corsair, Citation, Pacer, and Ranger.

Search For A Distinctive Style

Styling of the Edsel began in 1954. Stylists were asked to be both distinctive and discreet, in itself a rather tall order. The stylists studied existing cars and even scanned the tops of cars from the roof of a 10 story building to determine any distinguishing characteristics that might be used for the Edsel. Consumer research could provide some information as to image and personality desired, but furnished little guidance for the actual features and shape of the car. Groups of stylists considered various "themes" and boiled down hundreds of sketches to two dozen to show top management. Clay and plaster mock-ups were prepared so that three-dimensional highlights and flair could be observed. The final concept was satisfying to all 800 stylists.

The result was a unique vertical front grille—a horse-collar shape, set vertically in the center of a conventionally low, wide front end—push-button transmission, and luxury appointments. The vertical grille of the Edsel was compared by some executives to the classic cars of the 1930s, the LaSalle and Pierce Arrow. Push buttons were stressed as the epitome of engineering advancement and convenience. The hood and trunk lid were push–button; the parking brake lever was push–button; the transmission was push–button. Edsel salespersons could demonstrate the ease of operation by depressing the transmission buttons with a toothpick.

The Edsel was not a small car. The two largest series, the Corsair and the Citation, were 2 in. longer than the biggest Oldsmobile. It was a powerful car, one of the most powerful made, with a 345 horsepower engine. The high performance possible from such horsepower was thought to be a key element in the sporty, youthful image that was to be projected.

A Separate Division For Edsel

Instead of distributing the new Edsel through established Ford, Mercury, and Lincoln dealers, a separate dealer organization was decided upon, to be controlled by a separate headquarters division. These new dealers were carefully selected from over 4600 enquiries for dealer franchises in every part of the United States. Most of the 1200 dealers chosen were to handle only Edsel, with dual dealerships restricted to small towns. Consequently, there were now five separate divisions for the Ford Motor Company: Ford, Mercury, Lincoln, Continental, and Edsel.

Although establishing Edsel as a separate division added to the fixed costs of operation, this was thought to be desirable in the long run. An independent division could stand alone as profit center, and this should encourage more aggressive performance than if Edsel were merely a second entry in some other division.

The dealer appointments were made after intensive study to learn where to place each dealer in the nation's 60 major metropolitan areas. Population shifts and trends were carefully considered, and the planned dealer points were matched with the 4600 enquiries for franchises. The Edsel was to have the best–located dealer body in the automobile industry. Applicants for dealerships were carefully screened, of course. Guides used in selection included: reputation, adequate finances, adequate facilities, demonstrated management ability, the ability to attract and direct good people, sales ability, proper attitude toward ethical and competitive matters, and type of person to give proper consideration to customers in sales and service.[3] The average dealer had at least $100,000 committed to this agency. Edsel Division was prepared to supply skilled assistance to dealers so that each could operate as effectively and profitably as possible and also provide good service to customers.

Promotional Efforts

July 22, 1957, was the kickoff for the first consumer advertising. It was a two-page spread in *Life* magazine in plain black and white, and showed a car whooshing down a country highway at such speed it was a blur. The copy read: "Lately some mysterious automobiles have been seen on the roads." It went on to say that the blur was an Edsel and was on its way. Other "pre-announcement" ads showed only photographs of covered cars. Not until late August were pictures of the actual cars released.

The company looked beyond their regular advertising agencies to find a

---

[3] Baker, p. 143.

separate one for the Edsel. Foote, Cone and Belding was selected, this being one of the two in the top ten who did not have any other automobile clients. The campaign designed was a quiet, self-assured one that avoided as much as possible the use of the adjective "new," because this was seen as commonplace and not distinctive enough. The advertising was intended to be calm, not to overshadow the car.

The General Sales and Marketing Manager, J. C. Doyle, insisted on keeping Edsel's appearance one of the best-kept secrets of the auto industry. Never before had an auto manufacturer gone to so much trouble to keep the appearance hidden. Advertising commercials were filmed behind closed doors: the cars were shipped with covers, and no press people were given photographs of the car before its introduction. The intent was to build up an overwhelming public interest in the Edsel, causing its arrival to be anticipated and the car itself to be the object of great curiosity. Some $50 million was allocated for this introductory period.

THE RESULTS

Introduction Day was September 4, 1957, and 1200 Edsel dealers eagerly opened their doors. And most found potential customers streaming in, out of curiosity, if nothing else. On the first day, more than 6500 orders were taken. This was considered reasonably satisfying. But there were isolated signs of resistance. One dealer selling Edsels in one showroom and Buicks in an adjacent showroom reported that some prospects walked into the Edsel showroom, looked at the Edsel, and placed orders for Buicks on the spot.

In the next few days, sales dropped sharply. For the first 10 days of October there were only 2751 sales, an average of just over 300 cars a day. To sell 200,000 cars per year (the minimum expectation), between 600 amd 700 would need to be sold each day.

On Sunday night, October 13th, the Ford Motor Company put on a mammoth television spectacular for Edsel. The show cost $400,000 and starred Bing Crosby and Frank Sinatra, two of the hottest names in show business at that time. Even this failed to cause any sharp spurt in sales. Things were not going well.

For all of 1958, only 34,481 Edsels were sold and registered with the motor vehicle bureaus, less than one-fifth the target sales. The picture looked a little brighter in November 1958 with the introduction of the second-year models. These Edsels were shorter, lighter, less powerful, and had a price range from $500 to $800 less than their predecessors.

Eventually, the Edsel Division was merged into a Lincoln-Mercury-Edsel Division. In mid-October 1959, a third series of annual models of Edsels was brought out. They aroused no particular excitement either, and on November 19, 1959, production was discontinued. The Edsel was dead.

Between 1957 and 1960, 109,466 Edsels were sold. Ford was able to recover $150 million of its investment by using Edsel plants and tools in other Ford divisions, leaving a nonrecoverable loss of more than $100 million on the original investment plus an estimated $100 million in operating losses.

WHAT WENT WRONG?

So carefully planned and organized. Such a major commitment of manpower and financial resources, supported by decades of experience in producing and marketing automobiles. How could this have happened? Where were the mistakes? Could they have been prevented? As with most problems, there is no one simple answer. The marketplace is complex. Many things contributed to the demise of the Edsel: among them, poor judgment by people who should have known better (except that they were so confident because of the abundance of planning) and economic conditions outside the company's control. We will examine some of the factors that have been blamed for the Edsel's failure. None of them alone would have been sufficient to destroy the Edsel; in combination, the car didn't have a chance.

Exogenous Factors

One article, in discussing the failure of the Edsel, said, "In addition to mistakes, real and alleged, the Edsel encountered incredibly bad luck. Unfortunately, it was introduced at the beginning of the 1958 recession. Few cars sold well in 1958; few middle-priced cars sold, even fewer Edsels."[4] A dealer in San Francisco summed it up this way: "The medium-priced market is extremely healthy in good times, but it is also the first market to be hurt when we tighten our belts during depression . . . when they dreamed up the Edsel, medium-priced cars were a big market, but by the time the baby was born, that market had gone "helter-skelter"."[5]

The stock market collapsed in 1957, marking the beginning of the recession of 1958. By early August of 1957, sales of medium-priced cars of all makes were declining. Dealers were ending their season with the second-largest number of unsold cars in history up to that time. Table 7.1 shows total U.S. car sales from 1948 (as the country was beginning production after World War II) until 1960. You can see from this table that 1958 sales were the lowest since 1948.

[4] William H. Reynolds, "The Edsel Ten Years Later," *Business Horizons*, Fall 1967, p. 44.

[5] "Edsel Gets a Frantic Push," *Business Week*, December 7, 1957, p. 35.

Table 7.1 U.S. Motor Vehicle Sales, 1948–1960

Year	Units Sold
1948	3,909,270
1949	5,119,466
1950	6,665,863
1951	5,338,436
1952	4,320,794
1953	6,116,948
1954	5,558,897
1955	7,920,186
1956	5,816,109
1957	6,113,344
1958	4,257,812
1959	5,591,243
1960	6,674,796

Source: 1973 Ward's Automotive Yearbook (Detroit: Ward's Communications), p.86.

Table 7.2 shows the production of the major makes of medium-priced cars from 1955 to 1960. Note the drastic drop-off of all makes of cars in 1958, but the trend had been downward since 1955.

The trend was changing from bigger cars to economy cars. American Motors had been pushing the compact Rambler, and, in the year the Edsel came on the market, sales of foreign cars more than doubled. This change in consumer preferences was not solely a product of the 1958 recession, which indicated that it would not reverse once the economy improved. Sales of small foreign cars continued to be very strong in the following years, reflecting public disillusionment with big cars and a desire for more economy and less showy transportation. Table 7.3 shows the phenomenal increase in import car sales during this period, a trend that should have alerted the Edsel planners.

Other exogenous factors were also coming into play at the time of the Edsel's introduction. The National Safety Council had become increasingly concerned with the "horsepower race" and the way speed and power were translating into highway accidents. In 1957, the Automobile Manufacturing Association, in deference to the criticisms of the National Safety Council, signed an agreement against advertising power and performance. But the Edsel had been designed with these two features uppermost: a big engine with 345 horsepower to support a high-performance, powerful car on the highways. Designed to handle well at high speeds, its speed, horsepower, and high-performance equipment could not even be advertised.

Consumer Reports was not overly thrilled about the Edsel. Its 800,000

Table 7.2   U.S. Medium-Priced Car Production, 1955–1959 (units)

	1955	1956	1957	1958	1959
Mercury	434,911	246,629	274,820	128,428	156,765
Edsel			54,607	26,563	29,677
Pontiac	581,860	332,268	343,298	219,823	388,856
Oldsmobile	643,460	432,903	390,091	310,795	366,305
Buick	781,296	535,364	407,283	257,124	232,579
Dodge	313,038	205,727	292,386	114,206	192,798
DeSoto	129,767	104,090	117,747	36,556	41,423

Source: 1973 Ward's, pp. 112, 113.

subscribers found this as the first sentence in the magazine's evaluation of the Edsel: "The Edsel has no important basic advantage over the other brands." Negative articles and books regarding the "power merchants" of Detroit were also appearing about this time. John Keats published his *Insolent Chariots,* and the poet Robert Lowell condemned our "tailfin culture."[6]

Table 7.3   U.S. Sales of Import Cars, 1948–1960

Year	Units Sold
1948	28,047
1949	7,543
1950	21,287
1951	23,701
1952	33,312
1953	29,505
1954	34,555
1955	57,115
1956	107,675
1957	259,343
1958	430,808
1959	668,070
1960	444,474

Source: Automobile Facts and Figures, 1961 Edition (Detroit: Automobile Manufacturers Association), p. 5, compiled from U.S. Department of Commerce statistics.

[6] As reported in John Brooks, *The Fate of the Edsel and Other Business Adventures* (New York: Harper & Row, 1967), p. 57.

INFORMATION SIDELIGHT

SENSORING FOR ENVIRONMENTAL ALERTNESS

A firm must keep itself alert to changes in the environment of doing business: changes in customer preferences and needs, changes in competition, changes in the economy, and even changes in international aspects such as nationalism in Canada, OPEC machinations, or Japanese productivity and quality-control advances. Edsel, of course, failed in this respect by not recognizing the trend away from big, high-horsepower cars and toward smaller, more economical ones. Some of the other mistakes we encounter in this book also at least partially emanate from a lack of environmental alertness.

Now, how can a firm keep itself alert to subtle, insidious, as well as the more obvious changes? We use the term "sensors" here: a firm should have sensors monitoring the environment. Such sensors may be a marketing or economic research department. But, in many instances, such a formal organizational entity is not really necessary to provide primary monitoring. Executive alertness can help a great deal. Most changes do not occur suddenly and with no warning—one exception has been the OPEC dictation regarding oil prices, but even these could have been anticipated and the worst consequences appraised. By listening to feedback from customers, from sales representatives, from suppliers, by keeping abreast of the latest material and projections in business journals, and even by simple observation of what is happening in stores, in advertising, with prices, the introduction of new technologies, information about the environment and how it is changing should be readily available. Sensors of the environment can then be organized and formal; or they can be strictly informal and subjective. But it is surprising and a little disturbing how many executives overlook or disregard—or else are not even aware of—important changing environmental factors that augur effects on their present and future business.

Marketing Research

The failure of the Edsel cannot be attributed to a lack of marketing research. Indeed, large expenditures were devoted to this. However, these efforts can be faulted in three respects.

First, the research efforts directed to establishing a desirable image or "personality" for the new car were not all that helpful. Although they were of some value in determining how consumers viewed the owners of

Chevrolets, Fords, Mercurys, and other brands and led the Edsel executives into selecting the particular image for their car, in reality there was an inability to translate this desired image into tangible product features. For example, although upwardly mobile young executives and professionals seemed a desirable segment of consumers for Edsel to appeal to, was this best done through heavy horsepower and high-speed performance features, or might other characteristics have been more attractive to these consumers? (Many of these consumers were shifting their sentiments to the European compacts about this time, repudiating the "horsepower race" and the chrome-bedecked theme of bigness.)

Second, much of the research was conducted several years before the introduction of the Edsel in 1957. Although demand for medium-priced cars seemed strong at that time, the assumption that such attitudes would be static and unchanging was unwise. A strong shift in consumer preferences was undetected—and should have been noticed. The increasing demand for imported cars should have warranted further investigation and even a reexamination of plans in light of changing market conditions. At the very least, this should have led to some toning down of optimistic expectations for the Edsel and more conservative sales forecasts and budgets.

The last area where the marketing research efforts can be criticized is in the name itself, Edsel. Here the blame lies not so much with the marketing research, which never recommended the name in the first place, as with a Ford management that disregarded marketing research conclusions and opted for the name, regardless.

Much has been written about the negative impact of the name. Most of this may be unjustified. Many successful cars on the market today do not have what we would call winning names. For example, Buick, Oldsmobile, Chrysler, even Ford itself are hardly exciting names. A better name could have been chosen—and was, a few years later, with the Mustang, and also the Maverick—but it is doubtful that the Edsel's demise can justifiably be laid to the name.

The Product

Changing consumer preferences for smaller cars came about the time of the introduction of the Edsel. Disillusionment was setting in regarding large-sized, powerful cars. However, other characteristics of the car also hurt. The styling, especially the vertical grille, aroused both positive and negative impressions. Some liked its distinctiveness, seeing it as a restrained classic look without extremes. But the horse-collar shaped grille turned other people off.

The biggest product error had to do with quality control. There was a failure to adhere to quality standards; cars were released that should not have been. Production was rushed to get the Edsel to market on schedule and also to get as many Edsels as possible on the road so that people could see the car. But many bugs had not been cleared up. The array of models increased the production difficulties, with 18 models in the four series of Ranger, Pacer, Corsair, and Citation.

As a result, the first Edsels had brakes that failed, leaked oil, were besieged with rattles, and sometimes the dealers could not even start them. Before these problems could be cleared up, the car had gained the reputation of being a lemon, and this was a tough image to overcome. The car quickly became the butt of jokes.

The Separate Edsel Organization

A major mistake that can be singled out was the decision to go with a separate division and separate dealerships for Edsel. Although this separation was supposed to lead to greater dealer motivation and consequently stronger selling push than when such efforts are diluted among several makes of cars, the cost factors of such separation were disregarded. Having a separate division was expensive and raised breakeven points very high because of the additional personnel and facilities needed. Furthermore, Ford did not have ample management personnel to staff all its divisions adequately.

Despite the care used in selecting the new Edsel dealers, some of them were underfinanced, and many were underskilled in running automobile dealerships compared to the existing dealers selling regular Ford products. Other Edsel dealers were "dropouts" or the less successful dealers of other car makers.

An additional source of difficulty for the viability of the Edsel dealers was that they had nothing else to offer but Edsel sales and service. Dealers usually rely on the shop and maintenance sections of their businesses to cover some expenses. Edsel dealers not only did not have any other cars besides the Edsel to work on, but the work on the Edsel was usually a result of factory deficiencies; dealers could not charge for this work. Dealers quickly faced financial difficulties with sales not up to expectations and service business yielding little revenue.

Promotional Efforts

Contrary to what could be reasonably expected, the heavy promotional efforts before the Edsel was finally unveiled may have produced a negative effect. The general public had been built up to expect the Edsel to be a major step forward, a significant innovation. And many were disillusioned. They saw instead a new-styled luxury Ford, uselessly overpowered, gadget- and chrome-bedecked, but nothing really so very different; this car was not worth the buildup.

Another problem was that the Edsel came out too early in the new car model year—in early September—and had to suffer the consequences of competing with 1957 cars that were going through clearance sales. Not only did people shy away from the price of the Edsel, but in many instances they did not know if it was a 1957 or 1958 model. *Business Week* reported dealer complaints: "We've been selling against the clean-up of 1957 models. We were too far ahead of the 1958 market. Our big job is getting the original lookers back in the showrooms."[7]

Some dealers had complained about over-advertising too early, but now they were complaining of lack of promotion and advertising in October and November, when the other cars were being introduced. At the time when the Edsel was competing against other new models, advertising was cut back; Edsel executives saw little point in trying to steal attention normally focused on new models.

Finally, one of the more interesting explanations for the failure of the Edsel was:

> oral symbolism . . . responsible for the failure of the Edsel. The physical appearance was displeasing from a psychological and emotional point of view because the front grille looked like a high open mouth . . . Men do not want to associate oral qualities with their cars, for it does not fit their self-image of being strong and virile.[8]

WHAT CAN BE LEARNED?

Major miscalculations were made in estimating sales potential and in forecasting sales. Many of the other mistakes emanated from the unrealistic appraisal of potential sales. With more conservative estimates, the separate, dealer organization—which had a devastating effect on profitability—would not have been established. The Edsel could have been sold through existing Ford and Mercury dealers without greatly increasing the distribution costs of the new car and without subjecting dealers to high risks, because they would have had their other makes of cars to fall back on. Furthermore, the 18 models of Edsel, which made quality control and inventory handling and investments immeasurably more difficult, would have been cut back to a

[7] "Edsel Gets a Frantic Push," p. 35.
[8] Gene Rosenblum, *Is Your VW a Sex Symbol?* (New York: Hawthorn, 1972), p. 39.

more reasonable number, perhaps only 4 models. These two decisions alone would have had a major impact on the breakeven point, and perhaps sustained the Edsel until better economic times prevailed.

So, what can be learned? That optimistic forecasting should never be done? That confidently going ahead with an ambitious project is folly? No, not at all. But the decision maker must weigh carefully the risk/reward factors of costly and ambitious decisions. Mistakes will be made. The future is never certain, despite research into it, and despite the most careful planning. The environment is ever-changing, whether we consider customer attitudes and preferences, competitive efforts, or such completely unpredictable factors as OPEC-created petroleum shortages and skyrocketing energy prices.

When a decision involves high stakes and an uncertain future—which translates into high risks—is it not more prudent to approach the venture somewhat conservatively, not spurning it, but also not committing all resources and efforts until a more definitive idea of acceptance can be gained? It can be argued that with a new model of car—whether this be the Edsel, or more recently K-cars and X-cars—the huge start-up investment needed militates against any halfway measures. But still, a separate dealership need not be established; an array of models can be toned down; even advertising can be more conservatively placed.

Because this case is placed in the Organization Section, let us examine more specifically what we might carry with us from the Edsel case regarding organizational modifications for a new venture. When we consider product diversification, whether this be an Edsel or a new acquisition, one of the major considerations of such a decision should be how well the proposed venture fits in with present resources and facilities: Can the same dealers handle the proposed new product or operation, or will a separate organization have to be established? How about the sales force? The operating capacity? The know-how of present executives? Although these questions about the compatibility of a proposed venture do not exhaust the dimensions for such important decisions, they are examples of facets that need to be weighed. With the Edsel, of course, the requirement of a separate organization was hardly prudent, given the uncertain future and the fact that a capable dealer organization was already available. In general, it is folly to disrupt or bypass an existing and capable organization for a major and costly venture that is as yet unproven. The Korvette example illustrates the need for organizational change to keep up with a rapidly growing and getting-out-of-hand situation. This Edsel example represents the other end of the continuum: changing an organization, introducing a much more costly one, before the need for such a change is even hinted.

For Thought And Discussion

1. How would you have instituted environmental sensors to provide up-to-date information to Ford executives about changing exogenous conditions?
2. How would you respond to the comment that the failure of the Edsel, despite extensive planning (starting 10 years before the product finally was introduced), means that planning too far in advance is futile?
3. List as many pros and cons as possible for having Edsel as a separate division (with separate dealers) rather than as part of an existing division (and dealer organization) such as Lincoln-Mercury. Which of your pros and cons do you consider to be most important (which means that they deserve a higher weighting in the overall analytical process)?
4. How could the Edsel have been a more innovative entry into the medium-price market? What features might have made it successful?

Invitation To Role Play

Assume the role of the Ford executive responsible for the Edsel operation. What strategy would you have used both in the introductory period and in the subsequent several years to enable it to attain both viability and success? Be as specific and complete as you can and be prepared to defend your proposals against other alternatives. Be sure your recommendations are reasonable and practical.

CHAPTER 8

W. T. Grant—Wild and Unorganized Growth

In some respects, the mistakes of the W. T. Grant Company were not unlike those of Korvette: both involved a growth that could not be handled. But Korvette was a young company, the product of one man's creative and entrepreneurial talents, but a man who had poor organizational skills. Such was not the excuse for Grant. This was a long-established firm. It had already grown to relatively large size, so that an organization was well set and could presumably provide a solid foundation for the growth that was to come in the maturity of the company. But, as we will see, pell-mell growth can defeat even an established organization if it is not done prudently and with clearly defined objectives. Such growth efforts can outstrip the organizational capability, as well as the managerial and financial resources. The mistakes of the W. T. Grant Company did not result merely in a slap on the wrist and some retrenchment or decline in profits; instead, utter collapse and liquidation resulted.

In June 1975, James Kendrick, 62-year-old chief executive of the W. T. Grant Company, had his back to the wall. He was in charge of a retail giant of almost 1200 stores having sales of nearly $2 billion. But the company was in financial jeopardy, on the verge of bankruptcy. Grant owed $600 million in short-term loans and $100 million in long-term debt to 143 banks. Furthermore, it had just encountered a staggering $175 million loss for 1974. And the losses were continuing: in the first quarter of 1975, Grant's loss was $54 million. Dividends, which had proudly been paid for 69 years, were suspended. On June 2, 1975, Grant was to pay $57 million to retire its debt to 116 of the banks. Failure to do so might well have induced some of the creditors to push Grant into bankruptcy.

PRELUDE

The blame for this situation was not Kendrick's. The previous management had been deposed in a director's revolt in August 1974. Kendrick was a long-time Grant employee who had been running a subsidiary, Zeller's Ltd., in Canada. Seven years before, he had been a candidate for president of Grant; at the time he was Grant's first sales vice–president. But he was passed over then and exiled to Canada because he questioned certain policies of Edward Staley, chairman of the board. Now, Staley and the other top executives had been ousted and, for the company's greatest trial, Kendrick had at last been tapped.

Staley's influence came from his closeness with founder William T. Grant. Staley was Grant's brother-in-law, and as the aged Grant became less active, he turned increasingly to Staley to run the company. Staley was president from 1952 to 1959, but he remained in active control under various titles for over 20 years, until 1974. He supported Richard C. Mayer, the president of Grant from 1968 to 1974, who led Grant into an expansion course that was both heady and disastrous.

When Richard Mayer became Grant's president in 1968, he was culminating a 21-year career. He had set up the company's credit operation so successfully that it contributed 25 percent of sales in 1972. Mayer was interested in vigorous expansion. Shortly after he assumed the presidency, the company broke out of a 3-year earnings rut and joined the ranks of $1–billion–plus retail firms. Encouraged by this progress, Mayer set a goal of $2 billion in sales by 1972. Although this figure was never achieved in his reign, Grant embarked on one of the most ambitious expansion programs ever plotted by a retailer.

These are the principals of this case, except for one other, the founder of the W. T. Grant Company, whose influence came through his support of Staley.

HISTORY

"Looking back to the earliest days that I can remember, it seems to me that I always wanted to own a store," wrote William T. Grant. He sold shoes in his home town of Malden, Massachusetts, and headed the shoe department of a Boston department store when he was only 19. In 1906, taking his life savings of $1000, he opened his first store in Lynn, Massachusetts. This was successful; a second store was opened within 2 years, and the firm continued a steady growth.

Although his stores were similar to the five-and-tens of Woolworth and Kresge, William Grant saw an opportunity for prices above those of the five-and-tens and below the more expensive department stores. So his first stores carried the $0.25 price theme. As the company expanded through the years, it was thought of primarily as a variety store. Then, in the late 1960s, it went heavily into high-ticket durables such as TV sets, furniture, and appliances.

At age 48, Grant retired from active management of the company, but continued as chairman of the board until his 90th birthday in 1966. On his 50th anniversary with the company in 1956, Grant reiterated his childhood conviction about the thrill of retailing: "I know of no other business which could give a man so much action, so much challenge, so much satisfaction and so rich a reward for good service to the community than this wonderful business of ours. I have enjoyed every minute of it."[1]

THE GO-GO EXPANSION YEARS

As 1972 drew to a close, Richard Mayer, president of Grant, looked back with some satisfaction at the company's growth in the previous 10 years, and he ordered the record of this growth to be distributed to the financial community, company employees, interested vendors, and stockholders. The statistics were indeed impressive. Some of the more important ones are as follows:

	1962	1972	Percentage Increase in Ten Years
Total number of stores	1,032	1,208	17
Total sales	$686,263,000	$1,644,747,000	140
Credit sales	$ 97,478,000	$ 406,763,000	317
Net earnings	$ 9,004,000	$ 37,787,000	320
Net worth	$141,381,000	$ 334,339,000	137
Percentage earned on net worth	6.4	11.3	
Dividends paid on common stock	$ 6,997,000	$ 20,807,000	197

[1] Adapted from a publication of the W. T. Grant Company commemorating the decease of William T. Grant.

Mayer was particularly proud of the statistics on store growth since he had assumed the presidency in 1968:

	1963–1967	1968	1969	1970	1971	1972
New stores opened	202	41	52	65	83	92
Stores enlarged	55	11	3	8	5	5
Stores closed	148	35	49	44	31	52
Store space in thousands of square feet:						
Opened during period	10,933	3,205	3,950	5,360	7,254	7,070
Closed during period	(2,962)	(759)	(1,277)	(1,058)	(693)	(1,198)
At end of period	28,736	31,182	33,855	38,157	44,718	50,618

Source: . T. Grant Company, *Facts and Highlights, Ten Fiscal Years Ended January 31, 1973,* p. 5.

Given these comparative statistics, Grant looked like a winner, a true growth company, attractive both to investor and creditor.

However, one aspect of the operational performance nagged Mayer a bit and was gaining some attention from the investment community. Earnings were in a 3-year decline from a high of $41,809,000 in 1969, despite sales having risen by over $500 million in those 3 years. However, he had a ready explanation for this. He figured 3 to 5 years were necessary for a new store to "mature" before customer acceptance built a store's sales and profits to an acceptable level. Mayer was quick to assure his critics that he expected a couple of years of flat earnings as multiple openings caused start-up expenses to balloon at the same time that recently opened stores were still in the maturing period.

Certain other statistics should have given him some concern. Long-term debt had risen from $35 million to $126 million in the 10-year period, an increase of 377 percent. Furthermore, as we will examine later, the stock-to-sales ratio had risen sharply. Finally, sales per square foot between 1968 and 1972 dropped from $35.13 to $32.50. More important, Grant's sales per square foot remained less than half those of its major competitors. Yet, during this period, the company had closed over 6 million of its least productive square feet, mostly in marginal stores. This suggested that the new stores were not showing a very strong sales picture.

Table 8.1 compares the expansion efforts of Grant with the other major retailers during 1971 and 1972, as measured by square feet of space added each year.

As can be seen, Grant ranked a close second to Penney in 1971, and was third in 1972 behind Penney and Kresge. The expansion policies of Grant

Table 8.1 Retailing's Biggest Builders, 1971 and 1972

Space Rank		Company	1971 Added Space (sq. ft.)	1972 Added Space (sq. ft.)
1971	1972			
3	1	Kresge	6,532,500	9,602,000
1	2	Penney	7,634,000	7,630,000
2	3	Grant	7,283,000	7,280,000
5	4	Woolworth	5,000,000	5,860,000
4	5	Sears	5,450,000	5,150,000
11	6	Safeway	2,000,000 .	2,825,000
12	7	Kroger	1,877,000	2,717,000
10	8	A & P	2,136,000	2,678,000
13	9	City Products	1,378,000	2,493,000
6	10	Montgomery Ward	2,770,000	2,253,000

Source: Adapted from *Chain Store Age*, November, 1972, p. 22.

were more noteworthy when we consider how much larger Penney and Kresge were than Grant:

	Sales	
	1971	1972
Penney	$4,812,000,000	$5,530,000,000
Kresge	3,140,000,000	3,875,000,000
Grant	1,375,000,000	1,645,000,000

Furthermore, Grant was far exceeding the expansion efforts of Sears, the largest retailer, with sales about 10 times greater than Grant's.

The new stores Grant opened were more than twice the size of the average store of 1964, and some 75 percent were housed in suburban shopping centers. (The smaller stores that were being phased out were often located in deteriorating downtown locations.) Average sales per store had risen to about $1 million compared to $646,000 in 1964, reflecting the larger units.

Grant's expansion was highlighted by their "superstores," stores of 180,000 sq ft, although the size of other new stores ranged down to 60,000 sq ft. Two separate location strategies were in operation. The big stores, 120,000 to 180,000 sq ft, were being placed in medium-sized enclosed malls, with a Sears, Ward, or even a major discounter as a co-anchor. At the same time, the smaller stores that were being built in neighborhood and convenience centers were aimed at dominating a small market where there was no nearby competition from major general merchandisers.

The larger stores were necessitated by a vigorous effort to expand and upgrade the product lines. Emphasis was turning toward big-ticket items such as television sets, major appliances, power tools, automobile accessories, sporting goods, and camera equipment. The superstores even carried garden equipment, furniture, and auto servicing. By 1971, the product line was made up of about 25 percent family fashions, 50 percent hardgoods, and 25 percent small wares and services. This was a distinct change from the variety chain that once had 50 percent of its product line in family fashions, and very little in hardgoods. The average store now stocked over 21,000 items in all price ranges. About 70 percent of the merchandise carried the Grant private label; this permitted Grant to offer somewhat lower prices than if nationally advertised brands were handled.

As expansion was proceeding all-out, a program was designed to cut down the development time for the new stores from 90 days to 60 days. No longer was the developer's architect required to submit working drawings to the chain for final approval, provided the architect would certify that they conformed to Grant's specifications. Under the old method, plans were submitted to Grant, and many changes usually had to be made before final approval. Eliminating this review procedure resulted in widely fluctuating costs. But, with an objective of pell-mell expansion, shortcuts had to be taken.

APPROACHING DISASTER, 1973 AND 1974

Mayer's expansion plans continued unabated for most of 1973. Table 8.2 shows how Grant compared with other major retailers in 1973 construction.

Grant's operations were deep in the red for the first 9 months of 1973. But, because the last quarter of the year is the most crucial one for retail operations as a result of the peak November/December Christmas business, management waited until December to make any further decisions regarding the expansion program. In December, Grant had gains of 3.7 percent, the smallest of any major retailer. The expansion program had been a disaster. Management was now becoming aware that more stores do not necessarily mean profitable sales if they have low productivity. Although he remained as chief executive, Richard Mayer gave up the presidency to operations man Harry Pierson. The expansion program was over.

For the full year of 1973, sales rose to $1.8 billion. But profits dropped 78 percent, to $8,429,000, the lowest profits since 1962, when sales were only $575 million. And 1973 was a year when Sears, Penney, Kresge, and Woolworth all showed record earnings. Grant's return on equity, once a

Table 8.2   Retailing's Biggest Builders, 1973

Rank	Company	1973 Added Space (sq. ft.)
1	Kresge	10,000,000
2	Grant	6,300,000
3	Woolworth	4,782,000
4	Sears	4,014,000
5	Penney	4,000,000
6	Kroger	3,239,000
7	A & P	3,050,400
8	Safeway	2,832,000
9	City Products	2,780,000
10	Montgomery Ward	2,765,000

Source: Chain Store Age, November 1973, p. E22.

good 15 percent, dropped to under 5 percent. More ominous, however, was the rise in debt: long-term debt increased to $222 million, whereas short-term debt was up to $450 million. Table 8.3 shows the increase in long-term debt from 1970.

At this point, Grant's troubles were only beginning. The next year, 1974, found sales falling to $1.7 billion. And this was accompanied by a gargantuan loss of $175 million. Dividends were suspended for the first time in the 69-year history. And James Kendrick was brought in to engage in an 11th-hour effort to save the nation's 17th largest retailer from extinction.

To cut costs, Kendrick planned to close 126 stores in 1975, trim the payroll from 82,500 to 69,000, and pare the company's credit unit, which accounted for 62 percent of the 1974 losses. Also contributing to the

Table 8.3   Sales and Long-term Debt, 1970–1974

	Sales (000)	Long-term Debt (000)
1970	$1,214,666	$ 35,000
1971	1,259,117	131,526
1972	1,378,251	128,000
1973	1,648,500	126,000
1974	1,849,802	222,834

Source: Company Records.

staggering results was a loss of $24 million for store closing costs, heavy interest charges, and massive markdowns of slow-moving goods.

JUNE 1975

Finally, Kendrick was sweating out the June 2, 1975, payment of $57 million required to retire the company's debt to 116 of the 143 banks that had provided financing for the ill-fated expansion. Failure to pay these smaller creditors might well force bankruptcy. The bigger banks with more at stake in their loans to the company (for example, Chase Manhattan and First National City Banks of New York City each had $82 million loaned to Grant, and they were more willing to try to rescue the faltering firm and recoup their investments) would not be so inclined to sink the company in an effort to get a faster settlement. While the financial and investment community waited, the news finally hit the press and the market tape that Grant had somehow managed to come up with the $57 million. Kendrick now had a little breathing room.

Causes Of The Dilemma

Ill-conceived and too-vigorous expansion certainly must take the blame for many of the Grant problems. Kendrick said: "The expansion program placed a great strain on the physical and human capability of the company to cope with the program. These were all large stores we were opening, and the expansion of our management organization just did not match the expansion of our stores."[2] A former operations executive noted: "Our training program couldn't keep up with the explosion of stores, and it didn't take long for the mediocrity to begin to show."[3]

Another underlying factor also played a major role in the Grant dilemma. Although too rapid expansion causes assimilation problems, other firms have expanded rapidly in the past, such as the Penney Company and most of the other major chains in the 1920s; Kresge and their K mart stores have vigorously expanded for over a decade and have been the epitome of success. But Grant's expansion was hindered by a lack of a definable and distinctive image.

What was the image and how did customers see the store? As a variety chain? A discounter? A general-merchandise chain? This was the question, and the dilemma. What should Grant be? Or more realistically, what should

---

[2] As reported in "How W. T. Grant Lost $175 Million Last Year," *Business Week,* February 24, 1975, p. 75.

[3] Ibid.

INFORMATION SIDELIGHT

MANAGEMENT DEVELOPMENT

Any firm that is growing needs competent executives and staff professionals to step into newly opening slots. Such a managerial expansion can come in two ways:

1. From internal management development.
2. By recruiting from outside the organization.

Internal management development presumes a body of trainees who have the potential competence and motivation to fill important executive slots in the future. But time is needed to give such trainees the experience, coaching, and perhaps formal training programs to fulfill such expectations. For example, the S.S. Kresge Company at one time planned a 5-year program to develop new college graduates—whom they paid very competitive salaries to recruit—to become small variety-store managers.

The alternative is to conduct a vigorous recruiting campaign and obtain experienced executives from outside the organization. Unfortunately, such an approach, if relied upon primarily, can play havoc with the morale of present employees who see their chance of advancement as dim indeed. Furthermore, it requires that the firm's compensation package and reputation be attractive enough to woo outsiders. This may mean that the pay scale must be higher than that of competing firms, and this can place an organization at a cost disadvantage. Generally, we can say that a commitment to hiring from outside is hardly prudent for more than a nominal number of executive slots where, perhaps, special expertise or abilities not available in the present organization may be desirable.

Of course, there is another alternative to developing from within or hiring from without. People can be promoted quickly to fill slots, with the hope that they can develop on the job and not make too many mistakes in the process. This is akin to filling responsible positions with "bodies" and typified much of the expansion efforts of Korvette, as we described earlier. W. T. Grant also reached this situation in its vigorous growth efforts. The consequences of naively ignoring management development or of outpacing it can be dire indeed.

---

it strive to be? The company assumed some sort of mid-position between a discounter and a general-merchandise firm—neither fowl nor ass. As merchandise lines were expanded and prices upgraded, Grant veered strongly away from the variety-store image; yet, in some ways, it still retained it. For example, certain typical variety-store departments, such as candy, were still kept near the front of the stores. On the other hand, Grant did not try to keep up with K mart in being a discounter, although it was price competitive enough to be called promotional. Mayer coined the phrase ''one-stop family shopping stores,'' suggesting a general merchandiser such as Sears and Penney. However, Grant lacked the punch of either of these and was unable to offer the service or the established brands that Sears or Penney could. For example, Grant's major brand, Bradford, was practically unknown, and many people were reluctant to buy appliances and similar goods if quality and service were questionable. Given time, Grant could have established acceptance of its own brand, but problems were emerging too fast under its expansion policies.

Vigorous expansion, which led to inefficiencies and mediocre performance, added to an uncertain and murky image; it resulted in inventory problems, as some merchandise from the broadened product line—especially appliances—did not sell. Store buyers, in their eagerness to stock huge stores, often bought larger quantities than could be moved as seasons, styles, and tastes changed. But there was a reluctance to mark down and clear out this inventory. One merchandising executive recalled ''mounds of goods that just sat year to year collecting dust; they had so much stuff just sitting there they couldn't free up the dollars to do a good seasonal merchandising job.''[4]

Many of the new stores were not living up to expectations, and, with certain merchandise categories stagnant, Grant began a heavy credit promotion in an effort to move this merchandise. But too much leniency in granting credit led to disastrous uncollectable accounts and credit write-offs.

The mix of stores added to Grant's difficulties. The new stores were never really standardized. They came in sizes from 54,000 sq ft to 180,000, with different interiors and exteriors and different merchandise assortments. Some stores were free-standing, without other stores nearby; others were in malls; still others were in strip centers. Although K mart stores were standardized, such was not the case with Grant.

Now the flaws in Grant's planning began perpetuating. Because so many Grant stores had low sales productivity, developers often refused to give them choice locations. Consequently, many of the new stores were in

---

[4] Ibid., pp. 75, 76.

INFORMATION SIDELIGHT

WHAT SHOULD OUR BUSINESS BE?

An organization's business, its mission and purpose, should be thought through, spelled out clearly, and well communicated to those executives involved in policy-making. This is especially true for an organization endeavoring to grow, and grow rapidly. Otherwise, the organization lacks unified and coordinated goals and objectives. It is like trying to navigate unknown terrain without a map.

In setting goals, however, prudent judgment would opt for safe, rather than courageous, ones. Mayer, in his presidency of Grant's, wanted the company to grow from $1 billion in sales to $2 billion in barely 4 years— a courageous goal, but hardly safe and prudent.

Determining what a firm's business is or ought to be should be a starting point for specifying goals and objectives. Several elements should help determine this:

The *history* of the organization can hardly be disavowed, since it affects employees, suppliers, and customers alike. In view of its history, Grant could hardly translate its future business definition as a high-quality and fashion-oriented department store operation.

The firm's *resources* and *distinctive abilities and strengths* must play a major role in this determination. It is not enough to wish for a certain status or position if the resources and competence do not warrant this. To take an extreme example, a railroad company can hardly expect to transform itself into an airline, even though both may be in the transportation business.

Finally, *competitive and environmental opportunities* ought to be considered. The inroads of foreign car makers in the U. S. reflected environmental opportunities for energy-efficient vehicles and the lack of formidable U. S. competition in this area.

---

poor sites. On top of these problems, Grant filed a suit in February 1975 against three former employees charged with taking "hundreds of thousands of dollars in bribes in connection with store leases," which relegated Grant to many poor store locations. Lawsuits were pressed against the former real estate vice–president, the Southern real estate manager, and the Midwest real estate manager, alleging kickbacks and bribery: "some store sites and rental terms may not have been in our best interest and may have contributed to some of our problems."[5]

CLIMAX, 1975

The $57 million payment toward the debt reduction was made, even though the investment community had been holding its breath. Slender breathing room had been gained, but could Kendrick bring the company back to viability? There is something sad at contemplating the demise of an undertaking more than half a century old that owed its success to the dreams, hard work, and creative vision of a founder and his successors—and then suddenly to give this all up and succumb after only 5 years or so of misguided management.

Kendrick sought to undo the damages and move ahead. He proposed going after the same mass market as K mart and Woolco, to be competitive in price. He would deemphasize the big-ticket items, and strengthen infants' and children's wear, white goods, and curtains and draperies. He planned to spend $6 million on television spots in 35 major markets. Mayer had been a credit man, little versed in merchandising and operations. Now, Kendrick proposed stressing basic merchandising, such as keeping stocks fresh and clean and taking prompt markdowns. "We failed to stock staples, which in turn led to an overabundance of slow-selling items," Kendrick pointed out. He also recognized that Grant's merchandising program may have been too promotional-minded, and that not enough reliance was placed on national brands.[6]

In the next few years, Kendrick hoped to get down to a core group of 900 stores and stabilize sales volumes at about $1.5 billion. He intended to increase the use of brand-name goods and increase the dollar volume per square foot. Complicating the problem of streamlining, however, were the many long-term leases running anywhere from 10 to 20 years for some stores due to be closed because of poor locations. Unless these could be subleased, their expense drain would continue for some time.

As a further merchandising tool, Grant planned to accept Bank-Americard and Master Charge sales, thereby playing down its own dismal credit operation. Although it recognized the expenses involved in these bank cards, the company hoped to attract more customers.

Despite the efforts of Kendrick and the sharp reversal of previous policies, the picture steadily worsened during 1975. For the 6 months ending

[5] Ibid., p. 76.
[6] "It's Get Tough Time at W. T. Grant," *Business Week*, October 19, 1974, p. 46.

July 31, 1975, the chain lost $111.3 million, further straining financial resources. Landlords were asked to roll their store rents back 25 percent; some complied. Loan agreements were renegotiated with 27 banks headed by Morgan Guaranty, in which $300 million of the $640 million owed to the banks was subordinated (that is, given lower priority for repayment) to bills owing suppliers; and, in general, the loan provisions were moderated. Subordinating the bank loans was vital, because Grant had some $500 million worth of goods on order; but many suppliers were holding up deliveries for fear they would not be paid.

Grant was losing money faster than anticipated and was forced to announce that it was operating with a "negative net worth"; that is, that its debts exceeded its assets. This was the beginning of the end. On October 2, 1975, Grant entered bankruptcy proceedings, filing a petition under Chapter 11 of the Federal Bankruptcy Act. The W. T. Grant Company thus became the second biggest U. S. company ever to enter bankruptcy proceedings (the biggest was Penn Central Transportation Company in 1970), and the largest retailer ever to do so.

Under Chapter 11, a company continues to operate, but has court protection against creditors' lawsuits while working out a plan for paying its debts. Some shareholders, in a separate action, filed to have the proceedings converted to Chapter 10. This is a more drastic move in which control of the company passes to a court-appointed trustee whose interests are more with the creditors and who will try for a complete financial reorganization and, if necessary, may liquidate some or all of the company's assets to raise money to pay creditors.

In the fall of 1975, the company squeaked past the threat of complete liquidation, retrenching with hundreds of store closings, including most of those west of the Mississippi. If there was to be any chance for survival and eventual payment of creditors, strong Christmas sales were needed. However, with suppliers fearful of providing goods because of the bankruptcy proceedings, the chance of the company being adequately stocked for Christmas 1975 business was jeopardized. Thus, a major constraint on a faltering firm trying to maintain sufficient viability to work itself out of a constricting mess, that of difficulty in acquiring needed goods from suppliers for day-to-day business, remained a real concern and bleakly colored the future of Grant.

WHAT CAN BE LEARNED?

Even if Grant, with its huge debt and destroyed profits, could have survived and eventually become profitable, its excesses undoubtedly would have curbed growth for years to come. The only hope would lie in a retrenchment and assimilation of the better parts of the operation. Even with an old, established firm, management can make mistakes and lead it to the brink of disaster, to such an extent that no quick remedy is remotely possible. It is not unlike the diving accident that leaves a victim paralyzed: the momentary rash act may bring a lifetime of crippled consequences.

The mistakes reflect ignorance of the basic principle that growth should not be more rapid than organizational efforts to cope with expansion through training of managers and personnel, location research and analysis, judicious merchandising, and prudent financial considerations.

To be successful, a retailer needs to develop a distinctive image. Many years ago the problems of an image deficiency were cited:

> What happens to the retail store that lacks a sharp character, that does not stand for something special to any class of shoppers? It ends up as an alternative store in the customer's mind. The shopper does not head for such a store as the primary place to find what she wants. Without certain outstanding departments and lines of merchandise, without clear attraction for some group, it is like a dull person.[7]

The Grant Company had not really done this when the vigorous expansion effort was begun. It was like a voyager without a map, with no unified direction. Consequently, the stores varied greatly in size and location. Prices and quality were sometimes competitive and sometimes not. The guiding force of a unified image needed for coordination of expansion was not there.

Basic merchandising principles were violated in the rush toward expansion of square feet of selling space. Markdowns were not taken when needed, so merchandise was no longer fresh, clean, and attractive. Staple or basic merchandise should have been carefully maintained to avoid "out of stocks." New merchandise lines should have been carefully tested and planned, rather than being abruptly put in stock.

Finally, sensors of deteriorating situations should have been watched and corrective action taken quickly. The burgeoning debt, lessening merchandise turnover, the sorry sales/square foot ratio—all these should have alerted management that something was seriously amiss.

For example, the creeping problems of inventories becoming too heavy and out-of-line should have been detected and prompt action taken. The worsening position from 1969 on can be seen from the following table:

    [7] Pierre Martineau, "The Personality of the Retail Store," *Harvard Business Review*, January-February 1958, p. 50.

	Total Sales (000)	Year-end Inventory of Merchandise (000)	Inventory Percentage of Sales
1969	$1,210,918	$222,128	18.3
1970	1,254,131	260,492	20.8
1971	1,374,812	298,676	21.7
1972	1,644,747	399,533	24.3

In the 6 years before 1969, the stock-to-sales ratio had never been higher than 19.0 percent. When it reached 20.8 percent in 1970, and certainly when it reached 21.7 percent in 1971, corrective action should have been taken. (The argument that expanding merchandise lines and going into higher-priced items such as appliances and furniture justified the higher stock-to-sales ratio was hardly valid, because such diversification should have resulted in proportionately higher sales and should not have been at the expense of a worsening stock-to-sales ratio.)

Perhaps the major point to be learned from the experience of Grant is the fallacy of a growth-at-any-cost philosophy. In an effort to make the W. T. Grant Company a major factor in the general-merchandise market—and perhaps the siren call was to repeat Kresge's K mart success—stores were opened without regard for either sound location selection or an adequately trained organization. Adding millions of square feet of selling space each year was bound to increase sales. But at what cost? A growth-at-any-cost philosophy usually has severe consequences for profits; in an extreme case, as with Grant, the very viability of the company can be jeopardized.

Update

The W. T. Grant Company, as we all know, did not make it. On February 9, 1976, six banks and one vendor on the creditors' committee that had been formed after Grant went into Chapter 11 bankruptcy proceedings voted for liquidation (four other creditors on the committee voted against the liquidation). On February 11, the Federal Bankruptcy Court in New York ordered the liquidation to begin. Some 1073 retail stores were closed, and 80,000 persons put out of work. Furthermore, Grant's banks had to write off approximately $234 million in bad loans, and its suppliers some $110 million in unpaid bills.

Kendrick was not present at the burial. With Grant so heavily in their debt, the banks began to play a bigger role in managing the company by late 1975. They wanted a new top executive to replace Kendrick, and they invested $2.5 million to guarantee the salary and pension to Robert Anderson, former vice–president of Sears. Anderson became chairman and chief executive in October 1975, as Grant filed for Chapter 11. He and the committee of creditors were empowered to direct the company. The task was to shrink Grant to manageable size by closing losing stores, reducing number of employees, getting inventory flowing, settling liens, and reducing losses. To reassure vendors who were fearful of shipping merchandise, the banks again agreed to subordinate their claims to those of suppliers. But all was to no avail. The behemoth, racked with losses, staggering debts, confused inventory and accounting records, and a scandalous lack of controls, ignominiously produced the biggest retailing mistake of all time.[8]

For Thought And Discussion

1. What image do you think Grant should have aimed for? How should Grant have gone about developing such an image?
2. How would you counter the argument that an increasing stock/sales ratio is necessary to diversify the merchandise mix and provide stock for new stores?
3. How do you think it might have been possible for Grant to expand as vigorously as they did and to do so successfully?

Invitation To Role Play

1. Place yourself in the role of Richard Mayer as he assumes the presidency in 1968. What growth strategy would you have pursued? Be as specific as you can.
2. You are a staff assistant to James Kendrick. He has just assumed leadership of the company. You have been asked by him to develop plans for a course of action to keep the company viable. Be as specific as you can, and be prepared to defend your recommendations.
3. You are the new vice–president in charge of personnel. You have been particularly charged with instituting a management development program to ensure enough trained people to support a vigorous expansion. How would you formulate such a program?

[8] For more details of the final steps leading up to the liquidation decision, see "Investigating the Collapse of W. T. Grant," *Business Week*, July 19, 1976, pp. 60–62; and "Notes of Grant Creditors' Panel Filed, Show Firm's Effort to Avoid Bankruptcy," *Wall Street Journal*, June 21, 1976, p. 5.

Three

FLAWED LEADERSHIP AND STRATEGY EXECUTION

9

Montgomery Ward— Dictatorial And Misguided Leadership

Firms can pursue diametrically opposite strategies to their detriment. Earlier, we saw how major errors in overly ambitious expansion have brought organizations to the edge of bankruptcy and beyond: for example, the World Football League, Korvette, and the W. T. Grant Company. And still to come is the Burger Chef case, in which a fast-food franchiser expanded with ill-defined policies, careless selection procedures, and weak controls; not surprisingly, it faltered.

There are fewer examples of firms that made mistakes at the other end of the spectrum: nil expansion. The Montgomery Ward Company from 1939 to 1955 is the foremost example of this, as it postponed all growth efforts "until conditions are more favorable."

Ward's no-growth mistake is included in this section on leadership because it primarily reflected the dictatorial and mistaken leadership of one man: Sewell Avery. He tolerated no dissension or deviations from his views. He ruled this billion-dollar firm as an old-fashioned tyrant, and in the process lost dozens of capable, high-level executives who found the management atmosphere he created intolerable. Mistaken though his ideas were, they dominated the company until he retired at the age of 83. The result of his leadership was an irretrievable loss of competitive position relative to arch rival Sears.

Table 9.1   Stores Operated by Ward, Sears, and Penney, 1938–1954

	1938	1946	1952	1954
Ward	600	632	605	568
Sears	496	610	684	718
Penney	1,539	1,601	1,632	1,644

Source: *Moody's* and company annual reports for respective years.

THE DECISION OF NO-GROWTH

From 1945 to 1952—the years following the curbs brought on by World War II—not a single new Ward store was opened. Actually, some 27 stores were closed, reducing the total number of Ward stores from 632 to 605; an additional 37 marginal stores were closed between 1952 and 1955. During all this time, Sears was vigorously expanding, from 610 stores in 1946 to 684 by 1952. Table 9.1 shows the number of stores operated by Ward, Sears, and Penney during various years from 1938 to 1955.

Historically, Ward had opened its stores in small rural communities. This was in keeping with the farmer-consumer who was considered to be the market during the pre-World War II period. However, after World War II, most population growth was taking place in major metropolitan areas, particularly in their suburbs. Shopping centers were burgeoning and were inevitably taking business from downtown and from smaller business districts. But Ward repudiated expansion during this period of major change in shopping patterns, deliberately leaving the field to Sears, Penney, and other competitors.

Why? Why this obsession with stability and opposition to growth? Was it because the company had inadequate financial resources to support a vigorous growth program? Was it short in managerial resources? No! Ward was short of neither financial nor of managerial resources. The company was squirreling away millions of dollars during this time, so much so that one of the vice–presidents made a widely quoted statement: "Ward's is one of the finest banks with a store front in the U. S. today."[1] Many able executives were also on the staff during the years immediately after World War II, although many were to leave in frustration. What, then, led to this durable decision for no-growth?

The answer was Sewell Avery, chairman of the board of Ward since 1932. He had an adamant belief that a depression was imminent after the

---

[1] As quoted in *Business Week*, September 27, 1952, p. 62.

cessation of hostilities in World War II. His basis for this was the depression that did occur after World War I. Avery foresaw that the nation would have difficulties trying to readjust to a peacetime economy, as industries halted production of war materials and reverted to peacetime production, and as millions of returning servicemen tried to find employment. He predicted that "economic conditions are terrorizing beyond what we have known before." And he noted, "We (Ward) are starting nothing of any size; we are being cautious."[2]

If the expectations of Avery had been correct—if a severe depression had come within 3 or 4 years of the ending of the war—he would have been a hero; he might have achieved fame as the "shrewdest businessman in the U. S." as *Business Week* magazine speculated.[3] The cash and liquid assets of Ward might have fostered expansion at bargain prices while everyone else was trying to retrench. But, with every passing year, the soundness of the strategy of standing pat became more suspect.

Sewell Avery

Sewell Avery was born in Saginaw, Michigan, in 1874, the son of a wealthy Michigan lumberman. For many years of his life his was an admirable success story. He graduated from Michigan State University Law School in 1894 and started at the bottom in a small gypsum plant owned by his father. By the time he was 22 he was manager of the plant. Then, in 1901, the small firm was absorbed by the U. S. Gypsum Company. Four years later, Avery was president of U. S. Gypsum. *Time* magazine described him as a "suave and brilliant supersalesman,"[4] and he built U. S. Gypsum into one of the largest purveyors of building materials in the United States.

In the deep depression year of 1932, salesman Avery was called on by Ward's directors and creditors to rescue the foundering company, which had suffered an $8.7 million deficit in 1931. Avery gathered around him sharp young executives. He added new luxury items to Ward's stock, and said, "We no longer depend on hicks and yokels. We sell more than overalls and manure-proof shoes."[5] He reentered the fashion merchandise field. He improved the catalog. He closed 70 unprofitable stores.

And he was successful. In 12 years he had changed a $5,700,000 loss (1932) into a $20,438,000 profit (1943). In 1932, the company lost 2.2 times as

[2] "Betting on a Depression . . . and What It Costs," *Business Week*, September 27, 1952, p. 61.
[3] Ibid., pp. 60–66.
[4] *Time*, May 8, 1944, p. 12.
[5] Ibid.

much money as Sears on a volume only 65 percent that of Sears; by 1939, Ward had 82 percent of Sears' business and 84 percent of Sears' profit.

Avery ruled Ward with an iron hand, with no regard for the feelings of employees or executives. He also earned a reputation as one of the nation's foremost Roosevelt-haters and labor-baiters. When he finally stepped down from active domination of the company in 1957, he was 83 years old.

BACKGROUND OF THE MONTGOMERY WARD COMPANY

In 1872, (Aaron) Montgomery Ward, former general-store manager, dry-goods salesman, and traveling salesman, opened in Chicago the first large business selling a wide variety of goods exclusively by mail.[6] Ward had worked among farmers for many years and knew of their dissatisfaction with the high cost of goods and the limited choices available from the inefficient general stores of the day. He was also familiar with an organization they had recently formed, the Grange, which advocated cooperative purchasing to save farmers money by eliminating the middleman.

Ward and his brother-in-law had amassed $2400. With this they established their business in a 12 by 14 room in Chicago. They listed the articles for sale and explained how to order on a single sheet of paper. By 1874, the price sheet had become an eight-page booklet. Growth was phenomenal. Later in the same year, the booklet became 72 pages; by 1884, a catalog of 240 pages listed nearly 10,000 items of merchandise.

At that time, Ward was the official supply house of the Grange, thus winning easy acceptance in the rural market. But even more important to the success was Ward's guarantee that goods could be returned to the company without transportation charges both ways if the customer was not satisfied. Montgomery Ward was not averse to using hoopla; as one promotional device he had barnstorming railroad cars displaying the firm's goods and offering entertainment of the minstrel variety. Customers were invited to visit the company's plant in Chicago, and during the Chicago World's Fair some 285,000 did so.

Sears was not established until 1886, and then its chief business was selling watches by mail order. The company did not become Sears, Roebuck and Company until 1893. By 1902, however, Sears had surpassed Ward in sales, although it was never able to far outdistance Ward until after World War II.

For virtually the first 50 years of operation, Ward was strictly a

---

[6] This section has been greatly condensed from Boris Emmet and John E. Jeuck, *Catalogs and Counters* (Chicago: University of Chicago Press, 1950).

mail-order firm, as was Sears. Montgomery Ward had tried one venture of a "branch store" in Milwaukee, Wisconsin, in 1880, but it failed within 2 years. Finally, in 1921, Ward began experimenting with "outlet stores" located in basements of its mail-order plants; these were primarily used to dispose of overstocks and discontinued goods. After a depression in 1920-1921, two additional outlet stores were opened to dispose of the distress goods, and these stores were not located in mail-order premises. The two stores were not identified with Ward, and higher prices were charged than through mail order. These stores, however, turned out to be complete failures, although the outlet stores in the mail-order plants were profitable.

By 1926, Ward had established "mail-order agencies" in small towns as a stimulant for the mail-order business. Similar to present-day catalog order offices, they displayed samples of merchandise, but only tires could be purchased on the spot. During this time there was a real reluctance to open retail stores that might take away business from the mail-order operation. Finally, an incident triggered the decision to go with retail stores; it illustrates how consumer demand can finally assert itself over obstacles placed by a firm:

> In the mail-order agency in Plymouth, Indiana, a would-be customer wanted to buy a certain saw which was on display, and he refused to take "No" for an answer. Finally, the agency manager in desperation allowed him to buy the saw. News of this transaction led to scores of persons clamoring to buy the other goods on display. Agency personnel gave in and sold everything; then they promptly reordered a full stock from the mail-order plant; just as promptly this was sold out.

> The extraordinary movement of goods to the Plymouth agency came to the attention of the president, and he was outraged when he discovered the agency was selling merchandise directly. But the evidence of the resulting profits of this course of action was overwhelming. Ward's top management soon became completely convinced. (Sears had opened retail stores a few years before and undoubtedly helped in convincing Ward's management of the wisdom of this move.)[7]

By the end of 1927, Sears had 27 stores in operation, three times the number of the previous year. Ward had moved even more rapidly and already had 37 open by the end of that year, in addition to the outlet stores in each of its seven mail-order plants.

The rate with which stores were opened by both Ward and Sears during

[7] Ibid., pp. 342, 343.

the next several years was amazing. Ward sought to get into "choice" towns before Sears did, even if some of the outlets were to prove to be mistakes. Two different location strategies were used by the mail-order giants: Ward favored going into towns with populations between 4000 and 75,000; Sears entered much larger towns. By the end of 1929, Ward had opened 500 stores; sometimes as many as 25 were opened in one week. Sears reached a total of 324 stores in this time. Then, the depression years of the early 1930s marked a period of consolidation by both Ward and Sears. Both firms eliminated marginal stores, and new units were more carefully planned and researched.

During the war, of course, expansion was thwarted. But when the war ended, Sears launched the greatest expansion drive since the late 1920s. Some $300 million was staked on the conviction that the postwar economy warranted immediate expansion, and, in the first 2 years after the war, Sears' sales zoomed from $1 billion to almost $2 billion. And Sewell Avery elected to sit tight and do nothing about expansion.

OTHER MISTAKES OF POSTWAR MONTGOMERY WARD

Of course, a major depression did not occur after World War II as Avery had expected. But, aside from sacrificing growth and not entering the thriving big city and shopping-center markets, Avery made other mistakes. Not the least of these was the creation of an organizational climate that led to the loss of key executives. Avery ran Ward with an iron hand and permitted no disagreements with his ideas. During his tenure, 3 presidents, more than 24 vice–presidents, and numerous other high-level executives left. Among them were men who later became presidents of Lord & Taylor and W. T. Grant. The dictatorship of Avery was not conducive to retaining able executives who wanted freedom to make aggressive decisions.

In the process of standing pat and building up huge cash reserves, there was an overzealousness in paring expenses. Overhead in stores was minimized, and no expenditures were made for improvement. As an example of the pinch-penny philosophy existing at this time, Avery ordered that no professional models be used to show the clothes and accessories in the publication of the $6,000,000 catalog. By doing this, $60,000 in modeling fees was saved, or one percent of the total cost of the catalog. But the quality of the catalog and the resulting lack of adequate display and dramatizing of clothing adversely affected mail-order sales.

A parsimony regarding payrolls led to a confrontation with an aroused union membership representing Ward's numerous facilities. Union members felt they were being treated unfairly, but they received no satisfaction on what they considered to be valid grievances. After months of negotiations, Avery declared that the union did not represent the majority of employees

---

INFORMATION SIDELIGHT

LEADERSHIP STYLES

The leadership style that an executive uses can be viewed along a continuum, ranging from a very dictatorial style such as that of Sewell Avery to a participative style in which subordinates share in the planning and decision-making[8]:

dictatorial	authoritative	consultative	participative

none ⟵ degree of employee involvement ⟶ maximum
in decisions

According to Likert, the dictatorial style is based on mistrust and even fear of subordinates; the authoritative style may allow individual subordinates some decision-making within prescribed frameworks; consultative allows moderate interaction and encouragement of ideas from subordinates; and, in participative, employees are involved fully in all decisions related to their work—there is mutual confidence and trust and high morale.

Lest we be carried away, however, with the allure of the participative leadership approach, let us recognize that such delegation of authority and sharing of decision-making assumes that the subordinates are able and experienced, that the action or decision to be made is not urgent (because it takes time to invite participation in any decision), and that there is sufficient monitoring to ensure that, if things go wrong, they will be quickly recognized and corrected. Not all situations permit the judicious use of full subordinate participation.

---

and that Ward would no longer recognize the union. The result was that the union petitioned the National War Labor Board for clarification and threatened to violate the no-strike clause.

Avery refused government intervention in the labor-management conflict, and the union struck. Other unions honored the picket lines, and the Federal government was placed in a quandary: if National War Labor Board recommendations were not complied with, this could lead to severe erosion

---

[8] This classification is the classic one of Rensis Likert, *The Human Organization in Management and Value* (New York: McGraw-Hill, 1967), pp. 4–10.

Table 9.2   Sales/Inventory Ratio for Ward and Sears, 1942–1956

	Ward	Sears
1942	5.14	5.22
1948	4.18	5.65
1952	4.23	6.03
1956	3.47	6.44

Source: Moody's and company annual reports for the respective years.

of its effectiveness and result in an increase in labor unrest across the country. The time was 1944, and the nation was at its maximum war effort.

The Federal government finally ordered a takeover of Ward by the Army in order to force compliance with NWLB recommendations. Avery challenged the authority of the President of the United States to seize the Chicago plant. In a celebrated action, Avery was removed bodily from his office by two Army men.

Along with Avery's other "cost-saving" strategies in the years following the end of the war came an increasing reluctance to write off (or mark down) inventories as they became dated and unsalable. Table 9.2 shows the sales/inventory ratio[9] for Ward and for Sears from 1942 to 1956. As this ratio goes down, more money is tied up in merchandise relative to sales.

Although this ratio had been declining for Ward, it was steadily improving for Sears and almost doubled that of Ward by 1956. A heavy investment in merchandise relative to sales generally reflects poor merchandise control in the sense that slow-selling goods are not weeded out fast enough and marginal items are stocked too heavily. Good merchandising policies and tight controls should eliminate these deficiencies. Obviously, from the statistics in Table 9.2, Ward was seriously lacking here compared to Sears. But then, Sewell Avery was not really a merchant; his experience had been in sales, manufacturing, and general management.

CONSEQUENCES OF THE NO-GROWTH DECISION AND RELATED MISTAKES

Table 9.3 shows the sales and net income statistics for Ward versus those of the Sears and the J. C. Penney Company. Notice that sales and profits increased after the war until 1948, but began leveling off and declining for

---

[9] Although technically different (in that merchandising turnover is based on average stock throughout the year), we will consider the sales/inventory ratio (the sales/stock ratio as of the end of the year) as essentially the same as merchandise turnover.

Table 9.3 Sales and Income Statistics for Ward, Sears, and Penney, 1938–1954

Years	Ward Sales (000)	Ward Net Income (000)	Sears Sales (000)	Sears Net Income (000)	Penney Sales (000)	Penney Net Income (000)
1938	$ 414,091	$19,210	$ 537,242	$ 30,828	$ 257,971	$13,799
1942	632,709	22,353	915,058	29,934	490,356	18,058
1944	595,933	20,677	852,597	33,866	533,374	17,159
1946	654,779	22,932	1,045,259	35,835	676,570	35,495
1948	1,158,675	59,050	1,981,536	107,740	885,195	47,754
1950	1,084,436	47,788	2,168,928	108,207	949,712	44,931
1952	1,106,157	54,342	2,657,408	111,895	1,072,266	37,170
1954	999,123	41,195	2,981,925	117,882	1,107,157	43,617

Source: *Moody's* and company annual reports for respective years.

Ward after that. But compared with the growth of Sears during this period, Ward's performance shows up poorly.

However, there were other costs of conservatism:

1. Market share eroded badly. For example, in mail-order business among the four major mail-order houses, Ward did 41.7 percent in 1945, while Sears had 50.7 percent of this total business; in 1951, Ward did 28.3 percent, while Sears' share had risen to 66.1 percent.
2. Loss of profits that might have been earned with reasonable expansion. In 1939, just before World War II, Ward was closing in on Sears. By 1952, Sears did almost two and a half times the volume and over twice the net profits.

From 1946 through 1951, Sears spent $305 million on 304 new or modernized stores, warehouses, and mail-order plants. Ward spent practically nothing for such improvements during this time. Table

Table 9.4 Current Ratio for Ward and Sears, 1942–1956

	Ward	Sears
1942	4.49	3.57
1948	4.46	2.55
1952	5.43	3.13
1956	7.29	3.58

Source: Annual Reports, respective years.

9.4 shows the current ratio (the ratio of current assets divided by current liabilities) during this period.

The current ratio is a measure of liquidity, and a ratio of 2.0 is acceptable by most creditors; that is, that current assets are twice as much as current liabilities. As you can see, Ward was well above this and rose to the astronomical high of 7.29 by the end of Avery's tenure, reflecting idle assets that could be reinvested to the amount of $325 million in cash and securities. Sears, on the other hand, with its rapid expansion, was approaching the 2.0 minimally acceptable level of liquidity in 1948.

THE TURNABOUT

In 1955, Louis Wolfson attempted a raid on Ward to gain control, but was unsuccessful. John Barr, the legal counsel for Ward, led the fight against Wolfson. His successful defense led to his succeeding the aged Avery as chief executive.

Barr attempted to put Ward back on the growth trail, and he opened 58 new stores between 1957 and 1961. But Barr was a lawyer and not an operating man. He could not resolve the problem of maintaining profits while vigorously opening new stores. As profits eroded, he decided to cancel the new-store program and thereby eliminate the costs of new store openings.

Profits continued to diminish in 1960–1961. At that point, Barr recognized his deficiencies and brought a strong operating man into the firm: Robert Brooker, who had been a major executive with Sears from 1944-1958, and who was the president of Whirlpool Corporation, a major appliance manufacturer.

Brooker was given a free hand in the reconstruction, and he promptly enticed a number of management people from Sears to work for him. Gradually, the emphasis on small-town locations was changed to big stores. With a $500 million expansion, he began opening new or renovated outlets in heavily populated urban areas. The *cluster concept* was utilized, with "clusters" of stores opened in such major urban areas as Chicago and Los Angeles. A major advantage of clusters is that such groupings of stores provide sales volume needed to sustain the high cost of advertising in major urban newspapers: heavy advertising costs can be spread over a number of stores, thus permitting overall advertising expenditures to be increased without putting a severe strain on profits of any individual store.

The results of the store construction on Ward's operations were clearly evident. Between 1957 and 1965, 182 new stores were built. They accounted for 72 percent of 1965 sales, and 73 percent of pretax profits.

Ward had also been slow in modernizing its catalog operations, which contributed from 30 to 40 percent of sales. In the first year after Brooker had taken over, this part of the business had been in the red. The manually operated mail-order system was so backward that the volume of orders during Christmas 1965 overwhelmed facilities and resulted in monumental delays and shipping errors. After this, the mail-order part of the business was mechanized and computerized. Brooker noted in 1967, "We have lost none of our enthusiasm for the catalog business." And he pointed out that this type of selling was growing faster than conventional retailing.[10]

INFORMATION SIDELIGHT

CONCENTRATION OF VENDORS

The supplier/customer relationship functions best when each is important to the other. This is true whether we are talking about retailers as customers (as in the Ward case) or industrial firms or institutional organizations. There are strong advantages in concentrating buying efforts with a few top-notch vendors:

1. The customer becomes important to the supplier, and vice versa. The rapport and cooperation thus gained may become manifest in many ways, from priority with new merchandise and filling of orders to prompt, cooperative attention given to servicing and to damaged merchandise. With a good relationship, a vendor may even help out a buyer or purchasing agent who made a bad or ill-timed purchase, and arrange to take back the goods or have them transferred to another customer.
2. Costs can be lessened. Less search time is needed on the part of the purchaser. Ordering and processing of goods are easier when fewer invoices and fewer shipments are involved.

Brooker initiated merchandising policy changes as well as an expansion and modernization program. He reduced the number of vendors that Ward did business with from 15,000 to 7200. Of these, 200 supplied half the goods flowing into Ward stores. Under Avery and Barr, Ward did not enforce a system of aging inventories and writing off older and slow-selling stock. This now became vigorously enforced, even though profitability of some stores was temporarily reduced by heavy markdowns. Before, Ward buyers were

---

[10] "Somebody Loves Ward's," *Business Week*, April 1, 1967, p. 34.

not allowed to make long-term contracts with manufacturers; they could only make one-time commitments. The effect of this was to deny manufacturers the assurances they needed of continued sales. Consequently, Ward was often unable to get a sufficient supply of some goods and lowest prices and was not able to exercise demands for quality controls. Transportation charges were often higher because of the diversity of suppliers and the necessity of frantically seeking rush orders and fill-in merchandise.

Ward's fortunes at last began to experience a reversal as profits and sales rose. Share of the market also began to increase, and, although this did not regain pre-war competitive levels with Sears, at least the disadvantage was lessened. Then, in 1968, Ward merged with Container Corporation to form Marcor Corporation. Sales of the joint undertaking rose to over $4 billion in 1973, while net income was almost $100 million, with Ward contributing 55 percent of total earnings.

WHAT CAN BE LEARNED?

The no-growth philosophy of Ward points out a fundamental principle of American enterprise: a firm cannot stand still; it must grow if it is to stay viable. Customers, suppliers, executives, all are attracted to the firm that is growth-minded, because all stand to benefit from a firm's increasing growth and prosperity. Although growth can be over-emphasized to the extent that a firm has neither the finances nor the management resources to handle it, the opposite is just as dangerous. Moderation in expansion is to be desired.

A firm should be willing to shift strategies. It cannot remain wedded to a mistake, even for the sake of principles. Avery's strategy after World War II might have been correct; however, after half a decade had passed without the expected economic collapse taking place, the time was overdue for reevaluation and refocusing of strategy. The competitive environment is dynamic; continual reassessment is needed if a firm is to be aggressive and successful.

The action of competitors cannot be disregarded. Although Ward disdained expansion under the mistaken impression that its strategy would prove correct eventually, there was still a need to counter competitive actions; they should not be permitted to expand unchallenged, as Sears did for too many years. Eventually, it becomes impossible to catch up.

Dictatorship in any organization is questionable at best: everything depends on the correctness of the judgment of the sole decision maker. Far better is a more flexible approach, one that is alert to feedback about the marketplace and to the ideas put out by associates and subordinates.

For retailing firms, sound merchandising principles should never be overlooked. The importance of merchandise turnover, prompt markdowns, fresh and clean stocks, and being important to vendors—these cannot be spurned. And yet, they sometimes are, when the top executives have not come out of the ranks of merchandising (as Avery had not).

A leader can be outstandingly successful at one stage of his or her career, as Sewell Avery certainly was in his years as president of U. S. Gypsum Company and in his early leadership of a badly floundering Ward in the 1930s. Yet, in another age, the formerly successful leader may lead an organization to a debacle. (Another great business leader was Henry Ford, who, in the early decades of the motorcar, pioneered the assembly line, mass distribution, and cost economies never before realized, only to succumb to a myopic and unbending refusal to recognize changing conditions and lose market position for good to the General Motors Corporation in the 1920s.) The great leader who is rigid and unbending often becomes error-prone in later years and intolerant toward capable subordinates who do not accept all of his views.

Eventually, after Avery, Ward pulled itself around and tried to resurrect a growth pattern. However, the lost years could never be regained. Poor judgment, which permitted no deviating opinions, cast a sorry spell over the company. A man who, for much of his life, had evinced outstanding success led Ward down the wrong path and was too stubborn to admit it.

Update

In 1974, the Mobil Corporation, its coffers bulging with oil profits, bought control of Marcor and Montgomery Ward for $1.7 billion. This move was widely criticized by the government and public interest groups, for it smacked of a disdain for what most perceived as the urgent national need for such profits to be invested in more petroleum and energy exploration and development.

In addition to public criticism, however, Mobil's stockholders were not benefited either profitwise. For example, in 1978, Mobil's energy and chemicals business earned 14 percent on stockholders' equity. Ward earned only 9.3 percent, and the Container Corporation of Marcor earned only 2.4 percent. This Ward profitability compared poorly with 5-year average returns on equity for K mart of 18.2 percent, for Dayton-Hudson of 17.8 percent, for J. C. Penney of 13.0 percent, and for Sears of 11.9 percent.[11]

The situation was to worsen in the 1980s, with Ward suffering losses totaling $336 million from 1980 to 1983. The chain owed its survival to $609 million in debt forgiveness and cash infusions from Mobil in the early 1980s.

Finally, on May 6, 1985, Mobil announced that it would take a $500

[11] Statistics are from the various companies' annual reports and other public statements.

million write-down on Ward's assets, "loss-plagued parts" of the chain, so that it could become "a freestanding, profitable retail company without Mobil ownership or financial guarantees."[12] The implication was that Ward might be headed for sale or spinoff.

For Thought And Discussion

1. How would you go about evaluating vendors for possible weeding out? Be as specific as you can.
2. Is dictatorial leadership necessarily bad? Discuss possible advantages or circumstances for dictatorial leadership. (In the discussion, make the assumption that the leader was correct in major policy decisions.)
3. What do you see as the relative merits of Ward's expansion into small towns during the late 1920s, rather than into larger cities, as Sears did? How valid would such a strategy have been in the 1940s and 1950s?
4. Why should a firm be "growth-minded" rather than content with the status quo? Be as specific as you can.

Invitation To Role Play

Assume the role of vice–president to Sewell Avery after World War II. What arguments would you give that some expansion efforts should still be made, even if his prediction of a major depression were eventually to come true? Be as persuasive as you can, and be prepared to counter the objections.

---

[12] "Mobil Tries to Make the Best of a Bad Buy," *Business Week,* May 20, 1985, p. 61.

10

Gillette—"We Don't Want To Cannibalize"

Even firms whose past performances have been beyond reproach, and whose profits are the envy of American industry, can succumb to mistakes and leave themselves vulnerable to competitive inroads, inroads that need never have happened. In the early 1960s, venerable Gillette erred in assessing the impact of a new product in its industry: the stainless steel blade. It was reluctant to cannibalize (take sales away from) the major product in its line, the Super Blue blade, and procrastinated in introducing its own stainless steel blade. It thereby gave competitors the opportunity to wrest away some of its dominance. The result was a loss in market share never to be fully regained. How could such a thing happen to a shrewd and aggressive firm?

THE PROFIT MACHINE, 1962

Through the years, the Gillette Company had compiled one of the best profit records in American industry. In 1962, the company racked up its fourth consecutive record year, with sales of $276 million and net earnings of $45 million—a profit margin of 16.4 percent. This was the fourth best return on sales of all corporations on *Fortune's* list of the 500 largest industrial corporations. Even more noteworthy, Gillette was number one in return on invested capital, with a whopping 40 percent—no other major firm in the U.S. could claim such profitability.

INFORMATION SIDELIGHT

THE KEY INDICATOR OF PROFITABILITY:
RETURN ON INVESTMENT

The true measure of the profitability of any investment is the return—the interest, dividends, or profits—we get for the money invested. This is true whether the money is in a savings and loan association paying 5½ percent interest or in a business, where it may realize more. But note that in the examples below return on investment is not the same as net profit percentage of sales.

	Firm A	*Firm B*
Sales	$100,000,000	$100,000,000
Investment in plant and equipment, inventories, etc.	30,000,000	90,000,000
Net profit %	10%	12%
Net profit dollars	10,000,000	12,000,000
Return on investment (profit divided by investment)	33%	13.33%

In this example, Firm A is much more profitable, despite its lower net profit, than Firm B, because the money needed for investment in the plant, equipment, raw materials and other inventories, etc., is so much less than that required for Firm B.

In its primary business of manufacturing and selling razor blades, Gillette dominated the market. In 1962, it had 70 percent of the $175 million retail blade market, up from 40 percent of an $86 million blade market in 1946. Of the total razor blade market, single-edge and injector blades accounted for 25 percent, whereas the double-edge segment was 75 percent of the market. And in this important double-edge segment, Gillette was even more dominant, holding an awesome 90 percent share of the market.

It is not surprising, then, that as a result of this market share and profit performance, the company had no debt of any kind. About 30 percent of its assets, some $56 million, were in cash and marketable securities. With highly automated machinery, efficiency and production costs continued to improve. For example, in 1952, 850 blades per man-hour were produced; by 1961, Gillette improved to 3100 blades per man-hour. A sharp eye was also kept on other costs, such as packaging costs, which accounted for about half the factory costs of blades—all this while maintaining rigid quality control.

The Super Blue blade was the heart of the Gillette blade line, the top of the line, by far the biggest profit maker, and the one most sought after by consumers. The more economy-minded customers used the Thin or the Blue blade, both of which had been on the market much longer. The Super Blue was introduced in 1960 after 5 years of laboratory research aimed at developing a silicone coating that would prevent hair molecules from clinging to the blade and impeding the cutting. The much easier shaving with the Super Blue resulted in its immediate success, even though it was priced 40 percent higher than the old Blue blade. Despite the silicone coating and some necessary heat treatment, the production costs of the Super Blue were not appreciably higher than for the other blades. The Super Blue soon had a major impact on Gillette's profits. In 1962, it contributed some $15 million in profits, more than one-third of the company's total net profit.

As we come into the 1960s, two men were in charge of the company. Carl Gilbert had been chief executive since 1956. Silver-haired, genial, calm, and thoughtful, his areas of specialization were manufacturing and finance. The second man was Boone Gross, a direct descendant of Daniel Boone and a West Point graduate; he was president of the company. He had joined Gillette in 1946 as general sales manager, at which time he had launched a program that tripled the sales force and increased sales of blades 150 percent in 3 years. In contrast to Gilbert, he was dark-haired, aggressive, and restless, with expertise in sales and management.

EARLY HISTORY OF THE GILLETTE COMPANY

In the winter of 1901, a salesman named King C. Gillette and several associates rented a room over a fish market in Boston, where they made a shaving device invented by Gillette: a safety razor with thin replaceable blades. This was a far handier shaving tool than the old straight-edge razor that could even be used as a weapon. However, the results that first year were not very encouraging; only 51 razors and 163 blades were sold. But things slowly improved until, by 1917, annual razor sales were over 1 million, with 120 million blades being sold each year.

Then, the United States entered World War I, and almost all of the Boston factory's output went to the armed forces. Men who had never heard of a safety razor were issued a Gillette and began to shave regularly. Most continued with the practice when they returned home after the war, rather than going back to straight-edge razors or professional shaves by a barber. World War II introduced Gillette and self-shaving to millions more. By 1961, the shaving population was 61 million people in the United States, with 1,700,000 new shavers entering the market every year. Each year, $426 million was being spent for razors, blades, electric shavers, shaving creams, lotions, and talcums. This did not include the rapidly growing overseas market, where rising living standards and populations suggested greater potential markets for shaving products than in the United States.

As the Gillette Company grew in size and industry dominance, it expanded its research and development activities. By 1960, over 80 scientists and technicians were engaged in fundamental and applied research. Out of the research program had come the blade dispenser, developed at the close of World War II, which did away with paper-wrapped blades and permitted insertion of the blade directly into the razor; this eliminated most of the danger of being accidentally cut while handling a razor blade. The adjustable razor was brought out in 1957 and contributed to shaving comfort by permitting easy adjustment of blade angle and exposure to suit any combination of skin and beard. Then, in 1960, came the Super Blue blade. This was the company's first new blade product in 21 years and represented a major improvement in shaving ease (though not in blade longevity), by requiring 60 percent less cutting force for the average shaver than ordinary blades. Its edge was 750 times thinner than a newspaper page, so thin that it had to be measured by an electron microscope.

For decades, the company's product line had been limited to safety razors, double-edged blades, and shaving cream. Then, in 1948, it acquired the Toni Company, a leading manufacturer of women's hair preparations. Other acquisitions followed, most notably the Paper Mate Corporation in 1955. Although Gillette had marketed a brushless shaving cream in a tube for many years, it made a major thrust into the toiletries business with the introduction of Foamy Shave Cream in 1954, and Right Guard deodorant in 1960.

In the heady days as the company moved into the 1960s, it could look ahead with complete optimism. With a new plant in Boston and facilities abroad, it had all the capacity it would need for razor blade production for years to come. Its market seemed secure, unless the whiskered look were suddenly to become the universal mode, or unless a depilatory were to be invented that would banish the need for razors and blades—and no depilatory was on the horizon that could remove whiskers without damage to sensitive facial skin tissue.

THE STAINLESS STEEL BLADE

Wilkinson: Just a Gnat

Wilkinson Sword Ltd., headquartered in Chiswick, a London suburb, was a family-owned firm of swordsmiths, about 190 years old in 1961. Although the company still made ceremonial swords, its principal interest was a line of expensive garden tools (for example, a pair of its pruning shears retailed for $12.75, and this was in the days before inflation). Almost incidentally, Wilkinson began making a stainless steel razor blade, the Super Sword-Edge. Properly manufactured, the stainless steel blade is sharp, corrosion-free, and long-lasting—some men were getting more than 15 shaves per blade, versus an average of 3½ shaves for the regular carbon blades.

Of course, stainless steel blades cost more. Carbon steel strips, from which most double-edge blades were made, cost about $1900 a ton; the steel used for stainless blades, about $3700 a ton. The manufacturing process itself was also more expensive: grinding, stropping, special heat-treating, and quality control added to the costs and tended to limit production. Consequently, the Wilkinson blade was selling for about 15¢, versus about 6.9¢ for a Gillette Super Blue, 5¢ for the Blue, and 3.5¢ for the Thin.

In the summer of 1961, Wilkinson began marketing its tools in the United States. However, getting distribution for an unknown line that sold for two to three times American prices was difficult, at best. Wilkinson finally convinced some dealers and distributors to stock its products by placing the tools in garden shops on consignment (whereby Wilkinson kept title to the goods until they were sold by the dealer and bore all the risks and inventory costs).

In November 1961, the Wilkinson U.S. sales subsidiary got the first trickle of stainless steel razor blades from England. They were mentioned in promotional letters to the dealers, and there was an immediate reaction. By the spring of 1962, dealers were clamoring for more blades. Some were giving them away one at a time to customers for promotional purposes; others were selling them as fast as they could get them. About this time, a few small entrepreneurs who supplied sundries to tobacconists and druggists wandered into the cramped New York City sales office and cajoled them out of a few cartons of blades for resale. Macy's also heard about the blade and took six cartons a week.

As the blades moved irresistibly into distribution, word-of-mouth reports spread. Retail stocks were soon exhausted, and a new distribution policy was instituted. Blades henceforth were to be available only through authorized dealers; to be authorized, a dealer also had to stock the Wilkinson garden tool line. Consequently, garden supply shops and suburban hardware stores remained practically the only "authorized dealers" of Wilkinson blades. These stainless steel blades, then, in the midst of an insatiable demand, became the supreme promotional leader: customers were drawn to the garden shops—the only places they could get the blades—and they were sold the garden tools. As Wilkinson admitted, the profit on the blades was not very large; on the other hand, the tools were very profitable indeed.[1]

So, Wilkinson introduced the superior shaving product, stainless steel razor blades, to the market. By late 1962, it had already gained 15 percent of the British blade market, which Gillette had previously dominated with a 75 percent market share. Now, almost in spite of itself, the U.S. market was practically begging for this scarce item. But Wilkinson was such a gnat. In fact, in 1962, it exported about 7 million blades to the United States, less than one day's output for Gillette. It had limited blade-manufacturing capacity and was without the necessary mass distribution channels. Although Wilkinson intended to increase production, in no way was it in a position to match horns with the behemoth Gillette—nor, apparently, was it interested in doing so. But there were others who were!

U.S. Competitors: Hungry And Aggressive

Wilkinson, despite its heavily demanded new product, could hardly be depicted as either an aggressive competitor or a serious challenge to Gillette, but the publicity the Wilkinson blade engendered was not lost on Gillette's smaller and relatively unprosperous U.S. competitors. Indeed, the lack of interest by Gillette gave them the opening wedge they needed: a chance to bring out a stainless steel blade before Gillette.

Little Eversharp, Incorporated, with assets of $20 million, was already exploiting the opening. On January 26, 1963, it began marketing a stainless steel blade, priced at five for $0.79, under its Schick "Krona Plus" label in New York City and 11 Western states. "We're in heavy production," said its chairman, Patrick J. Frawley, Jr., "and we've already started shipping."[2] With 1962 sales of only $24.5 million against Gillette's sales of $276 million, this would hardly seem a formidable competitor. But . . .

Another competitor out to exploit the stainless steel breakthrough was the American Safety Razor division of Philip Morris. Its plans were to introduce its Personna, a stainless steel blade, in the early spring. "This will give us entry into the double-edge blade business which we have never been in before. We expect a tremendous improvement," proclaimed its president.[3]

Gillette's Position re Stainless Steel Blades, 1962-1963

So, where were Gillette's stainless blades? Why were its competitors given this opportunity? Boone Gross, Gillette's president, stoutly stated "We are

---

[1] "Cheek by Trowel," *Business Week*, December 22, 1962, p. 82.
[2] "Close Shave," *Forbes*, February 1, 1963, p. 14.
[3] Ibid., p. 15.

not inclined to use crash programs."[4] Technological reasons, particularly the production problems in getting a stainless steel blade into the kind of mass production Gillette needed, were cited for the delay. The company claimed, for instance, that it was much harder to get a proper cutting edge on a stainless steel blade than on a carbon steel blade, and that the rejection rate would consequently be considerably higher.

Chairman Gilbert admitted that the company did not particularly like having to put a stainless blade on the market at that time: "We're doing it primarily as a response. When other people come in, we have to join. But we wouldn't have chosen this route."[5] Part of the bearish thinking came from the fear that the Gillette stainless blade, although priced higher than the company's other blades, would yield so many more good shaves that the customer would end up spending less per shave—buying far fewer blades— thereby bringing Gillette's profits down. There was particular fear that the highly profitable Super Blue blade would be adversely affected—that its sales would be cannibalized.

Gillette's analysis of the situation involved three considerations other than the production and technological problems in starting up the mass production of the new blades:

1. Cost to Gillette of the stainless blade, relative to the price it could obtain.
2. Durability of the blade.
3. Kind of customer most attracted to the stainless blade.

Undoubtedly, there would be substantially higher costs in producing the new stainless steel blade. Not only would stainless steel costs be twice as much as carbon steel, but new production lines would have to be installed; there would have to be considerable training of technicians for the new process. However, some of these costs would be nonrecurring. The only cost that should continue to go higher would be the cost of the raw material, the new type of steel. At the same time the raw material costs would be increased, packaging costs would decline somewhat. By packaging the new stainless steel blades in the same kind of dispenser now used for the Super Blue blade, fewer packages would be needed to put a year's blade supply in the hands of the consumer. With the selling price two to four times the price of Gillette's other blades, the profit per blade should be higher.

A somewhat more difficult estimate to make was the durability of the blade—that is, how many shaves the average user would get from one

---

[4] "Women! God Bless 'Em," *Forbes*, May 15, 1965, p. 26.
[5] Walter Guzzardi, Jr., "Gillette Faces the Stainless Steel Dragon," *Fortune*, July 1963, p. 240.

Table 10.1 Cannibalization: Possible Consequences of the Stainless Steel Blade on
Gillette Profits

	Stainless	Super Blue
Retail selling price	15¢	7¢
Mark-up percentage for retailers	33%	33%
Gillette's revenue per blade	10¢	4⅔¢
Estimated cost to Gillette	4¢	2¢
Gross margin per blade	6¢	2⅔¢
Average use of blade	unknown, but probably between 7 to 16 shaves	3⅓ shaves
Approximate number of blades used in a year		100
If 8–shave average	45	
If 12–shave average	30	
If 16–shave average	22	
Profit margin per customer per year		$2.67
With 8–shave average	$2.70	
With 12–shave average	$1.80	
With 16–shave average	$1.32	

stainless blade. If the average man used the blade for about eight shaves,
which was twice as many as the average shaver got from a carbon-steel
blade, then Gillette would fare well. It would be offering a new blade that
would last twice as long as the Super Blue, that was priced twice as high, but
that cost less than twice as much to make. On the other hand, if the average
switcher from the Super Blue to the stainless blade used it for 16 shaves—
four times as many as the Super Blue—then Gillette's profits would drop by
as much as 25 percent. Table 10.1 shows the effects of cannibalization on
Gillette profits for several different rates of usage for the stainless blade.
Gross and Gilbert could hardly be unconcerned, knowing that some of the
early users were getting more than 15 shaves from each blade. Some even
gloated as to how many shaves they could eke out of a single blade, even to
the point of sacrificing some comfort. Were these to be typical?

The final unknown facing Gillette in the decision to go with the stainless
steel blade was what type of customer would be most attracted to it. If this
were the Super Blue blade user—if the stainless blade were to cannibalize
Gillette's most valuable property—then the firm should be reluctant to
embrace the new product. As we see in Table 10.1, only if a former Super
Blue user were to average eight shaves or less with the stainless blade would
the profit be maintained or improved, and this was by no means a certainty.

Yet, the company had some reason to hope the new blade would not cause many Super Blue users to switch. Laboratory tests had shown that the stainless steel blade, although it gave better third and fourth shaves than the Super Blue, did not give as good a first shave: stainless steel blades required 1½ lb of pressure to make the same cut as 1 lb by the Super Blue. Gillette, furthermore, based on some early sales data in England, had reason to believe that once the inital glamour wore off, the man most interested in the stainless blade would be the economy-minded customer who wanted the cheapest shave possible, even at some sacrifice of comfort. This would be the man who used the Gillette Thin or the Blue, and not the Super Blue customer. Although Gillette might then experience some loss in sales, the switch to stainless steel would mean higher profit margins per blade, and as much or more profit. And the Super Blue blade, the real profit-maker for Gillette, would not be imperiled.

Such reasoning finally assuaged some of Gillette's fears and hesitation in starting production on its own stainless steel blades. However, there still were enough unknowns for Gillette to procrastinate; it entered the market months after its competitors had moved aggressively.

Gillette finally brought its own version of the stainless steel blade to market in the fall of 1963, a good 6 months after Eversharp and American Safety Razor had introduced theirs. Once the decision to market the stainless blade was made, Gillette moved with its customary aggressiveness. First introduced in the New York and Philadelphia markets in early September, nationwide distribution had been achieved to over 500,000 retail outlets by October. The blades were competitively priced at six for $0.89.

Gillette supported its new production with $4 million of promotional and advertising funds. About 80 percent of the budget was diverted from other Gillette blade lines, notably from the Super Blue blade, which previously had received most of Gillette's promotional push. Because of the market-by-market introduction, the advertising campaign included intensive television spot (local) advertising. The exposure was soon broadened to include the traditional Gillette-sponsored telecasts of the World Series, Fight of the Week, American Football League games, Wide World of Sports, and the Rose Bowl.

The Result

During the next few years, Gillette paid the price of being the last company to the market with the stainless blade. Profits declined badly in 1963 and 1964. See Table 10.2. The effect on profitability is even more striking when we consider the return on investment (the real measure of profitability). Table 10.3 shows how the lofty 40 percent that made Gillette the most profitable of all U.S. firms dropped precipitously to below 30 percent by 1964, and was not regained.

Table 10.2   Gillette Company Sales and Profits, 1955–1964

Year	Net Sales	Net Income (after taxes)
1955	$176,928,594	$28,378,393
1956	200,714,707	28,726,938
1957	194,929,175	23,312,315
1958	193,865,095	25,593,990
1959	209,276,635	31,151,623
1960	224,737,000	37,123,000
1961	253,502,000	42,761,000
1962	276,159,000	45,274,000
1963	295,700,000	41,545,000
1964	298,956,000	37,673,000

Source: Published company records.

But more damaging by far was the loss of market share. This fell from 70 percent of the wet shaving market to 55 percent, while share of the double-edge blade market declined from 90 percent to 70 percent. With the situation stabilized as of October 1965, Gillette had obtained about 45 percent of the stainless blade market. However, Schick could claim 35 percent, American Safety Razor 15 percent, and little Wilkinson had about 5 percent of the market.

Table 10.3   Gillette's Return on Investment, 1960–1967

Year	(1) Stockholder's Equity (000)	(2) Net Income (000)	(3) Return on Investment (2)÷(1)
1960	$ 94,436	$37,123	39.3%
1961	106,601	42,761	40.1
1962	113,065	45,274	40.0
1963	121,918	41,545	34.1
1964	126,265	37,673	29.8
1965	136,346	42,330	31.0
1966	153,145	49,866	32.6
1967	186,721	56,615	30.3

Source: Calculated from published company records.

ANALYSIS OF GILLETTE'S DELAY WITH THE STAINLESS STEEL BLADE

Perhaps this was a "small" mistake. Certainly, the viability of the company was not jeopardized, nor was the mistake to result in monumental cost write-offs, as experienced by some of the other firms in this book. Rather, here we have only a hesitation, a missed step perhaps, resulting in a somewhat lower profit showing for a few years than might otherwise have been the case. What is so bad about this, you might ask, to merit its being included in a book of classic mistakes?

But here we are exposed to the importance of market share, something that ought to be zealously guarded and maintained, even though the slippage of a few percentage points may not always seem so crucial, especially if sales and profits are still maintained at comfortable levels. But market-share erosion means a shifting of customers to competitors. These customers may never be regained. There's the rub, and the critical importance of market share.

Whatever its reasons, Gillette tarried too long in introducing the stainless steel blade. In so doing, competitors were given a chance to gain a niche they probably could not have gained otherwise; the precious market share was ill-protected. It can be argued that there really was no mistake. Hesitating to introduce the new blade can be supported as a calculated effort to let competitors face the risks inherent in bringing out a new product; only if it turned out to be successful would Gillette step in.

Charitably, we can find rationale for hesitating with the stainless steel blade. Procrastination by Gillette's management can be supported. But, can a reluctance to embrace innovation really be condoned? For any firm or organization? Whatever the rationale, Gillette erred in taking a back seat with this promising innovation in shaving. Gillette was the industry leader, and it should have led with this. Sure, it misjudged the eagerness and the effectiveness with which its smaller competitors were able to develop their production capabilities. But, in whatever industry, when the dominant firm is willing to take a back seat, to let some other firm gain the initiative . . . this is hardly the mark of aggressive and effective management.

WHAT CAN BE LEARNED?

Successful management is alert to opportunities, quick to note them, quick to pursue them. Of course, not all innovations will be successful. But there is usually less risk in trying an innovation, even if it fails, than in not trying and letting another firm have a roaring success and a consequent competitive advantage.

There is the serious temptation for the dominant and successful firm in

INFORMATION SIDELIGHT

BOSTON CONSULTING GROUP'S APPROACH TO STRATEGY IMPLEMENTATION

The Boston Consulting Group, a leading management consulting firm, has boiled down the major strategy decisions a firm faces to only four, depending on a firm's competitive position in a particular industry and the growth of that industry. Accordingly, a firm's major business categories can be classified as: Stars, Question Marks, Cash Cows, and Dogs. Figure 10.1 presents a matrix of this concept.

A different strategy implementation is recommended for each of these business categories, as follows:

Category	Strategy Implementation
Stars	*Build.* In a dominant market position and a rapidly growing industry, more investment and long-term profit goals are recommended, even if they come at the expense of short-term profitability.
Question Marks	*Build or Divest.* The decision as to whether to commit more resources to trying to build such products into leaders or whether to divest and use company resources elsewhere is not clear-cut and easily made. It may depend on the strength of major competitors and how well-heeled the company is: e.g., it may decide it cannot provide sufficient financing to achieve the growth needed vis-à-vis competition.
Cash Cows	*Harvest.* When in a dominant position in a low-growth industry, the recommended strategy implementation is to reap the harvest of a strong cash flow. Only enough resources should be reinvested to maintain competitive position.
Dogs	*Divest.* There is no use wasting resources on poor competitive positions in low-growth industries. The recommended strategy is to sell or liquidate this business.[6]

[6] For additional reading, see Philip Kotler, *Principles of Marketing* (Englewood Cliffs, N.J.: Prentice-Hall, 1980), p. 80–82; Charles W. Hofer and Dan Schendel, *Strategy Formulation: Analytical Concepts* (St. Paul, Minn.: West Publishing, 1978), pp. 30–32; and George S. Day, "Diagnosing the Product Portfolio," *Journal of Marketing*, April 1977, pp. 29–38.

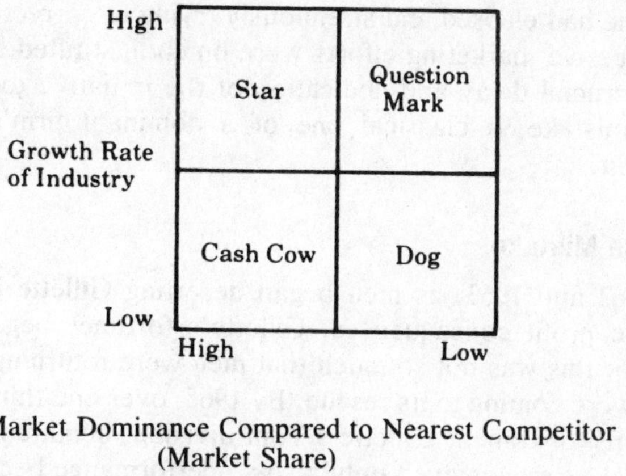

Relative Market Dominance Compared to Nearest Competitor
(Market Share)

Figure 10-1. Matrix of a firm's major business categories

Star = Dominant market position in a high-growth industry
Question Mark = Weak market position in a high-growth industry
Cash Cow = Dominant market position in a low-growth industry
Dog = Weak market position in a low-growth industry

Gillette, at the time of this mistake, was obviously in a cash cow situation, with high profits and minimum growth prospects facing it in its razor blade sector of business. It did not want to disrupt the harvesting of this business. But it became greedy in the sense of being reluctant to invest resources that might have resulted in diluting the beautiful cash flow. Unfortunately, a cash cow implementation strategy can leave a firm vulnerable to competitive inroads, despite the industry's lack of growth. High profits attract competition, especially when the total market is large, as the razor blade market was.

an industry to rest on its laurels, to be content with the status quo, to view significantly different products as disruptive and potentially cannibalizing, and therefore not worthy of support. There is also the temptation for the dominant firm to underestimate its competitors and what they are capable of doing: ". . . after all, they have not come close to matching our performance; they have proven themselves second rate; they are no threat." But such perceptions, comfortable though they may be, are often misleading, because downtrodden competitors tend to be more hungry, more willing to take risks, and more flexible in action than the large, complacent, and typically conservative industry leader.

In one sense, Gillette can be lauded for recognizing the error before much time had elapsed and strenuously trying to correct it. Decisive action and aggressive marketing efforts were finally instituted by the fall of 1963. But the crucial delay and abdication of the initiative to other firms was a serious mistake, a classical one of a dominant firm's unreceptivity to innovation.

After The Mistake

After 1962 and 1963, as men began deserting Gillette in droves with the inevitable profit consequences, Gillette's fortunes began improving. The reason for this was not so much that men were returning to Gillette as that women were coming to its rescue. By 1965, over one-third of Gillette's U.S. sales were to women. Gillette's Toni division, acquired in 1948, had for a number of years achieved only a so-so performance because of the decline of home permanents caused by the popularity of softer hair styles. Now it was becoming highly profitable with its Adorn hair spray, White Rain shampoo, Tame creme rinse, and Deep Magic facial cleansing lotion. In 1965, Toni contributed $10 million of Gillette's total profit of $42 million for that year. Even more spectacular was the success of Right Guard deodorant, again thanks to women. Right Guard had been introduced as a man's deodorant in 1960. But marketing surveys showed it to be very popular with women, too. Subsequently, Gillette used two cities as tests for an advertising theme of Right Guard as a family deodorant, rather than a man's deodorant. Sales doubled in those two cities in 4 months. By 1965, marketed as a family deodorant, Right Guard had become the number one deodorant in the United States, with sales over $17 million. (Recent advertising for Right Guard, however, has returned to the original target of men.)

In 1965, the double-edge market accounted for 75 percent of the $200 million razor blade market; single-edge and injector blades accounted for the other 25 percent of the market. Within the important double-edge segment, 50 percent of the dollar volume had now been captured by the stainless steel blade since its introduction less than 3 years before; carbon steel blades accounted for the other half of this market. The stainless steel blade was being used for an average of 10 shaves, and continued to be retailed at $0.15 each, versus $0.04 for regular carbon steel blades and $0.07 for Gillette's Super Blue.[7]

By 1965, Gillette's stainless steel blade had captured over half the stainless market. But Schick and Personna had firmly established their stainless steel blades in a way never possible with their regular blades.

[7] "Close Shave," p. 26.

Table 10.4   Gillette Company Sales and Profits, 1965–1970

Year	Net Sales	Net Income (after taxes)
1965	$339,064,000	$42,330,000
1966	396,190,000	49,866,000
1967	428,357,000	56,615,000
1968	553,174,000	62,278,000
1969	609,557,000	65,532,000
1970	672,669,000	66,075,000

Source: Published company records.

Although its diversification kept its profits from sinking abysmally, Gillette's overall earnings still declined for 2 years; not until 1966 were they to equal the net income of 1962. Table 10.4 shows the sales and profit performance for 1965 through 1970.

Update

In the 1970s, sales and profits marched inexorably ahead—the stainless steel blade miscalculation had seemingly long since been shrugged off. By 1973, Gillette's worldwide corporate net sales exceeded the billion dollar mark for the first time, reaching $1,064,427,000. Net profits were $86,665,000, also the highest in the company's history.

By 1984, sales were $2,288,600,000 with profits of $159,300,000. Return on investment (or equity), however, lagged far behind the 30 to 40 percent returns in the decade of the 1960s, as shown in Table 10.3. The 5-year average ending in 1984 was 19.6 percent.

For Thought And Discussion

1. Using an analysis similar to that of Table 10.1 calculate the effect on profits of cannibalization of the Gillette Thin blades, assuming that the selling price is 4¢, the retail markup is 33 percent, and the cost to Gillette is 1¾¢. What do you conclude from this analysis as to the desirability of marketing the stainless steel blade?
2. Critique the Wilkinson distribution strategy with its stainless steel blade. What rationale can you give for its nonaggressive efforts with its blade?
3. What rationale can you give for divesting or abandoning a product that is in a rapidly growing industry, but in which you have only a meager competitive position? What arguments can you give for trying to strengthen the competitive position?

Invitation To Role Play

Assume the role of vocal and critical stockholder at the annual meeting of the Gillette Company in early 1963. What arguments would you introduce for the company to bring out its own stainless steel blade without delay? How would you counter contrary arguments from Messrs. Gross and Gilbert?

11

Coors—"We Are Immune To Competition"

A tragedy occurred in the winter of 1960 that was to have an impact on the fortunes of the Adolph Coors Company, brewers, some 15 years later. On the morning of February 9, Adolph Coors III, 44-year-old chairman of the board of the brewing empire, kissed his wife and four children goodbye and drove off for the plant 12 miles away. He was never seen alive again.

For months, one of the most intensive manhunts in Colorado history took place. Finally, on September 26, more than 7 months later, tattered clothing and scattered bones were accidentally discovered in a desolate, heavily wooded area of aspen and pine about 40 miles southeast of Denver. Apparently, after the body had been dumped, the remains were scattered by coyotes or hogs. Dental charts confirmed the identification of Coors.

THE GOLDEN YEARS

Adolph Coors III had been sharing leadership responsibilities with his father, Adolph Coors II. After the murder, the father again assumed the sole leadership mantle, even though his official title was treasurer, until he died in 1970 at the age of 86. The elder of the two surviving sons, William H. Coors, became the chairman and chief executive; the other son, Joseph, was president. There were no formal lines of authority, although Bill generally handled the technical side of brewing and Joe the financial and administrative functions.

Both Bill and Joe (employees called them by their first names) were lean, tall, and rugged outdoorsmen. In fact, they regarded physical fitness and athletic recreation as so important for their employees that executives and workers were sent to outdoor-survival schools. Golf was subsidized for employees. Ski trips were underwritten. But Bill and Joe were concerned with more than the therapeutic benefits of fresh air for their employees: they encouraged them not only to participate in these programs but also to compete. "If you can't fight competition, you don't need to survive," Bill Coors asserted.[1]

Sensational Growth

By 1970, Coors' accomplishments in the brewing industry were awesome— all the more so in light of Coors' nonconformity to existing industry practices. The company produced only one kind of beer, and this in a single brewery, albeit the largest in the world. It sold its beer in only 11 Western states, most of them the most sparsely populated areas of the United States. It refused to build branch plants and had not expanded its territory in 22 years. The one brewery in Golden, Colorado, was not even close to its biggest market, California—indeed, the average barrel of Coors traveled over 900 miles. Finally, its ads featuring rushing mountains streams, and the slogan "Brewed with pure Rocky Mountain Spring Water" had not been changed in 33 years.

Yet, Bill and Joe Coors' little regional brewery had moved up to the big time. With a 19 percent increase in production in 1969 over 1968, it moved into fourth place in the national beer rankings, the only regional brewer to come close to the national brewers. In 1969, the production of the top four breweries was as follows:

Anheuser-Busch	18.8 million barrels
Joseph Schlitz	13.7 million barrels
Pabst	10.2 million barrels
Coors	6.4 million barrels

Furthermore, in 9 of the 11 states where it had distribution, Coors topped all other brands in sales. Among the full 11 states, Coors' market share was 30 percent. In California, it had 41 percent of the market by 1973, compared with only 18 percent for the industry leader, Anheuser-Busch; in Oklahoma, almost 70 percent of all beer sold was Coors. Overall demand was so

---

[1] "Colorado's Coors Family Has Built an Empire on One Brand of Beer," *Wall Street Journal,* October 26, 1973, p. 1.

outstripping supply that the company was forced to ration its product among distributors.

In compiling this performance record, the brothers eschewed a marketing orientation. Bill Coors stated this succinctly: "Our top management thrust is on engineering and production . . . we're production-oriented. Nobody knows more about production than I do."[2] Emphasis was on making a quality beer in terms of processing and raw materials. The product was a mild, light-bodied beer, scientifically tested and brewed, using hops, rice, Rocky Mountain spring water, and a specially developed strain of barley grown by contract farmers.

Great pains were taken to preserve the flavor. Pasteurization, which would add to the ease of preserving, was shunned, because it would slightly affect the taste. To give the best quality assurance, the beer was canned at near-freezing temperatures and shipped under refrigeration to refrigerated warehouses. To ensure perfection of taste further, distributors were required to pull Coors cans off the shelves in 60 days, lest there be some fading of the flavor.

Coors had become the beer of celebrities, from President Ford, who packed Coors on Air Force One, to Henry Kissinger, as well as such actors as Paul Newman (who, in an *Esquire* interview, claimed, "The best domestic beer, bar none, is Coors") and Clint Eastwood. In these years, the famous, as well as the rank and file, were all contributing to the Coors "mystique." Some 300,000 Coors fans a year toured the brewery; others made "pilgrimages" to a waterfall near Grand Lake, Colorado, which was supposed to be the one pictured on Coors bottles and cans. T-shirts and sweatshirts emblazoned with "Coors—Breakfast of Champions" were being sold by entrepreneurs hoping to cash in on the Coors mystique. And in the East, where Coors was not directly distributed, it could sell for three times the regular price.

Besides the product, the company was unique from the rest of the industry in certain other respects. In the heady years of the 1960s and early 1970s, Bill and Joe shunned outside expertise. Advertising and promotion were handled by inside staff, and total expenditures averaged only one-quarter those of major competitors. Construction at the brewery was done by Coors' own construction crews. Company engineers designed machinery for the can plant. Management talent was developed and promoted from within the organization, rather than brought in from outside.

The guiding philosophy of the company since it was founded by a German orphan who stowed away on a U.S.–bound ship to avoid conscrip-

---

[2] "The Brewery That Breaks All the Rules," *Business Week*, August 22, 1970, p. 60.

tion into the German army—the first Adolph Coors, in 1873—was to refuse to go to a bank for a loan. Such fiscal conservatism led the company to reject some seemingly attractive expansion possibilities. For example, the company's can-manufacturing subsidiary, Coors Container Company, was instrumental in developing the technical process for making a two-piece aluminum can. Coors, however, sold the process to Continental Can Company and American Can Company: "We could have dominated the industry, but we would have had to borrow from the banks, and Coors doesn't do that."[3] Between 1970 and 1974, to keep up with the burgeoning demand for Coors beer, some $276 million was spent on plant expansion. And how was this financed? All of it from cash flow.

How Come The Mystique?

What was the magic of Coors? How durable was this magic or mystique likely to be? Perhaps part of the mystique was accidental and fortuitous: being a Western-made brew at a time when the freedom and environmental purity of the West—emphasized by Coors' slogan, "Pure Rocky Mountain Spring Water"—was seen by many consumers as contrasting sharply with the degradation of the industrial centers of population. But was it a better beer—better tasting, higher quality? There were many who said it was. Whether real or imagined, Coors offered a "unique selling proposition" that distinguished it from other beers. One could claim that coming from a single brewery ensured better quality control and uniformity of ingredients and flavor. The company liked to boast that Coors was the most expensively brewed beer in the world. A plant geneticist was employed full-time to develop improved strains of barley for malting. Most hops were imported from Germany. And, as noted before, great pains were taken to prevent any deterioration of the flavor in shipping and handling.

Undoubtedly, part of the mystique came from the contagion generated by the aficionados, those famous and not so famous. A Western image conveying the out-of-doors and environmental purity, a light-tasting beer . . . perhaps the timing could not have been better in the 1960s and the early 1970s. (In the cigarette industry, Marlboro rose to become the top seller on a somewhat similar advertising and image thrust: The Marlboro man.)

It hardly seemed to Bill and Joe that the golden image of their beer could in the span of just a few years fade drastically. How could it help but be enduring?

---

[3] "Colorado's Coors Family," p. 27.

Going Public

For 103 years, ever since the first Adolph Coors opened his brewery on the trail to the Colorado gold camps, the company stayed private—talks of having public or outside shareholders were anathema to the Coors family. And it seemed that the company could indeed finance large-scale capital expenditures internally. Throughout the decade of the 1960s, its average rate of growth was over 10 percent, all this without turning to outside stock ownership or borrowing. In 1975, Coors had only $2 million in long-term debt on its books, against $375 million in equity.

But, in 1975, the proud family tradition had to be abandoned. With the death of Bill and Joe's parents, the Internal Revenue Service presented a bill for $50 million in inheritance taxes. Many companies would have solved such a problem by going into debt, but Bill and Joe decided to go public as the lesser of two evils. To avoid the risk of relinquishing control of the company to outsiders, they would offer only nonvoting shares. Furthermore, to avoid diluting the equity, no more than five percent of net income would be paid as dividends.

The time for such a stock offering was not very propitious. The Dow Jones Industrial Average was then moving between 620 and 690, and many were the investors who thought it would go still lower. Added to a sick stock market, the restrictions placed on this new stock venture were hardly likely to appeal to many investors. Because the shares would be nonvoting, this precluded listing on the New York Stock Exchange, as well as being offered for sale in many states, including California, where Coors' stock could otherwise have had a warm reception. The nonvoting feature would also make the stock offering unattractive to many large institutional investors.

In the end, Coors lucked out. When the offering finally reached the market, the stock market was beginning to rebound. Coors' investment bankers found so much interest in the stock in the last days before the offering that they raised the price to $31 a share. And it was a sellout the first afternoon. Not only was $50 million raised to pay off the inheritance taxes, but an additional $77 million went into company coffers. This $127 million offering was the first major new stock issue to come to market since 1973 and the fourth largest offering by industrial companies in the previous 10 years. The mystique of the company and its beer mitigated all the negative factors impinging on demand.

Geographical Expansion

Bill Coors now turned his attention to geographical expansion. The first target was eastern and southern Texas. Prior to this, the only Texas inroads were in the northern part of the state around Dallas, and the western part.

Eager to jump on a lucrative bandwagon, potential distributors lined up like beauty queen candidates, vying for selection by Coors. The contest, however, was hardly for the weak or poorly financed, because Coors' distributors had to build refrigerated warehouses to keep the beer under 40 degrees until opened by customers. From 4000 "panting" contestants, Coors selected 29 distributors for the eastern Texas expansion.

By 1976, Coors was also invading Montana and looking closely at expansion into Washington State, Arkansas, Nebraska, and Missouri, the latter state being the home base of Anheuser-Busch, the largest brewer. Bill Coors was also laying plans for expanding to the heavily populated Eastern market: "I think we've got a good enough beer—the beer that won the West—to assure ourselves 20 percent to 25 percent of the nationwide market," he told *Forbes'* reporters in the summer of 1976.[4] A bold statement this, with Anheuser holding 24 percent of the total market, while Coors had only 8.2 percent—although admittedly on far less than national distribution, (in fact, on only 20 percent of the total national distribution).

The question of whether expansion could still be handled out of the one brewery in Golden seemed not particularly troublesome to Bill. The Golden brewery was already at an annual capacity of 12.3 million barrels, and about 1 million barrels of capacity was being added a year; Bill was aiming for a total of 25 million. "Eventually we might build other breweries," he said. "But if you take a circle up around from where we already ship to in Northern California, you hit Atlanta, Georgia."[5]

The growth and profitability picture—and the highly successful public stock offering—should have been cause for heady optimism and great satisfaction for the Coors brothers. Sales for 1975 were $520 million, up from $350 million just 4 years before. Operating margin on net sales had reached 28 percent, the highest in the industry. Profit per barrel averaged almost $9, about double that of Anheuser. But there were some ominous portents on the horizon.

STORM SIGNALS FOR COORS, 1975-1976

Although the successful public stock float spurred new ambitions, trouble was brewing in the California market—a key market that accounted for almost 40 percent of all Coors' sales. In a bitter dispute with Coors' Oakland distributor, the California Teamsters called for a statewide boycott of the beer. At the same time, Anheuser was bringing on line a new 3.75 million

---

4 "Off Coors," *Forbes*, June 1, 1976, p. 60.
5 Ibid., p. 61.

barrel brewery in northern California. As a result, in this key market, Coors' sales dropped about 10 percent in 1975, while market share fell 4 percent to 36 percent. Anheuser picked up most of this, gaining 3 percent to a 23.2 percent share of the California market. Perhaps another contributor to the market share losses in California was a hefty price hike made in 1974 without first warning retailers.

Several other aggravations were also being encountered. In January 1975, the Federal Trade Commission was upheld by the Supreme Court in its efforts to loosen the tight grip Coors had held on its 167 distributors. Then, the Equal Opportunities Commission filed a suit against Coors alleging discrimination against minorities in hiring and in promotions. And the Colorado Health Department charged Coors with polluting Clear Creek, in the very same valley where the "Rocky Mountain Spring Water" rises.

Finally, brother Joe was embarrassed as the Senate Commerce Committee vetoed his nomination to the board of the Corporation for Public Broadcasting, citing Coors' ownership of a right-wing television news service as a conflict of interest. Joe had long been known locally as an archconservative, but his political views came to national attention in 1975 when the *Washington Post* ran four lengthy stories about his right-wing efforts in allegedly using Television News, Inc., a broadcast news agency subsidiary of the Coors Company, to further his own political views. This publicity, as well as the fact that the news subsidiary was losing money, induced the company to close down the TV news service. Whatever negative effect might have emanated from the unfavorable publicity could not be gauged.

Some dangers could be seen in the decision to push East, even though such a move, if successful, would greatly increase Coors' sales as well as lessen the risks inherent in relying on only a few markets—such as the California one—for maintenance of growth and even viability. To attempt to enter the Eastern markets would bring Coors face to face with entrenched major brewers: Schlitz, Pabst, and Philip Morris's Miller, in addition to Anheuser-Busch. Miller, in particular, looked like a most formidable competitor: it had become the nation's fastest-growing major beer company and, by the beginning of 1976, had moved to third place in the U.S. beer market, moving ahead of Coors in the process. Undoubtedly, Coors move to the East would necessitate massive additional advertising expenditures. Although sales might be increased by such expansion efforts, more questionable was what effect such expansion would have on profits. Furthermore, despite optimism by Bill Coors about their one brewery being adequate to supply their entire national market, rather serious logistical problems could be expected.

THE BREWING INDUSTRY

Concentration has increasingly characterized the brewing industry. In the last several decades, the number of beer firms dropped from 900 to 50. The smaller local and regional brewers just could not match the economies of scale of the big brewers, nor could they match their aggressive marketing efforts. In the span of only 8 years, from 1970 to 1978, the combined market share of the five largest brewers increased from 49 percent to 74 percent of total industry sales.

The hottest product in the brewing industry by the mid-1970s had become light beer, or low-calorie beer. About 10 percent of industry sales were accounted for by lights, and 30 percent of Miller's, with the trend rising rapidly. Initial introductions of low-calorie beers had failed because they were marketed as diet drinks to consumers who did not drink much beer in the first place. Miller changed the thrust by positioning its Lite to heavy drinkers, with the theme that they could drink as much beer as before without feeling so filled (a subtle inference was that they could thereby consume more beer). Profitably speaking, the lights are good business: they sell for more than premium beers, and they cost less to make.

The other growth area is super-premium beers, so called because they sell for higher prices. For years, Anheuser's Michelob had the market almost to itself, with its only real competition coming from imported beers. Miller was the first to intrude on Michelob's market niche by arranging first to import Lowenbrau from Germany, and then to produce a domestic version of Lowenbrau.

Table 11.1 shows the relative sales of the big five of the brewing industry from 1973 to 1977; Table 11.2 shows the relative profit perfomance for this period. Notice particularly the major burst of Miller both in sales and profits.

Anheuser-Busch, the industry leader, makes Budweiser, Budweiser malt liquor, Michelob, and Busch Bavarian. As Tables 11.1 and 11.2 show, its business was booming. It had 10 breweries operating full blast, yet could

Table 11.1 Relative Sales of Top Five U.S. Brewers, 1973–1977

	Sales (millions of dollars)				
	1973	1974	1975	1976	1977
Anheuser-Busch	1109.7	1413.1	1645.0	1441.2	1838.0
Miller	275.9	403.6	658.3	982.8	1327.6
Schlitz	703.0	814.5	923.0	1000.0	937.4
Pabst	355.4	431.3	525.0	600.5	582.9
Coors	378.8	467.8	520.0	593.6	593.1

Source: Company annual reports.

Table 11.2　Relative Profits of Top Five U.S. Brewers, 1973–1977

	Net Profits (millions of dollars)				
	1973	1974	1975	1976	1977
Anheuser-Busch	65.6	64.0	84.7	55.4	91.9
Miller	(2.4)	6.3	28.6	76.1	106.5
Schlitz	55.2	49.0	30.9	50.0	17.8
Pabst	23.8	18.3	20.7	32.4	21.8
Coors	47.5	41.1	59.5	76.5	67.7

Source: Company annual reports.

hardly keep up with demand. The meteoric rise of Miller had to cause concern, but Anheuser, it seems, had the marketing muscle and financial resources to more than match Miller's marketing efforts and building plans.

Miller Brewing Company makes Miller High Life, Miller malt liquor, Miller Lite, and Lowenbrau. Miller was a sickly company run by an aging management when it was acquired by Philip Morris, the tobacco company, in 1969. Philip Morris moved its tobacco executives in to run the brewing operations and found that beer and cigarettes have a great deal in common, both being low-priced, pleasurable products processed and packaged on high-speed machinery; they can be advertised and distributed similarly to many of the same end-use customers. With aggressive marketing efforts, Miller moved up from eighth to second place among U.S. brewers by 1977, and was trying hard to catch Anheuser. Its Lite beer, introduced in January 1975 with a blitz advertising campaign, was a marketing coup, and, by 1978, Miller was selling 10 million barrels of Lite, equal to its entire beer sales only 4 years before.

Joseph Schlitz Brewing Company—maker of Schlitz, Schlitz malt liquor, Old Milwaukee, Promo, and Schlitz Light—had staggered badly, both in sales and especially in profits, as Table 11.2 shows. After 15 years of uninterrupted growth, it lost second place to Miller in 1977. The product mix had proven weak, with sales of premium and light beers—the more profitable items in the line—falling off more than its lower-priced beers. In addition, Schlitz had problems coming up with a super-premium beer to compete with Michelob and Lowenbrau.

Pabst makes Pabst Blue Ribbon, Pabst Extra Light, and Andeker of America. It found it impossible to keep pace with Anheuser-Busch and Miller. Because of intense competition, it was forced to spend more and more for advertising, but volume continued to slide. Pabst Blue Ribbon lost considerable ground in certain major Midwestern markets; Pabst's light beer and Andeker, its super-premium beer, were both weak contenders.

TARNISH ON THE GOLDEN PROSPECTS, 1977-1978

In 1977, the boom lowered. Although Tables 11.1 and 11.2 show Coors as faltering considerably less than Schlitz and Pabst in sales and profits, 1977 marked a serious trend reversal after the heady years of growth. Furthermore, the reversal did not appear to be short-lived, but rather symptomatic of serious underlying problems.

In 1977, Coors earned $1.92 a share, down 12 percent from 1976. It shipped 12.8 million barrels of beer, down 5 percent from 1976. It lost market share in many of the 16 Western states where it had the bulk of its distribution. The problems continued into 1978. For the first half of 1978, barrelage was down another 12 percent; per-share earnings were down from $1.02 the year before to $0.56. In California, which had accounted for 39 percent of its sales, it had been surpassed by Anheuser-Busch. Coors' stock, which had been subscribed for $31 in 1975, was now hovering around $16, a loss of about 50 percent for the first public stockholders. Only a few years before, Coors had been selling its beer by allocation only; now, suddenly, it had to cut back production. Bill Coors was forced to admit: "Making the best beer we can make is no longer enough."[6]

The Eastern markets no longer beckoned, either. They were heavily saturated with strong, well-entrenched competitors. In fact, the big Eastern brewers were moving West because of this. Anheuser had built a new plant in California. Miller was building one. Schlitz had expanded its capacity in the West. Coors, with its single plant in the mountains of Colorado, faced exorbitant transportation costs in trying to reach the Eastern markets, all the more so because it wanted to ship its beer under refrigeration to preserve its quality. Unfortunately, the quality image of the beer had suffered from bootleggers bringing it into the East with careless handling and selling it at black-market prices. Coors had even been forced to take out newspaper ads in some Eastern cities advising beer drinkers not to drink Coors. But a negative image had been created in the minds of many Eastern beer drinkers.

Labor Problems

Labor problems exacerbated a deteriorating situation. On April 5, 1977, the brewery workers at the Golden, Colorado, plant walked out. A week after the walkout, the AFL-CIO approved a nationwide boycott of the company's beer.

---

[6] "A Test for the Coors Dynasty," *Business Week*, May 8, 1978, p. 69.

The company was unyielding and now raised the issue that all prospective employees take lie-detector tests. The idea of polygraph testing hearkens back to the kidnapping of Adolph Coors III and the family fears that this could happen again. Eventually, more than 1000 of the 1472 workers who walked out returned, and the rest were replaced. The strike lasted 15 months, and eventually the union was rejected by the employees. But the wrath of labor was incurred in the process, and Coors now ranked with J. P. Stevens Company on union hate lists.

Opinions differ as to the effects the union boycott had on Coors' sales and profits: how much of the decline was due to labor boycotting, and how

---

INFORMATION SIDELIGHT

AN INTERNAL VERSUS AN EXTERNAL ORIENTATION TO STRATEGY PLANNING AND EXECUTION[7]

A firm, in its strategy planning and execution, can primarily focus on internal factors, such as technology and cost cutting. The key to attracting customers is thereby seen in improving production and distribution efficiency and lowering costs if possible. Henry Ford pioneered this philosophy in the early 1900s with his Model T. Texas Instruments is a modern-day example, becoming dominant in pocket calculators and digital watches by improving its efficiency and bringing down prices.[8] Coors was certainly successful with such a management orientation up to about 1976. But then, conditions changed; the competitive environment became more hotly contested in Coors' markets, and consumers started switching their preferences to different types of beer, notably, light beers and premium beers. The internal or production orientation is most appropriate in two situations:[9]

1. Where demand for a product exceeds supply, such as in new technologies and in developing countries.
2. Where the product cost is high and the market can only be expanded if costs can be brought down as (Texas Instruments faced).

---

[7] Sometimes they are referred to as a production orientation (the internal focus) and a marketing orientation (the external emphasis).

[8] "Texas Instruments Shows U.S. Business How to Survive in the 1980s," *Business Week,* September 18, 1978, pp. 66 ff.

[9] Philip Kotler, *Marketing Management,* 4th Ed. (Englewood Cliffs, N.J.: Prentice-Hall, 1980), p. 27.

An external orientation recognizes the fallacy of the assumption that products will forever sell themselves, "if we can only maintain our production and technological superiority." Looking outside the firm to the business environment results in major priority given to determining customers' needs and wants, how these may be changing as evidenced by shifts in buying patterns, and adapting products and services accordingly. The external focus also permits more responsiveness to other external forces that may be factors, such as major competitive thrusts, changing governmental laws and regulations, economic conditions, trade union forces, and the like. With such an external orientation, attention will more likely be directed to locating new opportunities brought about by changing environmental conditions, rather than being engrossed with internal production and technological advances. Such an orientation is more geared to meeting and even anticipating change, and—like it or not—the environment for doing business is more and more dynamic today. Externally-oriented firms usually have the advantage.

much was due to intensified competition? Bill Coors blamed most on the boycott: "It was a shock for us to find that, as far as the union is concerned, anything goes. No lie is too great to tell if it accomplishes their boycott objectives. We view the boycott as a monument to immorality and dishonesty."[10]

The mystique of Coors, the image it had gloried in that seemed to give it a competitive edge over all other brews, was gone, abruptly, bewilderingly.

Competition

As evident from Table 11.1, the aggressive efforts of Anheuser and Miller were hurting the other members of the big five, not to mention the smaller regional brewers. The erosion of Coors' share of California, its biggest market, where previously it had 40 percent of the beer business, was particularly worrisome, especially as it hinted at a greater erosion to come. In the first 6 months of 1978, Anheuser took over first place with a 35 percent share, with Coors dropping to 25 percent. Even more threatening was the surging Miller. Although number two nationally, Miller was still a poor third in California, with less than 10 percent of the market. But Miller was building a brewery there, and Coors certainly had to expect that once its production

---

[10] "Coors Beer: What Hit Us?" *Forbes*, October 16, 1978, p. 71.

facilities were established at a sufficiently high level, Miller's aggressive thrust would be leveled at California. Coors would then be placed in the vulnerable position of trying to match the expenditures and the expertise of both Miller and Anheuser in a hotly contested market.

DEFENSIVE REACTIONS

The company turned to market research to determine where it had gone wrong. The answer was definitive. The beer industry was growing at only 3 percent a year, but almost all the growth was coming from two products: light or low-calorie beer, and super-premium beer. Coors offered neither of these, relying on its traditional one kind of beer. Furthermore, research revealed that 4 out of every 10 new light beer drinkers had switched from Coors. In addition to the lack of a responsive and aggressive product mix vis-à-vis competitors, Coors also had a hard-to-open press–tab can that hardly met consumers' desire for convenience and ease of operation.

Coors finally moved to rectify the product deficiencies of a single-beer strategy and, in the spring of 1978, introduced its first new product in 20 years, Coors Light. The company also began developing a super-premium beer, planning market tests in early 1980. It was considering naming this Herman Joseph's, after Coors founder Adolph Herman Joseph Coors, thereby emphasizing family name and tradition.[11] Coors' reluctance in expanding the product line is understandable, if not recommended: producing different kinds of beer in the same brewery poses serious production problems and results in sharply higher costs than if there is one long and unchanging production line.

Coors now began directing its geographical expansion to the Central states and those parts of the West it had not previously served. In 1978, it began distribution in Missouri, Iowa, and in parts of Washington State. In early 1978, it announced plans to begin distribution in Arkansas, which would bring to 17 the number of states in which it was now marketing its beer. The Coors brothers were reaching some painful conclusions, among them that the company must abandon its comfortable role as a regional brewer and emerge as a national power. "There'll be fewer than 10 breweries left in the United States in 10 years," predicted Bill Coors. "I don't say we have to be number one, but we do have to stay in the top five to survive."[12]

---

[11] "New Coors Brand Nears Test Stage," *Advertising Age*, December 10, 1979, pp. 2 and 86.

[12] As quoted in "Men at Coors Beer Find the Old Ways Don't Work Anymore," *Wall Street Journal*, January 19, 1979, pp. 1 and 24.

Table 11.3   Relative Advertising Expenditures for Top Eight Brewers, 1973–1976[a]

	Expenditures (millions of dollars)			
	1973	1974	1975	1976
Anheuser-Busch	20.5	17.8	27.4	28.5
Jos. Schlitz	19.7	20.9	26.5	34.1
Miller	10.9	13.6	21.3	29.1
Pabst	7.2	8.4	9.6	9.7
Coors	1.4	1.6	1.2	2.0
Olympia	3.3	3.9	5.8	5.7
Stroh	4.5	4.4	4.0	5.0
F. & M. Schaefer	4.4	4.3	2.7	2.5

[a] These expenditures are understated, because they do not include the large sums typically spent by brewers on point of purchase materials and other non-measured media.
Source: Advertising Age, September 26, 1977, p. 112.

Coors' promotional expenditures had been lagging far behind those of its major competitors, and even of some of the much smaller regional brewers. See Table 11.3. Accordingly, in 1976, Coors had hired the J. Walter Thompson agency to enhance its corporate image, and, in 1978, budgeted a whopping increase in the advertising budget to $15 million.

For the full year of 1978, Coors registered a small sales gain to $624.8 million. However, profits again declined to $54.8 million, almost 20 percent below 1977 profits and almost 29 percent under the peak year of 1976. Even back in 1975, profits had been higher. And Coors' stock had now declined to less than $14 a share by early 1978.

The question at this point was whether Coors waited far too long to awaken to a changing and much more aggressive marketplace. Deeply embedded policies of conservatism, misplaced confidence in the everlasting appeal of a beer and of an image that dispelled the need for aggressive or even conventional marketing efforts, and finally, a confrontation philosophy with union employees—all these factors may have brought the venerable Coors brewery to a point of no return. Not that the viability of the company was in jeopardy, but perhaps the golden, glory years were over for all time.

WHAT CAN BE LEARNED?

The Coors case evinces a classical disregard for external factors, especially present and potential competitive inroads, at least until great damage had been done to its positions in its markets and to its future promise. In particular, its marketing function was atrophied.

The problem was not that the company was not growth-minded; it was—if increasing the productive capacity of the single brewery and venturing into other geographical regions can be construed as growth-minded. However, this philosophy or policy of growth gave no recognition to changes in the environment, especially in the competitive picture— changes that necessitated adjustments and modification in business and marketing strategy. But alas, it is so tempting when things are going well, when a product is receiving accolades from ordinary people and from the famous, to be lulled into a sense of unrelieved complacency, to envision nothing going wrong, to see a favorable image as insulating the company and its brand from all competition and adversity. Such a perception of the environment tends to provoke less than desirable consequences. It tends to make a firm arbitrary and dictatorial in its relationship with dealers, employees, and even customers—in other words, it promotes a "take it or leave it" attitude. It can also induce a company to regard its situation as a "cash cow" from which the profits can be fully milked while investments in advertising, in new product planning, and other marketing activities are kept at a minimum. Certainly, as Table 11.3 reveals, Coors' expenditures for advertising were woefully below those of other brewers, even those much smaller than Coors.

We can also see from Coors' example the sad but nonetheless to-be-recognized fact of the impermanence of a good image. It is difficult to develop an image of quality and great desirability; even more difficult and time-consuming is the cultivation of a mystique. Although such an image can be a company's biggest asset while it lasts, it can be a fleeting thing. Coors' image of quality and great taste was lost in the Eastern markets because of bootleggers carrying the beer into these markets illegally and selling it at greatly inflated prices, while maintaining no quality care such as product rotation and adequate refrigeration. But we also see that consumer wants can be fickle and can change drastically: today's sought-after image may not necessarily be that of next year. The new sought-after image became light or low-calorie beer, and super-premium beer. Coors' brand image was dimmed.

A firm should not beguile itself into minimizing the threat of competition, both present and potential. Coors was guilty of this, under the illusion of the invincibility of their product vis-à-vis competing brands. Yet, we can see how easily such an entrapment could occur: during the heady days of the early 1970s, they dominated every market they were in. But the reality was soon to impose itself: without greatly increased marketing expenditures and, probably, the establishment of additional breweries closer to the market, there could be little chance of cracking the Eastern market against entrenched and powerful competitors. Furthermore, even Coors' captive and

cherished Western markets—particularly the important California market—
were vulnerable to the aggressive efforts of major competitors.

A firm has to be adaptable; it cannot expect the status quo to endure. It
has to be prepared to adjust to a changing environment. Ideally, a firm
should anticipate changes and make needed adjustments before it is forced
to. Otherwise, an initial advantage can be lost, never to be regained.

Update

By 1981, Coors was budgeting some $87 million for advertising and promo-
tion. This was nearly double what the company had spent 2 years before,
and compares with a bare $1.2 million spent in 1975. Coors Light was
running neck and neck with Miller's nationally dominant Lite in the 20 states
in which Coors was now selling. But its problems were hardly solved.

Both barrelage and income were down. Coors' share of the California
market had dropped to 20 percent in 1981. Anheuser was invading the Coors'
stronghold of Texas, and its Bud Light gained 3 percent of the total market
in 1 month. And Coors was still undecided whether to begin total distribution
of its Herman Joseph's of 1868, which it had been test marketing for a year
without making inroads against Anheuser's Michelob.

In 1984, however, Coors appeared to have honed its strategy. It moved
aggressively into the Southeast in 1983 and captured some 11 percent of the
market, with a good coordination of advertising and dealer incentives. But
Coors was still struggling to combat competitive erosion in its original
Western markets. In California, its competitive position had fallen to 16.1
percent by 1983; here, in the state with the highest beer consumption in the
nation, it had a 37.8 percent share of the market in 1972.

By 1984, Coors was in 26 states with its Coors Premium and Light
brands. But it was still testing Herman Joseph's of 1868, which had been in
and out of test since May 1980; it was also experimenting with another
potential premium beer, Golden Lager, with the results not suggesting a
strong "go." Coors was still clinging to its fifth place among all brewers and
had a 7.6 percent share of the market, exactly the same as it had had in 1978
with a much smaller geographic distribution.

For Thought And Discussion

1. How do you account for the fact that Coors beer achieved such a success despite
   the company's lack of advertising, new product development, and national
   distribution?
2. Discuss why an internal orientation is particularly unsuited for the brewing
   industry.

3. Do you think the company's fortunes would have remained strong and growing if advertising expenditures had been doubled or tripled during the late 1960s and early 1970s?
4. Is it likely that Coors' labor disputes had any serious effect on its fortunes? Why or why not?
5. At this time, 1986, should Coors plan to go national? Examine as many pros and cons as possible.

Invitation To Role Play

1. Place yourself in the role of Peter Coors, the young senior vice–president for sales and marketing. How would you attempt now (as of 1986) to reverse the company's fading performance? Be as specific as you can; also consider and identify any constraints to a corporate strategy that should be recognized. You might also want to consider how a mystique might again be built up for the Coors brand.
2. Place yourself in the role of a staff analyst. You have been asked to evaluate the desirability of opening another brewery in the East—perhaps in Virginia. Consider as many pros and cons as you can (you will, of course, have to make some assumptions, especially regarding construction costs). Develop a recommendation for a go/no-go decision, and be prepared to defend it before a top management committee.

12

Chrysler Corporation— "Can We Even Survive?"

On May 11, 1982, a headline in the business section of the Cleveland *Plain Dealer* stated, "Steel Imports Surge Aids Port." The article noted that a shipment of foreign steel was being unloaded on Cleveland docks the same day that domestic steel mills were reporting their lowest operating rate within recent memory. As many as 20 more ships carrying steel imports were expected to arrive in the next 30 days. The article further observed that the scene of imports unloading was nettling a domestic steel industry with 100,000 workers on layoffs and more than 30,000 on short workweeks.

In industry after industry, U. S. firms were finding it difficult to compete successfully against foreign competitors, not only in our own domestic market but in foreign markets as well. Business publications were calling for a reindustrialization of America,[1] which no one saw as being easily or quickly accomplished. No industry was more beset by foreign competition and by an inability to match foreign productivity and attractiveness of foreign-made products than the auto industry. And Chrysler was the most grievously beset.

IACOCCA TO THE RESCUE?

In November 1978, Lee A. Iacocca became president of the ailing Chrysler Corporation, at one time the fourth-largest industrial corporation in the

[1] For example, *Business Week*, June 30, 1980, entire issue.

United States. Iacocca brought to the enterprise and its hopes for survival his proven abilities of salesmanship, image-building, and cost-cutting. But many doubted that this would be enough to save the company—indeed, whether anything could. There was doubt that the entire U.S. auto industry could be saved—short of governmental subsidization, that is.

Iacocca embodied the great American success story. In an earlier era, his would have been dubbed a Horatio Alger tale, after the prominent fiction writer of rags-to-riches stories early in this century. Iacocca was the son of an Italian immigrant. He saw education as the route to success, and he went to Lehigh University and then on to Princeton for a master's degree in engineering. "In my day you went to college, not to go into government or to be a lawyer, but to embark on a career that paid you more money than the guy who didn't go. For 32 years I was motivated by money," said Iacocca.[2]

He started with the Ford Motor Company as a trainee in 1946 at $125 a week. As he moved upward through the Ford organization, Iacocca was responsible for introducing the trend-setting Mustang in 1964 (only a few years after the Edsel debacle), and followed up with the Maverick, Pinto, and Fiesta. By 1977, he was president of Ford, earning $978,000 that year. Then, in July 1978, Henry Ford abruptly fired him. The falling out has been attributed to basic disagreement between Ford and Iacocca over the pace of downsizing cars: Iacocca wanted to move fast, whereas Ford was worried about the impact of such additional investment on short-term profits and wanted to move more slowly.

After Iacocca left Ford, John J. Riccardo, chief executive of Chrysler, offered him the presidency. In accepting this, Iacocca turned down a dozen jobs that offered more money. But he was after a place in automotive history: "I might not only save a blue-chip company and 200,000 jobs, but also help the Big Three become an honest Big Three."[3]

THE CHRYSLER DILEMMA

Chrysler had long been the weak sister of the Big Three auto makers. Although a multibillion–dollar firm, it was smaller, less well financed, and less talented than General Motors (GM) and Ford. It had suffered major reversals in the early 1960s, in 1970, and in 1974–1975. The monumental problems affecting the very viability of the company in the later 1970s and early 1980s had their roots in the recession of 1974–1975. At that time, a severe drop in sales forced the company to make massive cuts in capital

---

[2] "Off to the Races Again," *Fortune*, December 4, 1978, p. 15.
[3] Ibid.

spending and, perhaps more serious, in engineers and designers. Delays in introducing new models and quality problems resulted. For example, Chrysler compacts, Volare and Aspen, were introduced in 1976, and subsequently went through eight recalls for defects. Many Chrysler fans who had been loyal through generations turned to other makes.

In 1978, Chrysler lost $205 million. By 1979, problems worsened as gasoline prices rose sharply and the public began demanding small fuel-efficient cars. Although Chrysler had some success with its subcompact Omnis and Horizons, losses were over $1 billion, and the future of the company was in doubt.

Lobbying In Washington

Iacocca turned to Washington to bail out the company. He sought Federal loan guarantees of $1.2 billion. Chrysler's lobbying had irresistible bipartisan appeal in a coming election because of the concentration of Chrysler workers and parts suppliers in such key states as Michigan, Ohio, Indiana, as well as five other states. The Carter Administration strongly supported the loan-guarantee legislation, and Congress finally authorized not $1.2 billion, but $1.5 billion. Chrysler immediately drew on $800 million to help it weather the coming months.

But Chrysler's problems continued, and its actual sales for 1980 were far worse than had been predicted, with the deficit an unbelievable $1.7 billion. Although the blame could be laid on such externals as a recession and mushrooming interest rates that affected consumers and dealers alike, the failure of the widely touted K-car was crucial.

The K-Cars

The Dodge Aries and the Plymouth Reliant were introduced in September 1980 with great fanfare. These were front-wheel drive compacts, somewhat roomier and a bit more fuel-efficient than GM's X-cars, introduced 18 months before. It was expected that sales would be about 70,000 for the introductory months of October and November 1980, and 492,000 for all of 1981. Instead, only 34,273 units were sold the first 2 months, and by the end of November, dealers had a 98-day supply of K-cars. GM, in contrast, had a 54-day supply of its older and virtually unchanged X-cars. Ford's new subcompacts, the Lynx and Escort, had also done considerably better than the K-cars during this period.

Thus, the poor showing of the K-cars could not be blamed solely on external factors. Chrysler had tried to price the K-car close to the X-car; it also loaded most cars with every conceivable option, consequently bringing the price from the basic $6100 car to about $8000.

The disappointment of the K-car introduction did not end Iacocca's troubles. By 1980, even the Omnis and Horizons that had done well the year before began to lose their luster. Chrysler had estimated sales of these cars at 394,000 for all of 1980; by the end of November, only 222,814 had been sold, and dealers' inventories had risen to a 134-day supply. Even Iacocca's hopes to reenter the luxury-car market were facing disappointment. The Imperial was again introduced—for the first time since 1976—with heavy advertising, even using Frank Sinatra to plug it. But sales of 1885 cars in October and November were less than half the forecast.

Iacocca's Defensive Moves

Iacocca's reaction to these disasters was to offer rebates of $380 to $1200 a car in December 1980 and in early 1981. An ambitious cost-cutting program was also announced that would save the company $1 billion in 1981. This involved four things:

1. A wage freeze for blue-collar workers.
2. A 5–percent reduction in prices charged by suppliers for 90 days and a freeze for the rest of 1981.
3. A $575–million cut in investment in new-plant capacity and new-product development.
4. Asking lenders to convert $572 million in debt to preferred stock, thereby reducing interest payments by $100 million a year.

And Chrysler went back to the loan-guarantee board for $400 million.

Although the Chrysler dilemma was unique and more serious than for other U. S auto makers, it was nonetheless symptomatic of the sorry straits confronting a major U. S. industry that had not adequately coped with foreign competition.

THE U. S. AUTO INDUSTRY—1970-1980

In the decade of the 1970s, U. S. automakers' share of the domestic U. S. market fell from 85 percent to 70 percent; in other words, by 1980, imports had captured almost 30 percent of the market, double that of a decade earlier. Import inroads intensified in the latter part of the 1970s. Table 12.1 shows the market share of all imports, as well as the units sold of the five leading ones from 1977 through 1980.

The vulnerability to imports came partly from Detroit's failure to build sufficient small-car capacity. American companies ignored the fact that many customers were returning to the idea of simple and efficient transportation. (This was the very idea that Henry Ford had pioneered with his

Table 12.1   Import Inroads in the U.S. Auto Market—1977–1980

	1980	1979	1978	1977
Total units sold—all makes	8,760,937	10,356,695	10,946,104	10,825,235
Total import units sold	2,469,180	2,351,053	1,946,094	1,976,512
Market share of imports (%)	28.2%	22.7%	17.8%	18.3%
Leading imports (units sold):				
Toyota	582,204	507,816	441,800	493,048
Datsun	516,890	472,252	338,096	388,378
Honda	375,388	353,291	274,876	223,633
VW	90,923	125,100	216,709	260,704
Mazda	161,623	156,533	75,309	50,609

Source: *Automotive News,* 1981 Market Data Book Issue.

Model T seven decades earlier.) When oil price increases made big cars all but obsolete, the foreign firms were ready and able to step in. Japan alone had a 22 percent share of the U. S. auto market by 1981. Only 3 years before, Japanese imports were 12 percent. As we can see from Table 12.1, sales volumes in 1980 were below a recession-level 9 million cars, and this included the major share carved out by imports. U. S. auto makers incurred some $5.5 billion in red ink in 1980 and 1981. About 2400 dealerships folded in these 2 years. The president of the 20,000-member National Automobile Dealers Association asserted that "dealers are holding on by their used-car departments."[4]

Another aspect contributing to Detroit's problems was a growing perception by the U. S. consumer that American-made cars were inferior in quality and workmanship to foreign-made, especially to Japanese-made cars. This perception was most difficult to overcome. In particular, Ford and Chrysler heavily advertised the improved quality of their cars. But consumers remained skeptical. Some experts predicted that 3 years of good word-of-mouth endorsements from happy owners would be needed to overcome the prejudices against the quality of U. S. cars.[5]

Sticker Shock

Detroit was blaming all its problems on high interest rates and the discouraging effect they were having on consumer willingness to buy high-ticket

---

[4] "Detroit's Struggle to Survive," *Business Week,* January 11, 1982, pp. 62–63.
[5] "Why Detroit Still Can't Get Going," *Business Week,* November 9, 1981, p. 110.

items. But a consumer survey by the Survey Research Center of the University of Michigan revealed that high car prices, not interest rates, were the biggest reasons for not planning to buy a new car.

Figures compiled by the National Automobile Dealers Association put the average selling price of a U. S.-made new car at $8900 by late 1981. Ten years before, the average price had been $3730. In the single year from 1980 to 1981, prices rose more than $1000. Even GM's Vice Chairman, Howard Kehrl, conceded, "If there's any sales problem, it's getting people to recognize that a very high-quality small car is not cheap."[6] The term "sticker shock" began to be heard in the land. And when a potential customer saw car prices 70 percent or more higher than the last car he bought, disinclination to buy a new car could readily set in.

Detroit's eagerness to embrace high prices was nothing new. Neither should there have been surprise at consumer reluctance to purchase at prices that were significantly higher than a few months before. The same thing happened earlier in the 1970s. For 15 months, from 1973 to late 1974, Detroit auto makers repeatedly increased the selling prices of their cars. This was a time of burgeoning inflation, with material and labor costs rising sharply. New government standards for safety and pollution control added other costs, and the auto makers themselves were incorporating more expensive equipment, such as radial tires.

In this period, the average price of a new car increased by $1000. And suddenly, sales plummeted 25 percent. Auto makers now began offering cash rebates for a limited time to reduce massive inventories of unsold cars. But the damage had been done, and the auto industry led the rest of the nation into a severe recession.

Did the U. S. automakers learn from this? Apparently not. Much the same thing was happening in late 1980 and 1981, when new economy-efficient cars were introduced to compete with foreign imports, but at prices that were far from "economy". By June 1981, used car sales were running 19 percent above the previous year, but domestic new car sales continued to plummet.

Detroit tried to ease buyers from their sticker shock by rebates, offering lower than market interest rates on new car purchases, and by some rollbacks of prices. But these were only temporary incentives, and they tended to borrow sales from future months when the rebates and other concessions ended. Even worse, the on-again, off-again bargains appeared to confuse some buyers, whereas others were convinced that special deals

[6] Ibid., p. 107.

INFORMATION SIDELIGHT

REBATES

A rebate is a promise by a manufacturer to return part of the purchase price directly to the purchaser. Usually, the rebate is given to consumers, although it can be offered to dealers instead in the expectation that they will pass some or all of the savings along to consumers.

Obviously, the objective of a rebate is to increase sales by giving purchasers essentially a lower price. But why not simply reduce prices? The rebate is used instead of a regular mark-down or price reduction because it is less permanent than cutting the list price. Rebates can be quite effective in generating short-term business. But they may affect business negatively once the rebate has been lifted.

were a routine part of car purchasing: demand dried up drastically during those periods when no concessions were in effect.

In defense of their higher sticker prices, Detroit maintained that the front-wheel drive they had adopted for most cars produced high re-tooling costs. And, with sales volume down, it became essential to squeeze as much profit from every car as possible. But the elasticity of demand could not accept higher prices, whatever the rationale, and demand dried up as sticker prices increased.

OPTIONS FOR CHRYSLER

By the end of 1980, the situation for Chrysler seemed bleak indeed, with sales declining badly and losses becoming astronomical, as shown below:

	1978	1979	1980
Sales (millions)	$13,618.3	$12,001.9	$9,225.3
Losses (millions)	$ 204.6	$ 1,097.3	$1,709.7

Source: Chrysler annual reports.

At this point, several options seemed available to Chrysler if it were to survive:

1. It could greatly pare its product line, and limit itself only to the small cars that seemed to comprise most of the market demand. By so doing, the full-sized and intermediate car lines would be discon-

tinued, and their factories either permanently closed or converted so that they could produce front-wheel-drive subcompacts.

2. Large chunks of the company could be sold off, such as the parts-making operation, which had been running in the red because of underutilization. Some or all of its profitable units, such as the military tank business, Chrysler Financial Corporation, and its electronics division might also be sold to provide needed funds to support the remaining auto operation.

3. The various lines of cars might be merged into a single nameplate. Thus, Chrysler-Plymouth and Dodge lines could be pared, thereby simplifying assembly, reducing inventory of duplicate parts, and concentrating selling efforts.

4. Augmenting its lines with "niche" cars that would be so distinctive they could command a high price and yield a good profit, even on low sales volume. This was a strategy that had revived BMW, the German sports car manufacturer.[7]

5. An affiliation might be established with another auto maker, such as Volkswagen. This might provide Chrysler with needed cash, as well as a product line expanded with foreign-designed cars. Unfortunately, Chrysler was hardly an attractive property for a foreign suitor. Although it had about $2 billion in tax losses that would shield future profits from taxes, it had a colossal drawback in its debt burden: $1.2 billion in guaranteed loans, almost $1 billion in other debts, in addition to $1.2 billion in unfunded pension liabilities.

6. Chapter 11 bankruptcy was the ultimate option. This would not necessarily lead to the company's demise and liquidation. Under Chapter 11, a company continues to operate, but has court protection against creditors' lawsuits while working out a plan for paying its debts. However, Iacocca was convinced that such a reorganization under the Federal bankruptcy code would quickly lead to total collapse, with car sales screeching to a halt as a result of what is termed the *orphan syndrome.* When potential customers fear that a firm may collapse, they see warranties as worthless; they suspect that dealers might not be around to handle problems, that resale value of cars will drastically decline, and that parts may become harder to find as years go by. Consequently, only a few die-hard loyalists might still be induced to buy. To some extent, the orphan

[7] "Could Bankruptcy Save Chrysler?" *Business Week,* December 24, 1979, p. 70.

syndrome was already affecting Chrysler because of its widely publicized difficulties.

Most of the preceding options were deemed by company executives to be hardly workable. Paring down to a profitable core, as American Motors had attempted to do, was ruled out, because it was thought that Chrysler dealers needed a full line of cars if they were to compete effectively with Ford and GM. In early 1982, however, Chrysler did sell its subsidiary, Chrysler Defense Corporation, to General Dynamics for about $350 million. This division produced the main tank for the U. S. Army, the M-1, and the sale provided a cash cushion against further operating losses.

So Iacocca and Chrysler were determined to maintain their role as a full-line auto manufacturer and to hang on doggedly until better times. One analyst criticized: "The problem is not that there aren't any alternatives, but rather the man at the helm . . . Lee's in a race to show Henry (Ford) what he can do. And in the process, he's likely to become a General Custer."[8]

WHAT WENT WRONG AT CHRYSLER?

Chrysler's basic problem had long been inadequate capital. This was aggravated by an acquisitions binge in the 1960s and early 1970s. Many of these acquisitions turned out to be lemons and had to be sold at losses to raise cash in the late 1970s. For example, European car companies were acquired as Chrysler attempted to build a foreign operation that could provide a sales cushion for the periodic downturns of the U. S. market. However, only failing companies were acquired: Simca in France, and Rootes Motor Ltd. in Britain. These companies turned into cash drains, siphoning off funds needed at home.

Lacking the capital and some of the creative talents of Ford and GM, Chrysler's products tended to be not innovative, but imitative, that is, "me-too" types of cars. Such cars, lacking in prestige and advanced styling, often had to be sold at lower prices than competing cars, and Chrysler had to be satisfied with lower profit margins. This situation was hardly likely to improve soon. For example, GM spent $8 billion in 1981 on plant and equipment; this was more than Chrysler planned to spend in 6 years.

The current problems stem more directly from 1970 when Lynn Townsend, then chairman, decided to squeeze the most out of existing plants and product lines rather than build for the future. Although the strategy seemed sound at the time for a cash-poor company, unforeseen world events sabotaged it. Notably, the Arab oil embargo brought a new

[8] Ibid., p. 72.

emphasis on economy and high mileage, and Federal legislation even made increased mileage standards mandatory. In 1970, subcompact cars accounted for only 3 percent of the U. S. market. And Townsend opted not to compete with the Vega and Pinto compact cars introduced in 1970 by GM and Ford. Instead, he chose to concentrate on restyling the more profitable big cars, in a $250 million model change. Just a few months later, the oil embargo destroyed the market for gas-guzzling big cars. And Chrysler did not have the smaller cars desperately sought by consumers. The 2 losing years of 1974 and 1975 brought the severe cutbacks in capital spending and in talented personnel that were to affect future operations.

John Riccardo, Townsend's successor, made another decision in 1975 that was to redound to the company's disadvantage. Facing the prospect of costly new Federal braking and noise rules, and recognizing—again—the limited cash resources, Riccardo decided to drop the profitable, heavy-duty truck business, and instead focus on vans and pickups. And sales of these products were the first to soften at the threat of fuel disruption and higher prices.

Can we fault Chrysler's management for failing to anticipate an oil embargo that was to bring gas lines and burgeoning prices, so that demand for big cars, vans, and the like all but dried up? Could any reasonable person have predicted such a situation? And can we fault Chrysler management for not having the same options available as the larger competitors with vastly superior financial resources? Where do we draw the line between prudent decisions and myopic ones?

The issue is complicated. And perhaps Chrysler's management was more the victim of circumstances. Perhaps the same can be said for GM and Ford management, and for that of the steel companies and the other industries vulnerable to foreign competition. Yet, some of the blame was simply an unwavering embracing of short-term profit objectives. Such objectives induce a firm to postpone plant modernization, to emphasize the most profitable products (in the case of U. S. automakers, and especially Chrysler, this meant big uneconomical cars, or small cars so loaded with expensive options that they cost as much as big cars), to cut back on research and development expenditures, and to seek maximum per unit profit, even if this meant increased inflation, not fully meeting the needs of consumers, and not even being competitive with foreign firms.

Chrysler blamed a lot of its troubles on costly government regulations imposed in the 1970s. For example, auto emission standards, fuel economy goals, passive seatbelt or air-bag systems—these were estimated to have cost Chrysler $1 billion extra in 1979 and 1980. Being the smallest of the major auto makers, it had fewer units to spread such costs over, and was thus more seriously affected than GM and Ford. The Reagan Administration

---

INFORMATION SIDELIGHT

SCRAPPING AUTO BUMPER STANDARDS

On May 14, 1982, the Federal government scrapped requirements that automobile bumpers must withstand a 5 mph crash without causing damage to the vehicle. Automobiles hereafter will be required to have bumpers that protect the vehicle only in crashes of up to 2.5 mph, and this may later be reduced to below 2.5 mph for some types of autos.

The bumper requirement had been highly criticized by the automobile industry as being unnecessary and adding $35 to $50 to the cost of a vehicle. On the other hand, consumer advocate Ralph Nader called the decision a "surrender to General Motors" that he claimed would cost motorists $400 million a year in added insurance premiums and repair costs. Industry experts confirmed this, estimating that insurance premiums could rise by 10 to 20 percent with the permission of weaker bumpers.[9]

In a pluralistic society in which many different interest groups are vying for legislation and regulations favorable to their position, it is impossible to satisfy all interests. However, in the early 1980s, the pendulum seemed to be swinging back to the side of management as it attempted to overcome foreign inroads.

---

brought a loosening of some of the regulations. As the "Information Sidelight" indicates, many regulations are extremely controversial, with different points of view creating almost irreconcilable issues.

WHAT CAN BE LEARNED?

We can draw some generalizations from the Chrysler problems that apply to the whole U. S. auto industry as well as such U. S. industries as steel, rubber, machine tools, and consumer electronics. The problems of Chrysler and the other Detroit automakers were symptomatic of problems facing other American industries as the decade of the 70s was ending: a substantial part of American industry was just not able to compete effectively against aggressive foreign competition, particularly the Japanese. A new assessment

---

[9] "U.S. Auto Bumper Standard Scrapped," *Cleveland Plain Dealer*, May 15, 1982, p. 4-A.

Table 12.2   Foreign Inroads in Key Industries in the U.S. Market, 1960–1980

Industry	Percentage of Total Industry Sales by Imports	
	1960	1979
Autos	4.1%	22.7%
Steel	4.2	14.0
Electrical components	.5	20.1
Farm machinery	7.2	15.3
Consumer electronics	5.6	50.6
Footwear	2.3	37.3
Metal-cutting machine tools	3.3	26.4
Textile machinery	6.6	45.5
Calculating and adding machines	5.0	43.1

Source: Commerce Department.

of American management philosophies seemed indicated. And a painful reevaluation of traditional ways of doing things and criteria for decision-making seemed essential if America were to regain its industrial dominance and if American jobs were to be saved.

Perhaps the major thing to be learned is that we in this country are not insulated from competition although we invented mass production and were in the vanguard of sophisticated management techniques. Nothing is guaranteed forever. The environment changes. Traditional ways of doing things can be vulnerable to fresh ideas. They need to be constantly appraised. We can learn from foreign competitors, just as they, for decades, have learned from us.

Table 12.2 shows the key industries hardest hit in the U. S. market by foreign competitors. This table shows the extent of foreign inroads in certain key industries from 1960 to 1980 (as we saw earlier, by 1981 the auto industry was in even worse shape, with imports in one year jumping from 22.7 percent to 28.2 percent of total U. S. auto sales). Although foreign inroads in the auto industry have received the most publicity, certain other industries have suffered even more—the trend over the last several decades has been disturbing indeed.

U.S. Disadvantage In Productivity

Productivity in the U. S. has been a nagging concern. It has been slipping relative to foreign industries, and by so doing has made many foreign products more attractive costwise and qualitywise than U. S. goods. The usual measure of productivity is output per hour, that is, how much an American worker produces in an hour compared, say, to a Japanese or West German worker. The calculation is made by dividing total output of goods and services by the number of hours or number of workers used to produce them. From 1966 to 1976, the U. S. had the lowest growth rate in productivity of the top 11 Western industrial nations.[10]

Productivity directly affects cost. In 1978, Japanese car companies had a $700 cost advantage per car over their U. S. counterparts. In other words, because of their greater productivity, Japanese carmakers could manufacture an equivalent car for $700 less than could be achieved in the U. S. Serious as this competitive disadvantage was to American firms, the difference had widened by 1981 to $1500 per car.[11]

Strong pressures began building to make American cars more competitive by reducing labor costs; with U. S. car makers facing billion-dollar deficits, and with worker layoffs increasing, unions began making some concessions. But such efforts only chipped away at Japan's big manufacturing-cost advantage. Limiting Japan's imports through quotas was another often-mentioned recourse. But some feared that quotas might prompt Japan to shift efforts toward larger, more expensive models, an area where U. S. carmakers were not as severely challenged as with smaller cars. The prospect that Japan might soon be competing against Detroit's entire product line struck fear in the industry.

Factors In U. S. Productivity Problems

Fingers of blame for U. S. productivity problems pointed in all directions. Although some of these factors were interrelated and due to multiple causes, for the sake of simplicity we will examine them under: lack of sufficient investment in productive facilities; short-term profit-maximizing managerial goals; and adversarial (rather than cooperative) relationship of business with labor and with government.

Lack of Adequate Investment in Productive Facilities. Outdated plants typify some U. S. industries. A major example is the steel industry. U. S. firms were still building open-hearth furnaces in the late 1950s, whereas the Japanese were building more modern plants that used the basic oxygen process, a process that ironically was a U. S. invention. The U. S. agricultural machinery industry in all practicality excluded itself from growing markets in developing countries by concentrating on making big and

---

[10] Thomas W. Gerdel, "America's Dilemma of Poor Production," *Cleveland Plain Dealer*, January 19, 1981, p. 1-D.
[11] "Why Detroit Still Can't Get Going," p. 109.

expensive machinery appropriate only for the U. S. market. For example, no American firm still makes a farm tractor under 35 horsepower. The failure of the U. S. machine tool industry to meet domestic market needs, because of a reluctance to build enough capacity to serve the needs of the market in periods of peak demand, simply invited foreign competition. And in consumer electronics, as we all know, most TVs, radios, stereos, and the like are now made by the Japanese; in 1960, about 95 percent of these products were supplied by domestic manufacturers. The Japanese secret: not so much lower labor costs, but superior technology and management.

Along with the sag in investment in modern plant and equipment, compared especially to Germany and Japan, has been a decline in research and development spending since the mid-1960s. This has resulted in the U.S. lagging behind in applying technology to commercial products. For example, robots were an American invention, but now Japan has taken the lead in applying robots to a variety of manufacturing processes.

Government regulations and a punitive tax system that penalized savings have also been blamed for a reluctance to invest in capital equipment. And, undeniably, our society in recent decades has been more oriented to spending than to savings, with interest payments on loans being fully tax-deductible, whereas interest on savings is taxed as ordinary income. The last 15 years have seen a heavy imposition of regulations dealing with environmental protection, safety, health, equal employment, energy efficiency, and the like. Such regulations and the bureaucracy that interprets and enforces them have sometimes placed major obstacles in the way of investing in new plants and even in maintaining present ones. For example, the Environmental Protection Agency has forced some industries, such as steel, to invest millions of dollars—which might have gone to modernizing facilities—into pollution control devices.

Faltering investment in productive facilities has also been blamed on the huge increases in the service industries, such as health and social services, which have absorbed resources that might have gone into productive areas. Others have blamed the deteriorating rate of productivity on a shortage of engineers and too many bureaucrats, staff people, and lawyers. Even the introduction of computer technology and sophisticated office systems has been blamed. These accouterments of modern business management have been seen by some as soaking up resources that might have been better used in more directly productive facilities, and also in providing more information to management than is really needed: that is, they have placed more people in paper-shuffling roles rather than in more productive activities, and in the process added greatly to the overhead burden.

Short-sighted Management. Major reasons for the decline of U.S. industry must point more directly to management deficiencies. A major orientation of American managers has been and continues to be maximizing profits. Performance is measured by reaching profit objectives, and promotion and compensation are tied to it. The executive who does not achieve profit goals is unlikely to advance very far. Is it any wonder that all levels of executives are thinking about profits and how to get more of them? And what, really, is wrong with this? The answer lies in what kind of profits we are talking about: short-term immediate profits, or profits over the longer run. Long-range goals have tended to be sacrificed for short-run profits—in Chrysler, the rest of the U.S. auto industry, the steel industry, and in many other industries as well. Consequently, if heavy investment is needed in research, retooling, and other efforts to reach long-term goals, they tend to be postponed because such programs hurt profits in the short run.

And the fallacy of such short-sighted strategies can be clearly seen. The auto industry's postponement of the need to develop high-quality, fuel-efficient vehicles the car-buying market really wanted gave a big hunk of this business to the imports. Likewise, the steel industry postponed for decades the shifting of production from outmoded facilities, and now lacks the capital to do so. (There are exceptions to this. Standard Oil of Ohio (Sohio) made huge investments in Alaskan oil development, even to the point of facing formidable debts a decade before any returns from the investment could be expected. Eventually, the payoff came, and Sohio was flooded with profits: it earned $1.2 billion on sales of $7.9 billion in 1979.)

Adversarial Relationships of Business. Some of the blame for poor productivity is laid at labor's door. Some people maintain that lazy workers who take too many coffee breaks and who have lost their forebears' zeal for work are to blame—not only for poor productivity with its high costs, but also for an uncaring and careless attitude toward quality. Sometimes this is seen as resulting from the growth of unions with their emphasis on seniority at the expense of capability. Unions have been criticized as too greedy, too uncaring, too rigid in adhering to old ways that curb efficiency and protect the status quo. Usually, collective bargaining has taken place in an adversarial rather than a cooperative environment. This contrasts sharply with the labor-management situation in Japan, where most workers stay with the same firm for life and enjoy almost a family relationship and certainly one of teamwork and cooperation toward common objectives. Quality circles as described in the information sidelight below are a major component of the close and cooperative management and labor relations of Japanese firms.

Management is certainly far from blameless in its labor relations, in the acceptance of inflationary wage settlements, and in the tolerance of mediocre quality. It has often been the easier course of action to make contract

---

INFORMATION SIDELIGHT

QUALITY CIRCLES

Quality circles were adopted by Japan in an effort to rid its industries of poor quality control and junkiness after World War II. Quality circles are worker-manager committees that meet regularly, usually weekly, to talk about production problems, plan ways to improve productivity and quality, and resolve job-related gripes on both sides. They have been described as "the single most significant explanation for the truly outstanding quality of goods and services produced in Japan."[12] For example, Mazda has 2147 circles with over 16,000 employees involved. They usually consist of seven to eight volunteer members who meet on their own time to discuss and solve the issues they are concerned with. In addition to making major contributions to increased productivity and quality, they have provided employees with an opportunity to participate and gain a sense of accomplishment.[13]

The idea—like so many ideas adopted by the Japanese—did not originate with them: it came from two American personnel consultants. The Japanese refined the idea and ran with it. Now, American industry is rediscovering quality circles and finding them a desirable way to promote teamwork, good feelings, and to avoid at least some of the adversarial relations stemming from collective bargaining matters or union grievances that must be negotiated.

---

concessions and pass the inflationary costs on to customers by raising prices, rather than suffer a lengthy strike. Eventually, the productivity and competitiveness of domestic industries have been diminished. Now, the challenge is to develop a framework within which labor and management can work together toward a common objective. Both have a stake in the competitive productivity of U.S. industries, because not only profits but jobs are truly at stake. Management has the challenge to offer new incentives to motivate workers to higher levels of productivity.

Government has also tended to take an adversarial stance toward U. S. business. As we have noted before, regulation has tended to be obstructive, even though some regulation is clearly needed. But an explosion of regula-

---

[12] "A Partnership; to Build the New Workplace," *Business Week,* June 30, 1980, p. 101.
[13] As described in a Mazda ad in *Forbes,* May 24, 1982, p. 5.

tions placed on business to achieve social goals, such as equal employment, a cleaner environment, and a safer workplace, have undeniably diverted vast amounts of capital from more productive avenues. A teamwork approach, a spirit of more cooperation and a less adversarial and litigious relationship may be essential if U.S. productivity is to be competitive. Japan and West Germany certainly have, for the most part, a harmonious and supportive relationship of government and business.

Update

Of course, we know what happened to Chrysler. It became perhaps the most notable success of the half century. Even supplier firms attempted to participate in the glory, as an ad by Control Data in the *Wall Street Journal* of February 8, 1985 (page 8) headlined: "Chrysler Shaped the Greatest Turnaround in Automotive History . . . with Help from Proven Technologies of Control Data." And Iacocca's autobiography became the number one nonfiction best seller for many weeks.

For Thought And Discussion

1. What incentives would you propose to motivate workers to higher productivity?
2. Discuss in what ways the Japanese worker differs from the typical U.S. worker. (You may need to do some research on this.) How do these dissimilarities affect labor-management relations in the two countries?
3. Quality circles have been praised by some experts as a breakthrough in management-labor relations and in improving productivity and quality. Do you see any problems with these quality circles?
4. Discuss the pros and cons of rebates versus reductions of list prices for stimulating demand.

Invitation To Role Play

1. How would you recommend to the executive committee a commitment to long-range profitability objectives, rather than short-term profit goals, in your organization? Discuss any difficulties you see in getting such a commitment from top management and in fostering it throughout the organization? How would you reconcile these?
2. Place yourself in the position of Iacocca. You have weathered the initial financial crunch and now have some breathing room. Your task, as you see it, is to bring Chrysler now to at least a strong third position behind GM and Ford in the next ten years. Ideally, you would like to wrest second place in the industry from Ford— you would like nothing better. Discuss how you would plan to achieve this growth objective, recognizing Chrysler's resource constraints.

CHAPTER 13

A. C. Gilbert—Frenetic Reactions To Emerging Problems

The A. C. Gilbert Company was not a youngster, having had some 58 years of toymaking experience at the time it failed. For years its name had been respected and well known, and it signified quality.

In a mere 5 years, all this was to end. Almost incredibly, bad judgment replaced the solid achievements of the past. Changing environmental conditions were ignored for too long. Rash, frantic decisions were then substituted for a well-planned, corrective strategy that could have built on the strengths of the company.

BACKGROUND

The A. C. Gilbert Company was the product of one imaginative man's inventiveness and willingness to back his ideas himself rather than selling out. Alfred Carlton Gilbert, after graduation from Yale, established the Mysto Manufacturing Company in 1909 to make the Erector set, which he had perfected. In 1916, this company became the A. C. Gilbert Company. In time, the son, A. C. Jr., joined the company as assistant to his father and became president in 1954. In 1961, the senior Gilbert died, and the son became chairman of the board. Gilbert Jr. was a respected figure in the toy industry, serving as president of the Toys Manufacturers of the U.S.A. in 1962–1963.

Although the company never became a large firm, it was solidly in the top ten of toy manufacturers in the 1950s, with sales reaching over $17 million. It was strong in science toys—chemistry sets, microscopes, and Erector "engineering" sets—at a time when science was becoming important as a national priority. Gilbert had the reputation of a quality toymaker, and its American Flyer trains and Erector sets were known by generations of boys and their parents.

This was the situation as the company entered the 1960s. However, the environment for selling toys was changing. The 1960s, with their attendant prosperity, brought a booming toy market. But it was different from what Gilbert was familiar with. A new promotional medium, television, had become important for toy marketing and was superseding catalogs and window displays. But television was expensive and made the breakeven point on toy sales much higher. It also enabled many items, from hula hoops to Batmobiles, to attain quick popularity. The market was changing rapidly, and a firm had to be nimble to tap the sales potential and not be caught with too heavy an inventory when demand was superseded by another fad item.

The toy market was also changing in that traditional toy stores, hobby shops, and department stores were being bypassed for self-service, high-volume supermarkets and discount stores. These new dealers were mainly interested in low-priced, heavily advertised toys with attractive packages that could act as selling tools.

So the old, successful, well-entrenched company entered the 1960s rather complacent and content with the status quo.

PROBLEMS

Anson Isaacson, president of Gilbert, had a desperate task before him. In April of 1966 he was searching frantically among financial circles to raise the money needed to operate another year, after suffering losses of $2.9 million in 1965.

Mr. Isaacson had assumed the presidency in June 1964, after A. C. Gilbert, Jr. died. He was a former vice–president of Ideal Toy Company, a larger toymaker, and had been brought into the company to straighten out serious sales and profit problems that had been getting worse since 1961.

After 3 weeks of scouring for financial aid, Anson Isaacson was successful. Pledging most of the remaining unpledged assets of the company, he was able to obtain a loan of $6,250,000, of which he himself put up $250,000 to show creditors his faith in the company and his confidence in his ability to straighten out the problems. There was one frightening stipulation in the loan agreement, however. The loan was contingent on the company's making a profit in 1966. If Gilbert failed to do so, the loan would be called and the assets liquidated to satisfy the indebtedness. Isaacson was not bargaining from a position of strength and had to accept the condition. Although he did feel that, under his management, the condition would not pose a particular problem, still it lurked in the background, ominous and threatening.

PRELUDE

Now let us examine how Gilbert got into this mess. The company did not really recognize a problem until the end of 1961, at which time sales dropped from $12,600,000 in 1960 to $11,600,000. In 1961, the company counted a mere $20,011 in profits. The company was obviously facing serious problems, and a program was hastily devised to correct the situation.

In early 1962, with stock prices down, the company became attractive to Jack Wrather, president of a West Coast holding company that owned the "Lassie" and "Lone Ranger" television programs, the Disneyland Hotel, Muzak Corporation (piped-in music), and a boatyard. He acquired a 52 percent interest in the Gilbert Company for some $4,000,000. He then replaced Gilbert top executives with his own people. Although A. C. Gibert Jr. remained as board chairman, his power was substantially lessened.

The 1961 sales drop was attributed to two factors: insufficient new products and insufficient advertising. Plans were formulated to boost sales to $20,000,000 with the addition of new "hot items." The sales staff was increased 50 percent, because more aggressive selling and more frequent contacts with retailers were assumed to be directly correlated with increasing sales. After expanding the sales staff, a new general sales manager and a new director of international sales were appointed.

But this strategy proved of no avail. In 1962, sales dropped to $10,900,000, with a $281,000 loss. This loss was attributed to the cost of preparing the new, greatly expanded 1963 line and the scrapping of obsolete materials. The company was pinning its great expectations on the 1963 selling season. A major effort had been made to expand the line. For the first time, the company was offering toys for preschool children, and for girls in the 6- to 14-year-old bracket in addition to boys, who had been the traditional market segment. More than 50 new items boosted the line to 307 items, by far the largest in the company's history. The ambitious expansion program seemed fully justified and badly needed; now the market was 35,000,000 boys and girls, instead of just 9,000,000 boys.

Modern Packaging magazine hailed the package revitalization program in 1963.[1] Upwards of $1 million was spent to repackage the entire line.

---

[1] "Saving a $500,000 Investment," *Modern Packaging,* August 1963, pp. 97–98.

Packages for Erector sets and other long-established toys had been virtually unchanged for many years; now they were given an "exciting" new full-color pictorial treatment illustrating the models in action.

The future looked bright at this time, and such an aggressive approach was viewed badly overdue in an old, conservatively managed family business. Officials confidently predicted record sales and earnings.

It must have been a bitter pill when sales results finally came in (in the toy business, the Christmas selling season is crucial for the year's performance; until the results of this business season are tabulated late in the year, no one really knows how successful a year has been). Incredibly, sales continued to slide in 1963, to $10,700,000; worse, instead of a profit, there was a whopping $5,700,000 loss, stemming mostly from huge returns of low-priced toys shipped on a guaranteed sale basis to supermarkets. After Christmas, Gilbert had an inventory of almost $3,500,000 in unsold toys.

Corrective Efforts

At this point, Jack Wrather decided that a toymaking company needed more expert toymaking experience. He fired most of the top managment he had brought in nearly 2 years before. A. C. Gilbert, Jr. reassumed the presidency, but Anson Isaacson, former Ideal Toy Company vice–president, was brought in as chief operating officer and chairman of the executive committee.

In 2 years, losses had reached almost $6,000,000. This was a terrible drain on a firm whose revenues were not much more than $10,000,000 a year. But loans were renegotiated at higher interest rates, and major creditors agreed to a delay in payment over a 3-year period. After the last several years of profligate expansion of sales staff and product lines, Isaacson began a strong economy drive.

He made a major change in the selling mechanism. In place of company salespeople, he fired the sales staff and switched to manufacturers' representatives. Manufacturers' representatives are independent sales representatives who handle a number of noncompeting lines of various manufacturers and charge a fixed commission, usually 5 or 6 percent on all sales made. They are somewhat less expensive than a company sales force and should be able to contact more dealers. Gilbert had less control over them, however, and their customer service for Gilbert could be erratic. In addition, major cuts were made in factory personnel, with the result that administrative and operating expenses were reduced from $10,000,000 to $4,700,000 for 1964. In June of 1964, A. C. Gilbert, Jr. died; Mr. Wrather became chairman of the board, and Mr. Isaacson president.

For the 1964 Christmas season, 20 new toys were added to the depleted line. Encouragingly, sales picked up almost 7 percent, to $11,400,000. The company would have registered a profit for the year, but Isaacson insisted on dumping excess inventory to enhance future years' profits, so a loss was registered of $1,900,000.

The expectations of Isaacson and the Gilbert Company now rested on the fall and Christmas selling season of 1965. This was to be the year the company turned around and reached for its new potential. To this end, the product line was again revamped and a heavy advertising and point-of-purchase display program budgeted. Television advertising centered on a 52-week schedule of Saturday morning Beatles cartoon shows, and $2,000,000 was committed for this. In addition, the Gilbert Company furnished some 65,000 animated displays free to dealers at a cost of $1,000,000.

Early indications for 1965 were favorable. By July, Isaacson predicted a net profit for the year. The order backlog was $12,000,000 in July, and losses for the first 6 months of the year (toymakers characteristically incur losses through most of the year until the peak Christmas business is realized) were only half those for the same period in 1964.

Isaacson's optimistic prediction, however, proved wrong. The heavy promotional expenditures did bring sales of $14.9 million, the best since the early 1950s, and a 30 percent increase over the preceding year. However, losses were up to $2,900,000, mostly because of heavy returns on a 007 racing auto set, which was then handled exclusively by Sears, as well as other racing sets. These racing sets turned out to be poorly engineered and constructed, poorly packaged, and overpriced.

As the company's financial condition continued to worsen. Anson Isaacson began his rounds to find the financing necessary to keep the company alive. The multimillion–dollar rescue loan that he finally obtained made virtually all the assets subject to liens to secure such indebtedness and was contingent on the company's making a profit in 1966.

It did not make a profit in 1966. Instead, the announced loss was $12,872,000. The once proud A. C. Gilbert Company went out of business in February 1967. Gabriel Industries acquired certain of Gilbert's assets, including Erector sets and chemistry sets, for about $17 million. This was paid to the financial institutions holding Gilbert's indebtedness.

Figure 13.1 depicts Gilbert's last 6 years.

HOW DID IT HAPPEN?

We can group the mistakes that Gilbert made into two broad categories: lack of recognition of the problem until late, and frantic reactions once the problem was recognized, resulting in successive mistakes until the end.

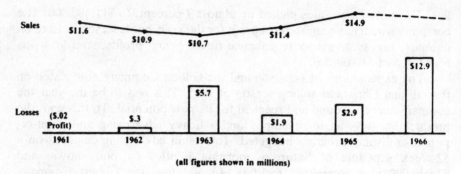

(all figures shown in millions)

Figure 13-1.

Each of these will be discussed in more detail, and the specific mistakes under these categories identified.

Gilbert failed to recognize that the toy environment was changing, and that the changes were causing an ever-worsening problem. Diminishing sales from the peak years of the 1950s apparently did not alert the company that there was a problem needing investigation and some adjustment in business strategy.

We have previously noted how major changes in advertising and distribution of toys were occurring and were only belatedly recognized by Gilbert. One change in toy demand that should have been quickly detected was that table-top slot-car auto racing sets, almost unknown 10 years before, were now outselling toy trains. Gilbert should have been in this market near the outset. Instead, not until the mid-1960s were its racing sets introduced. And these were poorly engineered, fragile, and overpriced—their returns in 1965 practically scuttled the company.

Apparently, not until the end of the 1961 selling season, when the company barely made a profit, was there any awareness of a possible problem. At this point, frantic and poorly thought-out actions were commenced. With the serious loss of 1962, there was no longer any doubt that there was a problem.

Frantic actions took place with the product line. This had remained relatively unchanged for decades. Suddenly, in 1 year, the line was greatly expanded—more than 50 new toys were added, not only directed to the traditional target market of 6- to 14-year-old boys, but now also for girls and for preschool children. Furthermore, the toys were different from what the company had been used to making—lower-priced, lower quality, and geared to large-volume sales. This placed great strains on the company's engineering and production capabilities. The almost inevitable result was poorly designed toys of not very good quality and of disappointing customer appeal.

INFORMATION SIDELIGHT

THE PROCESS OF CHANGE IN ORGANIZATIONS

We can identify certain steps that should normally be followed by top management in responding to major forces dictating change:[2]

1. Awareness of a problem
2. Diagnosing the cause of the problem
3. Examining alternative solutions to the problem
4. Making a preliminary choice for a new course of action
5. Testing the preliminary choice on a small scale before making a permanent choice
6. As a result of the test results or pilot run, the proposed solution is either accepted and adopted on a wider scale, or rejected and another alternative is considered

Effective management is quick to recognize emerging problems, hopefully before they have become serious and are drastically affecting sales and profits. Considerable attention is given to determining the cause(s) of the problems. This may involve collecting more information, perhaps through a research study or various internal analyses. After determining cause, alternative solutions can then be identified, their pros and cons evaluated in view of the resources of the organization, and one selected. If there are doubts concerning the chosen alternative, it may be introduced on a small scale—perhaps in one or two departments or locations—before proceeding further with it or else testing another alternative.

These, then, are the steps for prudently coping with major change. Crises develop when the first step is not recognized early enough, before sales and profits are drastically affected. Therefore, crisis management can usually be avoided. But if a crisis should develop, the other steps represent the most systematic and effective approach to dealing with it.

More than this, the company's unique niche as a quality toy maker of high-level educational toys was abandoned, and the company flung itself into the fiercely competitive marketplace against better experienced and mostly larger competitors.

Subsequent actions did nothing to restore the image of the reputable

---

[2] For more discussion of such steps, see Larry Greiner, "Patterns of Organization Change," *Harvard Business Review*, May-June 1967, pp. 119–130; and William F. Glueck, *Management*, 2nd Ed. (Hinsdale, Ill.: Dryden, 1980), pp. 418–442.

toymaker. A company and brand image is precious; a good image is not easily developed but can be torn down rather quickly.

Toy buyers were critical of the company's product changes and of its packaging:

> Gilbert had a natural in its Erector sets. Instead, they neglected it. They used to offer sets up to $75 packaged in metal boxes. Now the most expensive is only $20, the parts are flimsy, and it's in an oversized cardboard box. They did the same thing to their chemistry sets. You can't store anything in those oversize see-through packages.[3]

Gilbert had high hopes for its new All Aboard series, consisting of landscaped panels that fit together to form a tabletop train layout. But:

> It's a real good idea, but the quality is poor. The locomotive and cars are cheap and lack detail.[4]

Gilbert's doll series was overpriced, poorly made, and incomplete, because no changes of clothes were offered. This was at the time when additional wardrobes were the major appeal of many dolls, as well as a source of extra profits.

Incredibly poor timing was the lot of the company in attempting to compete with fad items. For example, in 1965, spy items were especially popular, with spy and secret agent movies and television series having high audience ratings. So Gilbert introduced such spy figures as Man from U.N.C.L.E., James Bond, and Honey West. The only trouble was that they did not reach the market until after Christmas Day in 1965, obviously too late for the selling season. Such timing was inexcusable and reflected drastic problems in the planning and operations of the company; the ground had been laid for this situation in 1964.

Successive errors were piled on each other. After the ill-conceived product line expansion of 1963 that resulted in $5.7 million in losses, an austerity campaign was put in effect in 1964, with major cutbacks made in engineering and production—expenses were consequently reduced more than 50 percent for 1964. But such austerity hardly led to the planning and production efficiencies needed for the quick introduction of fad items.

Other aspects of the austerity were less obvious but consequential. The company switched from having its own sales force to contracting for independent manufacturers' representatives to handle its selling efforts.

---

[3] "Toymaker A. C. Gilbert Co., Poor Loser?" *Sales Management,* May 1, 1966, p. 27.
[4] Ibid., p. 28.

Although this move was expected to increase dealer coverage while not adding to the cost of selling, dealers did not like the new arrangement: "It used to be that you could call a Gilbert salesman and get service on a problem. Now the reps just want to get the order," disgruntled dealers were saying.[5]

In attempting to widen its distribution to supermarkets, discount stores, and other aggressive promotional retailers, Gilbert made certain concessions that were to cost dearly, such as guaranteeing the sales of its products to some of these demanding outlets. By guaranteeing sales, the company assumed the burden of poor selling efforts, markdowns, and product write-offs of anything unsold after the Christmas season. Guaranteeing sales is usually a last-ditch effort by a new manufacturer trying to gain entry in the marketplace. Offering an unknown brand, such a supplier is totally dependent on retailers and may be forced to accept the conditions demanded by some. Gilbert was not a small unknown firm trying to crack the marketplace. In 1963, it still had a quality image, was widely known, and had good distribution, even though not as wide as desired.

A final dramatic mistake came in 1965. After the austerity of 1964, the spigots were reopened, and with a vengeance. More new toys were added. Of more significance, a massive television advertising campaign and point-of-purchase display program were instituted. Here was a company with sales of just over $11 million facing the specter of insolvency; yet, almost 30 percent of sales was budgeted for a massive promotion effort. The lack of success, resulting from poor judgment of products, distribution, and timing, laid the groundwork for the company's demise. The image of a reliable producer of high-quality toys had been lost. The $6,250,000 last-resort financing that Isaacson managed to come up with in 1966 could no longer support the company's efforts to regain a viable niche in the market.

WHAT CAN BE LEARNED?

Perhaps the first thing to be learned from Gilbert's experience is that it does not take long for a supposedly healthy and long-experienced company to come to its end. A series of successive bad decisions coming in the space of a few years can destroy all the gains built up by decades of successful operation.

Certainly, the need for better attention to and sensoring of the environment for doing business is evident. Gilbert needed to assess changing conditions better and more quickly, both in consumer demand and in competitive actions. The changes occurring were not difficult to detect; they

[5] Ibid.

were obvious to all—consumers, retailers, and manufacturers alike. But Gilbert continued to operate as if the status quo could be maintained, as if everything were unchanging. If nothing else, this case should point out the need to be constantly alert and responsive to change.

But a firm must also beware of reacting too quickly, without careful analysis of alternatives. This is the height of misguided crisis management. Problems need to be carefully identified, and probable solutions or adjustments to them weighed in view of the particular strengths and resources of the firm. In Gilbert's case, hasty actions only compounded past mistakes. To be specific, the major strength of the firm was its quality image; this should not have been sacrificed to bring out a hasty proliferation of "cheap" new products similar to competitors'. By expanding hastily with new products, the company's capabilities were disregarded, and a flood of poorly made products resulted.

Update

Although the Gilbert Company has folded, never to return to life, we can happily note that the Erector set has survived. As described earlier, Gabriel Industries, a large toy manufacturer that also makes Tinker Toys, acquired the Erector asset at the liquidation of Gilbert. In 1977, nearly 600,000 Erector sets, ranging in price from $1 for a 45-piece pocket set to $40 for a deluxe 450-piece set, were sold around the world.

In August of 1978, Gabriel and its Erector set subsidiary were purchased by CBS for $27.1 million. The senior vice–president of Gabriel predicted: "A hundred years from now, I think you'll still be able to buy an Erector set . . . long after everyone here is gone."[6]

For Thought And Discussion

1. What controls should Gilbert have had to remain alert to changing market conditions? What research would have helped?
2. Do you think Gilbert was right in expanding its target market in 1963? Why or why not?
3. Evaluate the advertising efforts of 1965 and the point-of-purchase display expenditures.
4. Discuss the pros and cons of changing management quickly when adversity sets in.

[6] "The Nuts and Bolts of Erector Set Firm," *Cleveland Plain Dealer*, September 10, 1978, Sec. 2–1.

Invitation To Role Play

1. As an assistant to the president, what would you have advised Gilbert to do at the end of 1961 when the first drastic decline in profit (to a $20,011 profit) occurred?
2. As a management consultant, what would you have advised at the end of 1963?

PART Four
LACK OF ADEQUATE CONTROLS

CHAPTER **14**

Burger Chef—
Repudiation of
Standards

In 1967, the General Foods Corporation (GF) acquired Burger Chef Systems, a fast-food franchising operation of some 700 units, for $16 million. In less than 4 years, GF amassed a pre-tax loss of $83 million in this venture. During this same time, 1967–1971, McDonald's net income rose from $7,072,000 to $27,248,000, for a 285 percent increase. Although some marginal fast-food franchisers collapsed during this period, when there appeared to be a saturation of hamburger, chicken, and other restaurants, GF was no marginal firm. It was the nation's largest manufacturer of convenience foods, with sales approaching $3 billion. It was an astute and aggressive marketer and the country's third-largest national advertiser (behind only Procter & Gamble and American Home Products), spending over $150 million a year. It had had an unbroken string of annual increases in sales dating back to 1935, and its last decline in net earnings had been in 1962. With such backing for an already established and growing franchise chain, how could disaster strike, and in just a few years?

FRANCHISING

Franchising is a contractual arrangement in which the franchiser extends to independent franchisees the right to conduct a certain kind of business according to a particular format. Although the franchising arrangement may involve a product, a common type of franchise today involves a service rather than a product: the major contribution of the franchiser is a carefully developed, promoted, and controlled operation, both through external signing and commonality of physical plant to internal standards and procedures, such as provided by McDonald's, Howard Johnson, Kentucky Fried Chicken, and Burger Chef.

Franchising dates back to at least 1898, when General Motors established its first independent dealer to sell and service automobiles. By 1910, franchising was the principal method of marketing automobiles and petroleum products. By 1920, it was being used by food, drug, variety, hardware, and automotive-parts firms. The major growth of franchising began after World War II. Soft ice cream outlets typify this growth: in 1945, there were 100 soft ice cream stands in the United States; by 1960, there were almost 18,000.

Franchise sales of goods and services by 1978 were about $275 billion, almost 30 percent of all retail sales. In 1978, there were almost half a million franchise establishments in the United States, and these employed over 4 million workers.[1]

Advantages Of Franchising

A firm has two major advantages in expanding through franchised outlets rather than with company-owned units. First, expansion can be very rapid, because the franchisees are putting up some or most of the money—almost the only limitations to growth are the need to screen applicants, to find suitable sites for new outlets, and to develop the managerial controls necessary to ensure consistency of performance. The other major advantage is that more conscientious people normally can be obtained to operate the outlets, because franchisees are entrepreneurs with a personal stake, rather than hired managers.

A potential franchisee or licensee finds the major advantage over other means of self-employment lies in the lower risk of business failure or, to say it positively, a greater chance of success. By going with an established franchiser, our entrepreneur will have a business that has a proven consumer acceptance and perhaps wide recognition. The franchisee can also benefit from well-developed managerial and promotional techniques and from the group buying power that is afforded.

---

[1] U.S. Department of Commerce, *Franchising in the Economy, 1977–1979* (Washington, D.C.: Superintendent of Documents, U.S. Government Printing Office, 1979), pp. vi, 1.

Fast–Food Restaurant Franchising

Franchised fast-food restaurants have made a major impact on the food service industry since the second World War. By the 1970's, employment in fast-food franchising accounted for almost 30 percent of total franchising employment, and over 30 percent of all persons employed in eating and drinking places in the United States.[2] To illustrate the successful growth of this industry, let us briefly look at two of the stars: Kentucky Fried Chicken and McDonald's.

Colonel Harland Sanders and Kentucky Fried Chicken. In 1955, Sanders was operating a moderately successful Southern fried chicken restaurant on a main highway in Kentucky on the north-south route from Detroit to Miami. But a new highway that bypassed his business by 7 miles was built, and he was forced to close. He was 65 years old, and all he had left was a 6th-grade education and $105, his first Social Security check.

On a hunch, he took five frozen frying chickens and a special cooker, along with some flour and spices, and began calling on restaurants in Indiana and Ohio. His method was to cook chickens at high temperatures for less than 8 minutes. After 3 years, he finally made some headway. He gave franchises away; he leased cookers or converted stoves for high temperature; he supplied at cost paper, napkins, and buckets with his image and the Kentucky Fried Chicken name—and he received $0.05 for each chicken sold by these restaurants.

Customers liked the product. In 8 years he had granted more than 500 franchises, and his revenues were over $2.3 million. He was his own sales force and he never had more than 18 employees. In 1962, then 72 years old, he expanded the business to include take-home sales. In 1964, he sold the entire business, including patents, to a group for $2 million, retaining for himself the lifetime job of goodwill ambassador. The new management concentrated on take-home sales. By 1968, sales were over $250 million and there were more than 1500 outlets.

Ray Kroc and McDonalds. In 1954, at age 51, Ray Kroc was the sole distributor for a Chicago firm making a multimixer for milk shakes (i.e., a mixer for six milk shakes at a time). He became excited when he received his largest order: eight multimixers from one store in San Bernardino, California, operated by Maurice and Dick McDonald. He flew out to California to see for himself this "super" restaurant, and found a clean, efficiently run, high-volume drive-in restaurant with a limited menu based around the hamburger. Kroc immediately thought that, if there were only 100 other such

[2] Ibid., p. 11.

200

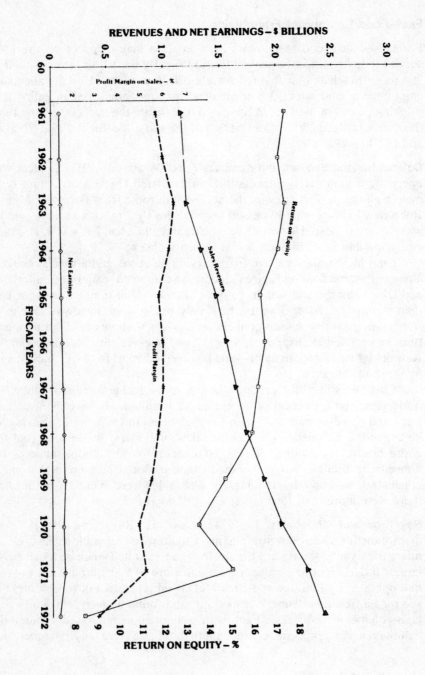

REVENUES AND NET EARNINGS – $ BILLIONS

0   0.5   1.0   1.5   2.0   2.5   3.0

Profit Margin on Sales – %

60   2   3   4   5   6   7

1961 1962 1963 1964 1965 1966 1967 1968 1969 1970 1971 1972

FISCAL YEARS

Returns on Equity

Net Earnings

Sales Revenues

Profit Margin

RETURN ON EQUITY – %

8   9   10   11   12   13   14   15   16   17   18

restaurants, he'd be rich (8 multimixers × 100 restaurants = 800 multimixers sold). He persuaded the McDonalds to let him franchise their outlet throughout the country, with *one-half of one* percent of the gross receipts going to them. Kroc opened the first franchise in Des Plaines, Illinois, in 1955. Five years later there were 228 restaurants. In 1961, Kroc bought out the McDonald brothers for $2.7 million. By 1966, McDonald's units were generating sales of $266 million; by 1971, $784 million; and by 1975, $2.5 billion.

THE GENERAL FOODS CORPORATION

GF can trace its beginnings back to C.W. Post Cereals in 1895. It was incorporated in 1922 as the Postum Cereal Company, manufacturers of Post cereals and Postum beverage. Then, in 1925, the firm began consolidating with certain other companies, among them the Jell-O Company and the Maxwell House Coffee Company. In 1929, the Postum Cereal Company changed its name to General Foods.

The company continued to grow and diversify, not only through internal development of many new products, but also by acquisition and mergers with other firms. By 1965, its sales were $1.5 billion, a 60 percent gain over 1956; during that same period, net earnings more than doubled to $177 million. Well-known brands of this major processor and marketer of packaged food products included: Maxwell House, Yuban, and Sanka coffees; Jell-O desserts; Bird's Eye frozen foods; Post cereals; Swans Down cake mixes; Baker's chocolate; Minute Rice; Kool-Aid soft drink mixes; Gaines pet foods; Tang breakfast drink; and Log Cabin syrup.

During the 1960s, however, some indicators of performance began showing deterioration. Although sales revenues increased steadily, net profits did not keep pace with sales. As a result, profit margins on sales began declining from the high of 6.5 percent in 1963. Furthermore, returns on stockholders' equity also began declining from the 17.5 percent of 1963. Figure 14.1 shows these trends graphically. Still, in 1966, when a new man, C. W. "Tex" Cook, came in as chairman and chief executive, and Arthur E. Larkin became president and chief operating officer, GF stood at the forefront of the packaged foods industry with net profits at 6 percent of sales, among the industry's highest. Furthermore, of six major food categories, GF led in all but cereals, with no competitor even close in instant coffee, desserts, and dog food.

More tangible problems emerged in 1968, when the Federal Trade Commission forced GF to divest its S.O.S. soap-pad business, which it had acquired in 1957. Chairman Cook bitterly took umbrage at this decision:

They laid down some pretty severe strictures regarding what we could and could not do for 'X' number of years. For instance, they made it very clear that we were precluded from touching anything of consequence that went through the supermarket on a national basis. Similarly, they would frown on something that depended very heavily on consumer advertising. So that we were almost directed away from the kinds of things where our experience and expertise had, over the years, given us most of our benefits.[3]

To add to the problems connected with antitrust action, three of GF's biggest divisions began running into trouble. The Bird's Eye Division lost ground to Green Giant Company, which had developed ready-to-cook vegetables in plastic bags that could be dropped directly into boiling water, thereby offering consumers a very attractive convenience. Furthermore, supermarkets were increasingly bringing out their own private branded products, which they could sell below the prices of GF national brands, and consumer acceptance of these was further cutting into GF's market share and profit margins.

The Maxwell House Division, which had been generating more than a third of GF's sales revenues, began finding sales leveling off. To a considerable extent, this reflected changing consumer tastes, particularly those of young adults, whose consumption of coffee was not matching that of their parents.

Probably for the same reason—a change in consumer tastes—the dry cereal market growth slowed markedly. Added to this, competitor General Mills was exerting a massive promotional push with the results that GF's Post Division (Post Toasties, Grape Nuts, 40% Bran Flakes, etc.) was displaced from second place behind Kellogg.

Faced with governmental constraints, a tangible loss of profit momentum, and an eroding competitive stance, GF began seeking diversification in directions that would at least have some compatibility with the company expertise: food-related activities. During the mid-1960s, fast-food restaurants—McDonald's and many others—had been experiencing burgeoning growth rates. In fact, food sold away from home was growing at twice the rate of food sold in stores for home consumption.[4]

In late 1967, the acquisition, for somewhat over $16 million, of Burger Chef Systems, an Indianapolis-based chain of 700 (mostly franchised) fast-food hamburger restaurants, seemed altogether reasonable and expeditious. Six Rix roast-beef sandwich restaurants were also acquired at that

---

[3] As quoted in "The Rebuilding Job at General Foods," *Business Week*, August 25, 1973, p. 50.

[4] "We've Turned a Corner," *Forbes*, March 15, 1969, p. 46.

time. The logic seemed inescapable. GF had great expertise in food processing; 1968 was a boom year, and companies like McDonald's were growing at rates in excess of 25 percent a year. Burger Chef was already operating in 39 states and was selling 1 million hamburgers a day. Needless to say, expectations for the fast-food business were high.

BURGER CHEF UNDER GENERAL FOODS

In an effort to capitalize on the opportunities of the times, a vigorous expansion program was undertaken for Burger Chef. By March 1969, not much more than a year after the acquisition, there were 900 outlets operating across the country. That same month, Burger Chef moved into Canada with the opening of an outlet in Toronto.

By December 1969, there were 1022 outlets in the United States and 29 in Canada. Exactly 1 year later, the totals were more than 1200 outlets in the United States and 36 in Canada, representing an increase of over 70 percent in 3 years. Some 84 percent of the outlets were franchised, with 16 percent operated by Burger Chef. Advertising expenditures averaged $2.5 million a year.

A complication for GF in its fast-food acquisitions was the loss of key executives from these operations. The founder of Burger Chef left to pursue other interests shortly after the acquisition. Another key executive had a heart attack. Other departures for various reasons resulted in an almost complete management turnover during the first 2 years. But this seemed to pose no severe problems, because GF supplied the new management for its acquisition from its own ranks.

The bad news, when it came, was sudden and shocking. In January 1972, GF announced a write-down amounting to $83 million pre-tax dollars, nearly $1 a share after taxes. GF informed its stockholders that it was cutting back, pruning rather drastically, after its ambitious expansion into fast food. It was closing all 70 of its Rix roast beef restaurants. Of some 1200 Burger Chef hamburger stands, it announced that it had already closed 100 and was writing off many more. The faster GF tried to expand its fast-food operation, the bigger the problems became.

Forbes magazine questioned how so big a company could go so wrong in so seemingly simple a business as frying hamburgers and slicing roast beef. In an interview with *Forbes* reporters, President Larkin explained: "We couldn't get enough people to come into our stores. The kids didn't want roast beef and, later, the adults didn't want it either. Roast beef was just a fad." Regarding the Burger Chef operation, Larkin admitted the problem was simply management: "The key man got a heart attack. We sent one of our own men, and he just did not know his way around this kind of operation."[5]

The heavy loss was a shocker. The original investment in Burger Chef had been $16 million. GF discovered, however, that long-term lease commitments are debts too, especially if an outlet goes bad. Then, the expansion of the two chains, neither one on sound footing, was like throwing good money after bad, so that the $16 million investment escalated into an $83 million loss.

Struggle For Survival

For 19 straight years, GF had managed to achieve gains in per-share earnings. But the hamburger and roast beef disaster broke the trend in 1972. The viability of the multibillion–dollar company was not in danger, and the company still made profits overall, despite the fast-food drain. Still, the heavy losses suffered with Burger Chef hurt the image of the company, especially with its major food chain customers. This image further suffered when GF cut back on some customer services to absorb the fast-food losses.

Arthur Larkin, who had been the heir apparent for the chairman's position, took an "early retirement." As part of a company-wide efficiency drive, salaried personnel were cut by 10 percent, and GF took a hard look at its total marketing operation.

Although some other aspects of the operation were also causing problems, the biggest rebuilding job continued to be the Burger Chef chain. The total number of units was pruned to about 1000, and more attention was given to clustering these in major markets to obtain a more efficient sharing of advertising expenditures. More thorough screening and training of franchise owners and managers was instituted. A new building design, new logo, more emphasis on product quality, a more varied menu, and even a new plastic wrapper to keep hamburgers warm longer, were belatedly introduced. Yet, it seemed likely the fast-food division would be years away from making a major contribution to GF's earnings. Table 14.1 shows how Burger Chef fared in these years against its major fast-food competitors. Notice that, although sales increased slightly each year, in no way did they match the increases of the major competitors—market share slipped every year.

[5] "The Bigger They Are. . ." *Forbes*, February 15, 1972, p. 21.

Table 14.1 Top 25 Fast Food Restaurants

	1974		1973		1972		1971	
	A	B	A	B	A	B	A	B
1. McDonald's	1,940,000	19.8	1,507,000	17.7	1,032,000	15.2	784,000	13.4
2. Kentucky Fried Chicken	1,150,000	11.7	1,000,000	11.8	840,000	12.4	900,000	15.4
3. International Dairy Queen	590,000	6.0	530,000	6.0	510,000	7.5	424,000	7.3
4. Burger King	466,500	4.8	388,600	4.0	270,700	4.0	226,000	3.9
5. Burger Chef	275,000	2.8	225,000	2.6	200,000	2.9	225,000	3.9
6. A & W International	265,000	2.7	264,000	3.1	241,000	3.5		
7. Hardee's	259,000	2.6	206,000	2.4	136,000	2.0	107,000	1.8
8. Denny's	252,964	2.6	204,016	2.4	163,411	2.4	132,332	2.3
9. Jack-in-the-Box	244,000	2.6	170,000	2.1	132,000	1.9		
10. Pizza Hut	242,000	2.5	160,000	2.0	115,000	1.7	77,680	1.3
11. Bonanza	193,000	1.9	140,700	1.7	92,846	1.4	64,000	1.1
12. Sambo's	190,000	1.9	138,000	1.7	92,152	1.4	61,582	1.1
13. Gino's	170,521	1.7	170,521	2.1	128,044	1.9	95,300	1.6
14. Dunkin Donuts	169,474	1.7	141,757	1.7	126,693	1.8	99,593	1.8
15. Ponderosa	155,000	1.6	96,552	1.1	96,552	1.8	64,065	1.1
16. Church's Fried Chicken	126,000	1.3	101,600	1.3	79,354	1.2	51,200	0.9
17. Shoney's	120,401	1.2	101,349	1.2				
18. Arby's International	120,175	1.2	100,000	1.2				
19. Jerrico	98,870	1.0	61,678	0.7				
20. Frisch's Big Boy	91,000	0.9	88,000	1.0	79,000	1.2	73,000	1.2
21. Morrison's	90,800	0.9	66,000	0.8	52,250	0.8		
22. Friendly Ice Cream	90,000	0.9	71,775	0.8	61,249	0.9	49,379	0.8
23. Shakey's	87,000	0.9	74,500	0.9	63,650	0.9	73,000	1.2
24. Mr. Steak	85,000	0.9	81,700	1.0	64,000	0.9	49,800	0.9
25. Sizzler	85,500	0.9	62,200	0.6	43,443	0.7		

Key: "A" represents Total Sales, given in $1000's (000).
"B" represents Market Share, given as a percentage (%).

Sources: Advertising Age, June 3, 1974, p. 52; May 14, 1973, p. 93; and June 30, 1975, p. 49.

INFORMATION SIDELIGHT

STEPS IN THE CONTROL PROCESS

Any control process has three basic steps:

1. Standards of performance need to be set and communicated to those persons involved.
2. Performance should be checked against these standards.
3. Corrective action should be taken as needed.

With Burger Chef, standards needed to be set as to quality and preparation of food, cleanliness and service, menus and general operations, and personnel—their qualifications for selection, and uniform and conduct requirements. Accounting standards also needed to be established regarding budgeted costs, size of servings, number of employees, payrolls, and the like. The better-run franchised operations, notably McDonald's, had extensive standards and specifications for all aspects of the operation drawn in minute detail.

Only when standards have been specifically designated and communicated to those responsible for adhering to them can the next step of the control process be imposed: measuring performance against these standards. Such measures of performance are best done by outside auditors, inspectors, or district executives coming on the premises unannounced, usually with a checklist, and grading actual against expected performance.

The final step in the control process involves identifying the deviations from the standards and, if serious, instituting measures to correct the situation, perhaps through better training, more motivation, or even threat of dismissal or demotion.

Although franchise operations involve independent owners of outlets, the franchiser, in this case, Burger Chef, still has authority to impose sanctions on deviant behavior. Such sanctions typically consist of warnings, placing on probation, and finally, if performance still does not meet standards, removing the franchise.

Only in this way can a far-flung operation have reasonable assurance that standards of quality and performance will be maintained. A few poorly performing outlets can hardly be tolerated, because their resulting customer dissatisfactions carry over to the detriment of other outlets as well.

POSTMORTEM

Evaluation of Strategy after General Foods Acquisition

Such a perfect acquisition it seemed in 1968. How could such a compatible union go wrong? In retrospect, a fast-food operation was vastly different from the marketing of packaged food sold in supermarkets, despite their both dealing with food. There were major differences in promotional efforts needed, in competition, in facilities required, and most important, in management controls needed. Unfortunately, GF did not realize this until much of the damage was done.

No single event can be selected as the cause of the Burger Chef debacle; rather, it was a combination of circumstances. These, however, were by no means hidden; they were obvious and should have been identified and corrected by an astute management.

At the time of the acquisition, Burger Chef suffered from a lack of distinction and identity. McDonald's had its golden arches, gaudy though they might be, but they readily identified an outlet; Kentucky Fried Chicken was easily recognized; so were most of the other successful fast-food establishments. But what did Burger Chef have: a red and yellow sign, of no particular distinction, not even universally used, and certainly inconspicuous among the multitude of other signs proliferating along commercial strips. The outlets themselves tended to be cheaply constructed gas station-quality buildings, some with walk-up windows, but few with sit-down accommodations. Furthermore, there was little uniformity in design among the mostly franchised operations.

Burger Chef faced a considerable disadvantage in that its 700 outlets at the time of acquisition were thinly dispersed and spread over 39 states. As a result, a major metropolitan area might have only a handful of restaurants, in contrast to McDonald's and some of the other major franchisers. Consequently, supervision was difficult and costly, and the benefits of concentrated promotional efforts, which could have been shared among a number of outlets at no prohibitive cost for any, had to be curbed, leaving the competitive advantage to those firms with more concentration of outlets. The better policy, then, would have been a slower geographical expansion, doing so on a market-by-market basis.

The quality of food and the limited assortment available also contributed to the poor performance. At a time when competitors were adding fish sandwiches, double- and triple-decker hamburgers, onion rings, and fruit pies to their food assortment, Burger Chef was standing pat. And the food quality, which varied with franchisee and area, was a major problem.

Company spokespersons admitted their selection and training of franchisees was questionable at best. Persons who expressed an interest in a Burger Chef franchise, and who had satisfactory character references and financial standing and some experience in running a filling station or whatever, were approved. Although these new franchise holders were then sent to a training school for a brief period, there was no on-the-job training to familiarize them with hiring people, to teach them how to be hospitable, how to handle the problems of a teen-age gathering place, and so on.

A further flaw became apparent in the Burger Chef operation. Emphasis was on expanding—expanding in number of outlets just as rapidly as possible. In the process, existing outlets and their problems were ignored. As a result, location mistakes, problems of controlling quality of product and service, and others were not corrected for the new units being established. Expansion was coming on top of an unstable and even wobbly base.

An economic recession in 1969–71 should have discouraged pellmell expansion, or at least caused some introspection and review of the overall growth strategy for this division. During this time, some of the marginal fast-food franchisers bit the dust. But the stronger ones survived with few ill effects. With the formidable resources of GF, Burger Chef should have strengthened its competitive position, focusing on upgrading and improving the outlets it had, instead of enlarging its mediocrity. As President Larkin said: "We moved too far, too fast, under the pressure of the times."[6]

Comparison Of Burger Chef With McDonald's

The deficiencies of the Burger Chef operation are more apparent when we compare it with the most successful in the industry, McDonald's. What was the key to the overwhelming McDonald's success?

This statement is widely quoted: "McDonald's success is based on the fact that it changed the smelly roadside hamburger stand into a clean, efficient family restaurant."[7] Kroc offered the public a clean, family atmosphere where service was quick and cheerful. Cleanliness of outlets, including the toilets, and friendliness of salespeople became major competitive advantages. Efficient speed, friendly service, and assured cleanliness were not maintained without great pains. At Hamburger University, a special McDonald's training school for managers and owners, heavy emphasis was given to customer service. A 350-page operating manual required adherence to strict standards, not only in preparation of food but also in care and maintenance of the facilities. For example, the manual called for door

---

[6] Marylin Bender, "At General Foods, Did Success Breed Failure?" *The New York Times*, June 11, 1972, p. III–18.

[7] "McDonald's Keeps Them Cooking," *Financial World*, August 28, 1974, p. 45.

windows to be washed twice daily. Similar tight standards concerned service, food, and cooking procedures. There was even an employee dress code, with men required to keep their hair cropped to military length and their shoes highly polished. Women had to wear dark, low shoes, hair nets, and only very light makeup. All employees wore prescribed uniforms.

The cooking was completely standardized. A pound of meat had to contain less than 19 percent fat. Buns had to measure 3½ in. wide; no more than ¼ oz of onions was permitted per hamburger, and so on. The holding time for each of the cooked products was set by corporate headquarters; for example, french fries, 7 minutes; burgers, 10 minutes; coffee, 30 minutes—after this time the products had to be thrown out. Company auditors closely scrutinized this part of the operation to ensure that all food served was of the same quality.

Consistency in adhering to the high standards was another notable mark of McDonald's. Close supervision of store operations by strong regional offices was maintained to prevent a weakness in one restaurant from having a detrimental effect on other stores in the system.

Franchises were granted store by store, and operators permitted to expand only if they satisfactorily met the stiff standards. This contrasted with most other franchisers, who granted area franchises to large investors who promised to put up a given number of outlets in a specified period. Although the rate of growth was rapid, there were few problems with substandard conditions at either company-owned or franchised outlets.

McDonald's rigorously analyzed potential sites to assure each unit of the maximum chance for success, and failures resulting from poor locations were few. The distinctive buildings and the arches, of course, made a McDonald's unit conspicuous from a distance.

McDonald's was one of the biggest users of mass media advertising of any retailer, budgeting over $50 million each year. Who is not familiar with the jingle "You Deserve a Break Today"? How successful has this mass advertising been? In a survey of school children in the early 1970s, 96 percent identified Ronald McDonald, ranking him second only to Santa Claus.[8]

Judiciously, and only after considerable testing, McDonald's began broadening its product line. In 1975, a new breakfast menu resulted in 5 to 10 percent sales increases for those outlets serving it.[9] Other kinds of sandwiches—for example, a quarter pounder with lettuce and tomato—were tested, as was the addition of chicken to the menu, a move estimated to

[8] "The Burger that Conquered the Country," *Time*, September 17, 1973, pp. 84–92.
[9] "Broader Menus for Fast Foods," *Business Week*, July 14, 1975, p. 118.

increase sales 15 percent, but requiring about $14,000 worth of additional equipment per store.[10]

In all these areas of operation, Burger Chef showed up poorly compared to McDonald's. It lacked image, consistency, a diversifying product line, and promotional expenditures—only $2.5 million annually during the growth years, versus $50 million for McDonald's—to bring it recognition, distinctiveness, and customer appeal. In addition, it lacked a well-planned and organized selection procedure for franchisees and a training program to ensure that desirable operational procedures would result. Finally, Burger Chef controls and auditing in no way compared with the thoroughness and strictness practiced by McDonald's.

Comparison Of Burger Chef With The Losers

Burger Chef was not quite a loser. Although it was trimmed in size, it did not go out of business (we can speculate, however, that GF might have been better off selling the division rather than continuing the drain on financial and managerial resources). A useful perspective can be gained by comparing it against the real losers in the industry, especially those franchise firms that faded in the late 1960s and early 1970s.

Some franchisers failed because of difficulty in obtaining qualified franchisees or licensees. McDonald's believed that a key factor for success was for a licensee initially to work full time in the business. The unsuccessful franchisers failed to attract or insist on licensees who met prescribed qualifications. They tended to be interested primarily in getting the initial franchise fee. Business was viewed as a quick-buck scheme, to be milked dry with the franchiser then exiting.

Poor site selection plagued some franchise operations. In eagerness to secure footholds in major markets, they failed to research satisfactory locations. Too fast an expansion led to indiscriminate site selection, sometimes influenced by opportunistic realtors. Another factor inducing poor locations was lack of capital to purchase the more desirable sites.

When business and the economy in general are going well, a lack of effective management controls is not always readily apparent. However, when the economy experiences a downturn and, more importantly, when competition intensifies, lack of effective controls can be fatal to these businesses.

To gain quick public attention and recognition, many fast-food franchisers in the 1960s used the name of either an entertainer or professional sports figure to lure potential licensees. For example, Minnie Pearl's Chicken,

---

[10] "For Ray Kroc, Life Began at 50, or Was It 60?" *Forbes*, January 15, 1973, pp. 24–30.

Here's Johnny Restaurant (Johnny Carson), Al Hirt Sandwich Saloon, Broadway Joe's (Joe Namath), Jerry Lucas Beef 'n Shake, and Mickey Mantle's Country Cookin' Restaurant. What soon became apparent, however, was that, although the public might pay to see the entertainer or sports figure perform, they would not necessarily be willing to frequent a fast-food outlet simply because of the famous name—unless the food and service warranted their patronage. And most of them did not. Two successful exceptions have been Gino's, primarily located on the East Coast, and owned by Gino Capelletti, former All-Pro defensive end for the Baltimore Colts, and Roy Rogers Restaurants, sponsored by the cowboy star. But both offer good food and amenities.

Deceptive advertising was sometimes used to vastly inflate profit claims, the better to attract investors. Sometimes the profit claims were based on questionable accounting procedures, as with Minnie Pearl's Chicken. In May 1968, there were 405 franchises, and stock was first issued at $20 a share: By December of that year, there were over 1200 franchises, and the stock reached a high of $68. Success appeared phenomenal. By the end of 1969, 1600 franchises had been sold, although only 263 stores were in operation. By 1970, there were only 183 stores operating out of 1840 franchises sold, and success was turning to failure. What happened? It became apparent that profits had been vastly inflated by counting the sale of franchises as current income, instead of conservatively taking this into income in increments from year to year. The stock that had reached $68 in 1968 plummeted to $0.50 in 1970.[11]

Burger Chef exhibited none of these irregularities of deceptive advertising and profits or opportunistic speculation. It was a solidly–backed operation, geared to playing a major role in the fast-food industry. Yet, its flawed operational procedures nullified its strengths. It had the ball and fumbled it.

WHAT CAN BE LEARNED?

Franchising presents some significant differences from the other business operations examined in this book. The major distinction is the very rapid growth possible through franchising—far more rapid than a firm can achieve on its own, even if it has substantial resources. Because somebody else is putting up most or all of the capital for an outlet, the major impediments to expansion are finding and wooing sufficient investor-licensees, as well as

[11] Reported in "Fried Chicken that Went into Politics," *Business Week*, September 19, 1970, p. 37; and Richard Elliott, Jr., "Home to Roost: Excesses of the Fast Food Franchisers are Catching Up with Some," *Barrons*, September 22, 1969, p. 5.

finding enough attractive sites for units to be placed. As we have just seen, both of these requirements can be carelessly done in the quest for wild expansion or, as with McDonald's, can be carefully adhered to for controlled expansion.

A further distinction of franchising is that a few poor operations can be detrimental to other outlets, because all are operating under the same format and logo. Although this is not dissimilar to any chain operation—a few bad stores can hurt the image of the rest of the chain—a franchise system is composed of independent entrepreneurs who will tend to be less controllable than the hired managers of a chain operation.

Illusion Of Rapid Growth

The great growth possible through a franchise system can be its downfall. Because growth in number of units can occur so easily and quickly, there is the temptation to be a slave to it, to rush headlong into opening ever more units to meet the clamoring demand of prospective licensees. Such emphasis on growth often means that existing operations will be largely ignored. As a consequence, they will be undercontrolled, with emerging problems not receiving adequate attention. Screening people and locations tends to become superficial. Eventually, the bubble bursts, and the firm is forced to recognize that many outlets are marginal at best and will have to be drastically pruned, if, indeed, the total operation can even survive. This was the scenario with Burger Chef, as well as others that failed. The growth an aggressive and ambitious firm seeks must be prudent and controlled—even if a slower growth rate must be tolerated to achieve adequate assimilation.

Necessity For Tight Controls

Any firm needs to maintain tight controls over far-flung outlets if it is to be sufficiently informed of emerging problems and opportunities, and if it is to maximize the resources of the firm and maintain a desired image and standard of performance. In a franchise operation this is all the more essential, as we have noted before, because we are dealing with independent entrepreneurs rather than hired managers, and because a few inferior units can adversely affect the others. Controls should mean not only prescribing standards—remember McDonald's 350-page operating manual—but also monitoring to ensure that the standards are maintained. Regional and/or home-office executives should make frequent, unscheduled calls on stores, preferably with a checklist in hand, and grade their performance according to the prescribed standards. All aspects of the operation should be checked, ranging from the grease content of french fries to the soap supply in the restrooms. When performance of a particular outlet deviates significantly from that prescribed, remedial action will have to be taken, from warnings even to taking a franchise away in the event of continuing deficiencies.

Other controls are needed for screening and selecting franchisees and for training them. Specifications should also be established for site selection and building standards. Only in this way can uniformity of operation at a desired quality level be achieved and maintained.

Need For A Distinctive Image

Any firm needs to develop a distinctive image, one that differs from that of competitors and is unique and identifiable. This is especially important in a highly competitive environment. Burger Chef failed badly here, in the midst of competitors who were highly effective in developing such distinctions. To this day, Burger Chef has not achieved a distinctive image.

Admittedly, uniqueness is not always easy to achieve, especially if many competitors have already adopted more obvious possibilities. But the search should go on. Uniqueness can come from a distinctive design or logo, or roof, or building style; it can come from a different menu, somewhat different services, a different promotional approach; it can even be achieved by appealing to a different customer segment.

Imitation Should Not Be Disdained

A willingness to imitate may seem a contradiction to the previous section, the need for a distinctive image. But not so. We are talking here about adopting proven successful business practices, not imitating a sign or a building style, or even a menu without any changes.

Burger Chef had the supremely successful example, McDonald's, to learn from. McDonald's management and operational procedures were not unknown; indeed, they were highly publicized. It required no genius to recognize the merits in what McDonald's was doing and put them into effect in another operation. But Burger Chef failed to do this; other franchisers— for example, even Burger King, a Pillsbury Company acquisition—also either failed to imitate the successful strategy fully, or did so belatedly, as Burger King finally began to do in the late 1970s.[12]

When a firm has developed a proven and successful format, why should other firms hesitate to imitate it? They can still maintain their own distinctive

[12] As reported in "The Man Who McDonaldized Burger King," *Business Week*, October 8, 1979, pp. 132–136.

images, but ones fully structured on successful management and control practices. Although imitation may be viewed as not creative, it represents sound and astute learning. Creativity can be reserved for other aspects of the operation.

Update

Late in 1981, GF agreed to sell the Burger Chef subsidiary to Hardee's, a Canadian-owned hamburger fast-food firm that had 1396 U.S. outlets. Burger Chef by now had been pruned to 679 units and, after 5 years of losses, was finally showing a small profit. The sale to Hardee's resulted in a charge against earnings for GF of $12.5 million. This loss was deemed acceptable to be rid of a burr that had plagued it and that now, while admittedly showing a profit, was still yielding a much lower return on investment than most of its other divisions. The acquisition was viewed by Hardee's as providing additional sales and earnings growth potential to its already substantial fast-food operation.

For Thought And Discussion

1. Playing the devil's advocate (one who takes the opposing viewpoint for argument's sake), criticize the acquisition of Burger Chef by GF as thoroughly as you can.
2. In an exercise in creativity, perhaps brainstorming,[13] offer suggestions for a distinctive image or format for Burger Chef.
3. Would you advocate changing the name of Burger Chef? Why or why not?
4. How do you account for the reluctance of competitors to imitate successful examples of other firms in their industry?
5. Do you think the FTC was justified in curbing GF's expansion in 1968? Discuss both sides of this action—that is, from the viewpoints of the FTC and GF.

Invitation To Role Play

Assume the role of the GF executive responsible for Burger Chef after the acquisition. Be as specific as you can in formulating a strategy for the growth of this venture.

---

[13] Brainstorming is a technique to stimulate group creativity. A group of persons (five to eight persons seems to be the best–sized group) are brought together for the sole purpose of producing ideas, with this best achieved when: criticism is ruled out; free-wheeling is welcomed; quantity of ideas is wanted, with no emphasis on quality at this point; participants are encouraged to build on and/or modify the ideas of others.

15

Osborne Computer— Trying For Rapid Growth Without Controls

Only rarely may a new firm hit the jackpot: a meteoric rise surpassing even the most optimistic expectations of founders and investors. In the heady excitement of great growth, anything seems possible. It is tantalizing to think that such an enterprise is invincible to competition. Alas, such stars can sometimes come tumbling back to earth, and reality. Perhaps no better example can be found in modern business annals than the almost vertical rise and collapse of Osborne Computer Corporation. Founded in 1981, the business was booming at a $100–million clip—in barely 18 months. But on September 14, 1983, the company sought protection from creditors under Chapter 11 of the Bankruptcy Code.

ADAM OSBORNE

Adam Osborne was born in Thailand, the son of a British professor, and spent his earliest years in India. His parents were disciples of a maharishi, although he was educated in Catholic schools. He was later sent to Britain for schooling, and in 1961, at the age of 22, he moved to the United States. He obtained a Ph.D. in chemical engineering at the University of Delaware and then worked for Shell Development Company in California.

Osborne and Shell soon parted company, the bureaucratic structure frustrating him. He became interested in computers, and in 1970 he set up his own computer consulting company. The market for personal computers began to mushroom in the mid-1970s, and he emerged as a guru. He had a computer column, "From the Fountainhead," for *Interface Age,* and he began making speeches and building a reputation. He wrote a book, *Introduction to Microcomputers,* geared to the mass market. But it was turned down by a publisher. So Osborne published it himself, and it sold 300,000 copies. By 1975, his publishing company had put out some 40 books on microcomputers, nearly a dozen of which he had written himself. In 1979, he sold his publishing company to McGraw-Hill, but agreed to stay as a consultant through May 1982.

Osborne was thus in a position to take full advantage of the growth of the microcomputer industry. But he had also angered many in the industry by his stinging criticisms and bold assertions. In particular, he spoke out sharply against the pricing strategies of the personal computer manufacturers, contending that they were ignoring the mass market by constantly raising prices with every new feature added.

Osborne himself came to be the subject of some of the most colorful copy of the industry. Tall and energetic, he possessed a strong British accent to go along with his volubility, his charm, and his supreme confidence. He seemed to epitomize the new breed of entrepreneurs drawn to the epicenter of the new high-tech industry, the so-called Silicon Valley in California.

Early in 1981, Osborne put his criticisms and assertions to the test. To a chorus of skeptics he announced plans to manufacture and market a new personal computer, one priced well below the competition. His first machines were ready for shipping by that July, and before long the skeptics were running for the hills. Now Osborne could prove that he was a doer, and not merely a talker.

INDUSTRY BACKGROUND

In the early 1970s, computers ranged from small units to the very large, with prices reaching limits only affordable to well-heeled firms. The industry was dominated by one company, IBM, which held 70 percent of the market. All the other firms in the industry were scrambling for small shares. IBM seemed to have an unassailable advantage, because it had the resources for the heaviest marketing expenditures in the industry as well as the best research and development. The firm with the masterful lead in a rapidly growing industry has ever-increasing resources over its lesser competitors, who can hardly hope to catch up and, it seems, must be content to chip away at the periphery of the total market.

The computer industry had been characterized by rapid technological changes since the early 1960s. By the early 1970s, however, the new technology being introduced generally involved peripheral accessories, and not further major changes in main units.

Before the advent of microelectronics technology, which makes smaller parts possible, computers were very costly and complicated. It was not economically feasible for one person to interact with one computer. The processing power at that time existed only in a central data processing installation, and, for those who could not afford to have their own computer, time-sharing services were available.

The "small" or minicomputer industry began in 1974, when a few small firms began using memory chips to produce small computer systems as do-it-yourself kits for as low as $400. These proved popular, and other companies began to build microcomputers designed for the affluent hobbyist and small businessperson.

In 1975, microcomputer and small business computer shipments went over the $1 billion mark. As the mainframe market began to mature, the microcomputer industry was starting its rocketing ascent. In 1975, the first personal computer reached the market.

Personal computers can be defined as easy-to-use desk-top machines that are microprocessor based, have their own power supply, and are priced below $10,000. By using various software packages, these computers can be customized to serve the needs of businesses and a variety of professionals, such as accountants, financial analysts, scientists, and educators, as well as the sophisticated individual at home. It should be noted that the minicomputer grew up without IBM, the company that dominated mainframe computers and accounted for two-thirds of all computer revenues in the mid-1970s. But one of the great success stories of the century had occurred with personal computers. Apple Computer was started in a family garage on $1300 capital in 1976. By 1982, sales were $583 million, and Steven Jobs, a college dropout who was the co-founder at age 21, had become one of the richest people in America with a net worth exceeding $225 million.[1]

Portable computers are a subset of personal computers, being, as the name implies, lightweight and relatively easy to carry. Actually, three categories of portable computers are recognized by the industry: 1) hand-held computers, 2) portable, which have a small display screen, limited memory, and weigh between 10 and 20 lb, and 3) transportable, which have bigger screens and memories, and weigh more than 20 lb. Osborne computer was in the third group.

THE OSBORNE STRATEGY

Osborne had discerned a significant niche in the portable computer market: "I saw a truck-size hole in the industry, and I plugged it," he said.[2] He hired

---

[1] For more details of the Apple success story, see Robert F. Hartley, *Marketing Successes*, (New York: John Wiley & Sons), 1985, pp. 200–213.

[2] "Osborne: From Brags to Riches," *Business Week*, February 22, 1982, p. 86.

Lee Felsenstein, a former Berkeley radical, to design a powerful unit that weighed only 24 lb and could be placed in a briefcase, small enough to fit under an airline seat. It was the first portable business computer, the only portable computers being of much more limited sophistication. And it sold for $1795, which was hundreds of dollars less than other business-oriented computers and half the price of an Apple. He was able to sell for this price by running a low-overhead operation. For example, he hired Georgette Psaris, then 25, and made her vice–president of sales and marketing. But her office was in a chilly former warehouse. He was able to achieve economies of scale, and also capitalized on the declining prices of semiconductor parts. The computers were assembled from standard industry components. The display screen was small, only 5 in. across, and there was no color graphics capability. Osborne himself admitted, "The Osborne 1 had no technology of consequence. We made the purchasing decision convenient by bundling hardware and needed software in one price."[3]

To cut costs on software, no programmers were employed, this being a drastic departure from other personal computer makers. Instead, independent software companies were relied on entirely to provide programs written in the popular programming language. To reduce software costs still further, Osborne gave some software suppliers equity in the company. The result was that Osborne was able to provide almost $1500 worth of software packages as part of the $1795 system price.

Osborne had a flair for showmanship. One of his first triumphs was at the 1981 West Coast Computer Fair in San Francisco. In place of the rather ordinary booths and displays of the other computer makers, he took a substantial part of his venture capital to build a Plexiglas booth that towered toward the ceiling. The Osborne Company logo, the "Flying O," dominated the show.

He believed that mass distribution was a key to success. By 1982, he had signed an agreement with Computerland Corporation, the largest computer retailer. This extended Osborne's distribution by doubling in one swoop the number of retail stores carrying his computer. The Osborne 1 was proving to be a hot item, with sales hitting $10 million by the end of 1981, the first year of operation, although the first computer had not even been shipped until July. By the end of 1982, after only 18 months of operation, annual sales were soaring to $100 million. Predictions were that "most of the Osborne management team would be millionaires by the time they're 40 or even 30."[4] And the bare-bones operating style had been forsaken.

---

[3] "Osborne Bytes the Distribution Bullet," *Sales & Marketing Management*, July 4, 1983, p. 34.

[4] Steve Fishman, "Facing Up to Failure," *Success*, November 1984, p. 48.

By 1983, some 750 retail outlets were stocking the company's portables: the Computerland chain, Xerox's retail stores, Sears' business centers, and such department stores as Macy. And early in 1983, 150 office-equipment dealers with experience in selling the most advanced copiers were also added, enabling Osborne to reach small- and medium–sized businesses.

In summary, Osborne was certainly not the originator of the portable computer, but he was the first to sell such computers in mass quantities. And he expanded the market greatly—every key person in data processing departments and every office desk were sales targets.

MARCHING INTO 1983

By early 1983, Osborne began to loosen his grip on the company, under pressure from his investors. It was felt that the growing operation—it already had 800 employees—required a professional management that Osborne and his early hirees were not. Osborne was an entrepreneur and not an administrator, and the two abilities were quite different. To protect the company's front-running position—estimated at an 80–90% market share—Robert Jaunich II, president of Consolidated Foods, was hired to head up Osborne Computer as president and chief executive officer. Adam Osborne moved up to chairman. Jaunich had turned down offers at Apple and Atari, because he felt that these firms would not give him enough control. He also sacrificed a $1–million incentive to remain at Consolidated Foods. So he must have strongly felt that the opportunities and potential of Osborne far surpassed his other options.

Jaunich moved quickly to decentralize the management structure. Georgette Psaris, vice–president of marketing, was moved into a newly created position as vice–president, strategic planning. She was replaced by Joseph Roebuck, lured from Apple Computer, where he was marketing director. Fred Brown, the director of sales for Osborne, was elevated to vice–president of sales, and David Lorenzen, a consultant for Osborne, was made director of marketing services, with responsibility for dealer-support programs.

The distribution strategy, in which Adam Osborne had prided himself as one of the strengths of the venture, was refined. The computer-store outlets were continued, but some alternative channels were instituted. A major addition was an affiliation with Harris Corporation's computer systems division to act as a national distributor for contacting major firms. Harris was a $1.7 billion minicomputer firm having in the computer systems division some 70 salespeople and 1200 support personnel, including systems analysts. To protect Osborne's smaller clients, Harris agreed to handle only large orders of 50 units and over.

Other sales targets were United Press International (UPI), the news service, to sell Osborne portables to its 1000 subscriber newspapers as a personal workstation. Brown, the vice–president of sales, also began exploring other distribution possibilities, including independent sales organizations, airlines, and hotel chains.

As competitors started to enter the portable market, offering cheaper and fancier machines than the Osborne 1, the firm began readying itself to broaden its product line. An even cheaper version of the Osborne 1, the Vixen, was being prepared. And an Executive 1 was unveiled in the spring of 1983, with an Executive 2 planned for late summer, these offering more storage capacity and larger screens than Osborne 1. The Executive 1 could serve as a terminal to communicate with a mainframe, enabling users to work with larger data bases and handle more complicated jobs. This was to have a $2495 price tag with some $2000 worth of software, including word processing, an electronic spread sheet, and data base management. The Executive 2, at $3195 was to be promoted as compatible with IBM's hot-selling personal computer, the IBM PC.

In 1982, Osborne spent $3.5 million on advertising. This included $1.5 million in consumer magazines and $500,000 on spot TV, with $1.5 million in business publications. Plans were laid to continue heavy advertising to reinforce product differentiation. The sales force was also being expanded to keep pace with the growing firm. An 8-person sales force was to be supplemented with an additional 30 to 40 people, permitting more specialized selling. Instead of being generalists selling to all types of customers, sales was to be organized by specialists concentrating either on retail or nonretail accounts. Brown explained this rationale: "Retailers . . . need help on such things as point-of-sale displays to stimulate the guy who comes in off the street. Dealers call on purchasing and data-processing departments and need advice on direct mail campaigns.[5]

The sky seemed to be the limit. Osborne was predicting revenues of $300 million for 1983. And, when he made one of his frequent trips abroad, he was received by ambassadors and prime ministers, most of whom wanted stock in his company. He was the head of the fastest-growing company Silicon Valley had ever seen—even faster growing than Apple.

PREMONITION

The first premonition of trouble came to Adam Osborne on April 26, 1983. He was giving a seminar in Colorado when he received a call. "Over the

[5] Osborne Bytes . . ." p. 36.

weekend considerable losses were discovered," he was told. "That's not possible," he is reported to have said.[6]

The news that earlier profit figures had been in error was particularly ominous because of its timing. On April 29, a public stock offering was planned. This was designed to raise about $50 million, and would have made the top executives of Osborne rich. How would this news of losses instead of profits affect the stock offering? Adam Osborne had to wonder.

Actually, in the few days Adam had been away from the office, the bad news had been building up. In the first 2 months of the fourth fiscal quarter (the fiscal year ended February 1983), pretax profits had been reported that ran $300,000 ahead of company projections. And in February, the company racked up an all-time high in shipments—all these with supposed very high profit margins. Projections had been that profits in February would be in the neighborhood of $750,000 for that month alone, and the future had seemed euphoric.

But the heady optimism was to disappear emphatically. By late March, the results for February showed, instead of the profit, a loss of more than $600,000 for the month, reflecting charges against new facilities as well as very heavy promotional spending. For the entire fiscal year, a loss of $1.5 million was incurred, despite revenues of slightly more than $100 million.

The worst was yet to come. On April 21, Jaunich, the CEO, had learned that later data showed that the company would have a $1.5 million loss for the February quarter and a $4 million loss for the full year. The chief reasons seemed to be excessive inventories of old stock that the company did not even realize it had, liabilities in software contracts, and the need for greater bad debt and warranty reserves. Jaunich still planned to move ahead with the filing for the stock offering, although, certainly, attractiveness of stock in the company was rapidly diminishing.

Unbelievably, worse was to come. On April 24, Jaunich was informed that the losses would be even greater: $5 million for the quarter and $8 million for the year, owing to further unrecorded liabilities and more inventory problems.

That same day Jaunich decided to scrap the offering, despite heavy pressure to find another underwriter to bring the stock to market. Now every report blackened the situation further. The final report for the year showed a loss of more than $12 million. Heavy losses continued over the next months, as further adjustments in inventories and reserves became necessary. Adam Osborne's house of cards was well–nigh collapsing.

Osborne had had no trouble attracting seed money from venture

[6] Fishman, "Facing Up to Failure," p. 51.

capitalists before—indeed, venture capital firms had been clamoring to participate. But now that the company's earnings problems had come to light, such funding was drying up. A few investors still had hopes, and Osborne found another $11 million in June. But an additional $20 million, which the company considered necessary to speed a needed competitive product from drawing board to market, could not be found.

Black Friday

Sporadic employee layoffs had been occurring since late spring as the company desperately tried to improve its cash flow. But the climax came on Friday, September 16. On the previous Tuesday, the company had filed for protection from creditor lawsuits under Chapter 11 of the Federal Bankruptcy Code. The company filed its petition after three creditors filed two lawsuits saying Osborne owed them a total of $4.7 million. Osborne's petition stated that it owed secured and unsecured creditors about $45 million, while its assets were $40 million.

Osborne's employees had to expect the worst when a meeting was abruptly called in the company cafeteria. They soberly listened as top management announced that more than 300, about 80 percent of the company staff still remaining, were to be immediately "furloughed." Final paychecks were issued, and the workers were given 2 hours to empty their desks and vacate the company offices.

News of the company's Chapter 11 filing and near total shutdown shocked the industry, although Osborne's recently sagging sales and the consequent need for cash were well known. The company had made strenuous efforts to raise money, especially after July shipments had turned soft, and the banks were pressing it to improve its shrinking capital base. But venture capitalists appeared to have fled the industry as a serious shakeout was occurring, not only for Osborne but for other personal computer firms as well. The market was just not able to support some 150-plus microcomputer companies.

POST MORTEM

Internal Factors

Adam Osborne was an entrepreneur, not a professional manager. Perhaps this accounted for most of the problems that were to befall his company. So often it seems that the entrepreneurial personality is incompatible with the manager-type of person who must necessarily be engrossed with the nitty–gritty of details and day-to-day controls over operations. Osborne had never managed more than 50 people, but the organization grew to almost 20 times that size. He operated under a "fire fighting" perspective, with no advanced planning and with problems being dealt with as they arose. "I had no professional training whatsoever in finance or business management," Osborne admitted.[7]

Osborne's board of directors and the venture capitalists who had contributed mightily to the fledgling enterprise certainly brought about sufficient pressure to persuade Adam Osborne to step aside and turn over operating responsibilities to a professional manager, Robert Jaunich, early in 1983. But this was apparently too late to rectify the damage that had already been done. Perhaps 6 months earlier . . . ?

Some of the mistakes are inexcusable from the standpoint of any prudently run operation. But perhaps they can be explained as a result of the heady excitement that can accompany geometrically rising sales and the euphoria that clouds rational judgments and expectations. Other mistakes can be credited to simple miscalculations—of which any firm could be guilty—as to the impact of competitors of all kinds, and particularly the rapidity with which the awesome IBM could enter the market and dominate it.

Lack of controls was the most obvious failing of the company. It had no efficient means of monitoring inventories of finished products. Consequently, managers did not know how much inventory they had. They did not know how much they were spending, or needed to spend. Information management was sorely lacking—and this in a company whose product was primarily geared to aiding information management. Although rapid growth can be accompanied by growing pains and some difficulty in keeping abreast of booming operations, in Osborne's case the lack was abysmal and accounted for supposed profits suddenly being revealed as devastating losses. Other examples of incompetence were: unrecorded liabilities, with some bills never handed over to the accounting department; no reserves established for the shutdown of a New Jersey plant that was producing computers with a 40% failure rate; not enough was set aside to pay for a new European headquarters on Lake Geneva in Switzerland.

Lack of controls permitted expenses to run rampant. "Everybody was trying to buy anything they wanted," said one former Osborne employee.[8] When Jaunich finally took over the managerial reins, he clamped down hard on expenses, but perhaps it was too late.

By spring of 1983, miscalculations had reduced cash flow to a trickle.

[7] Jaye Scholl, "Osborne's Back Byting," *Barron's*, July 26, 1984, p. 26.
[8] "Shaken Osborne Computer Seeking Suitor in the Face of Possible Failure," *Wall Street Journal*, September 12, 1983, p. 35.

INFORMATION SIDELIGHT

STRATEGY COUNTERING BY COMPETITORS

Some strategies are easily duplicated or countered by competitors. Of these, price is the most easily countered. It is easy to match a price cut, and it sometimes can be done within minutes. Similarly, if one firm offers a different package, such as bundling, or an extended warranty, such efforts can be easily matched by competitors so that the net effectiveness is nullified. Osborne's low price, its bundling of software, and even the portability of its product could be quickly and easily met by competitors, even though profits might be affected.

Other strategies are not so easily duplicated. Most such strategies pertain to either service considerations or a strong and positive company image. A reputation for quality and dependability is not easily countered, at least in the short run. A good company or brand image is hard to match, because it usually results from years of good service and satisfied customers—and here, of course, Osborne was hampered by its newness.

Strategies are best that can offer something not easily countered, that have some lasting effect, and that are reasonably compatible with the present image and resources of the company. But, alas, in a volatile industry comprised of mostly new and unproven firms, such insulation from competitors is rarely achieved. Strategy countering has to be expected, and euphoric expectations tempered.

Osborne had planned to introduce a new computer, the Executive, but he made the grievous mistake of announcing it too soon. Although the Executive was not supposed to compete against the original Osborne 1, many dealers saw it as doing just that. Upon learning of the new machine in April, many canceled their orders for the Osborne 1. This in itself necessitated heavy inventory writeoffs, as the Osborne was not planned to be phased out. Compounding the problems, the Executive was delayed and not ready for initial shipments until May. April was consequently a month with practically no sales.

Another major mistake was failing to realize just how quickly competitors could react and counter a successful strategy in this volatile industry, how quickly a competitive advantage—the low price, portability, and bundling of software—could be matched by competitors and even improved upon.

Other companies, notably Kapro and Compaq, entered the market with low-priced computers and at least as much bundled software. But the biggest impact was that of IBM. Its personal computer was introduced in late 1981, and it quickly became the industry standard against which other competitors were judged. And Osborne turned out to be slow in reacting and adopting IBM's state–of–the–art technology. Furthermore, Osborne was slow in coming up with a model that was compatible with the IBM personal computer at home or in the office. Scores of other computer companies jumped to produce IBM-compatible computers, while Osborne lagged, and suddenly its product was not selling. Hardly a year after coming to market, the formerly popular Osborne computer with its tiny screen was practically obsolete.

One new product developed by Osborne was obsolete before it was even introduced. The Vixen was originally scheduled for introduction in December 1982. It was 10 lb lighter and an even cheaper version of the Osborne 1. But a poorly designed circuit board caused production delays, and the project was finally scrapped as company resources were at last redirected to an Executive model, an IBM-compatible unit with a larger screen. But the Osborne production delays and the speed with which IBM took over the personal computer market were tough to cope with.

External Factors

The environment for personal computer makers was rapidly becoming unhealthy by 1983. A major shakeout for the more than 150 small manufacturers in this industry was inevitable. A major factor behind the proliferation of firms was a tidal wave of venture capital. Early winners like Apple Computer had dazzled investors and led to the perception of a "can't lose" industry. It became almost too easy to start a new computer company. "As a result, a whole series of 'me too' companies have been started. They are developing products that do not have a unique feature or competitive advantage. They don't stand a chance," one venture capitalist said.[9] Only the strongest firms were likely to survive. And yet, in size and with its headstart, Osborne should have been one of the survivors.

As demand by businesses and consumers alike for small computers was rapidly increasing, so was cutthroat competition. Price-cutting and shrinking profit margins were inevitable. And certainly, dealers' shelves could hardly accommodate more than a few brands.

The first presentiment of worsening problems for the industry came early in 1983, when three big manufacturers of low-priced home computers, Atari, Texas Instruments, and Mattel, reported first-half losses totaling more than half a billion dollars. Makers of higher-priced computers tried to

[9] "Trouble in Computer Land," *Newsweek*, September 26, 1983, p. 73.

dissociate themselves from this low-end calamitous environment. But other well-known companies such as Victor Technologies, Fortune Systems, and Vector Graphics all reported shocking losses for the second quarter. Even Apple Computer saw its stock price sink nearly 34 points between June and September 1983.

Indicative of the price-cutting going on, Texas Instruments' (TI) 99/4A home computer, which sold for $525 when introduced in 1981, was retailing for $100 by early 1983. Yet, each 99/4A cost about $80 in parts and labor, to which TI's overhead expenses, dealer profits, and marketing costs had to be added.[10]

Other computer makers were desperately struggling to revamp their production and marketing efforts. For example, Vector Graphic, after losing $1.7 million in the second quarter of 1983, obtained a new $7 million line of credit to help it tailor its computers to such specialty markets as meeting the accounting needs of farmers.[11]

Now the problems of the industry dried up venture capital. Osborne was partly the victim of an external situation over which it had no control. The external factors were unforgiving of its internal mistakes.

AFTERMATH

Under Chapter 11 of the Federal Bankruptcy Act, a company continues to operate but has court protection against creditors' lawsuits while working out a plan for paying its debts. By the end of 1984, Osborne was emerging from bankruptcy with most of its debts paid and two new machines to sell. Its retail network had shrunk from 800 dealers to about 50. Suppliers now demanded cash on delivery. And the firm was anathema to venture capitalists, who had lost $31 million when the company collapsed. Gone were the factories, the 1000-worker payroll, and the swank executive offices. But the lean, trimmed-down company had $10 to $30 million worth of tax-loss carryforwards. And its name and still-extant dealer network in Europe was a plus. Perhaps the biggest challenge it now faced was redeveloping its retail network: "Competition for shelf space is hot even for companies with no strikes against them. Retailers were left with a bad taste when the company went Chapter 11," noted the president of a 40-store chain.[12] The new

---

[10] "Behind the Shakeout in Personal Computers," *U. S. News & World Report*, June 27, 1983, pp. 59–60.

[11] "Trouble in Computer Land," p. 73.

[12] "Osborne Tries for Comeback in Computers," *Wall Street Journal*, October 12, 1984, p. 27.

president was Ronald J. Brown, the former vice–president of international operations who engineered the company's restructuring.

Adam Osborne had left the company. He was now trying his entrepreneurial talents in the marketing of software, as well as organizing a defense against investor lawsuits. He wrote a book (publishing it himself, because major publishers were reluctant), *Hypergrowth: The Rise and Fall of the Osborne Computer Corporation* (with John Dvorak) soundly criticizing Robert Jaunich. Georgette Psaris, Osborne's former vice–president noted: "I've gone from being a multimillionaire to being in the hole."[13] But she joined Adam Osborne in his new entrepreneurial endeavor.

WHAT CAN BE LEARNED?

Osborne's rapid rise, and even more rapid fall, has to be sobering to investors, executives, and employees alike—as well as to dealers and customers who may find themselves with no recourse for warranty and parts service. But inexperienced entrepreneurs tend to fall into the quicksand of expanding operations as fast as they can, without building up the organization and controls necessary for larger enterprises. As a result, costs get out of hand, inventory buildup becomes an albatross, customer accounts may imprudently be allowed to become excessive and overdue; in the excitement of increasing sales, profits may be assumed when, in reality, losses are being incurred. The caution is plain: beware of uncontrolled growth. Tight controls, especially over inventories and expenses, is essential.

New and rapidly growing industries present dangers far greater than those facing the entrant to more mature industries. Unless entry to the industry is exceedingly difficult because of high startup costs or secure technological expertise, the new, rapidly-growing industry is attractive to all kinds of firms and a host of investors. Such new industries are usually characterized by rapid product improvements and by severe price-cutting. A firm in such an industry must beware the shakeout. It may well have to resist expanding so fast as to leave itself vulnerable to overcapacity and excessive inventory when the trauma of price-cutting begins. Competition is almost surely going to be heavily involved on a price basis, as production efficiencies and technological improvements are advanced by the competing firms. When a large number of firms have entered the industry, it requires no great insight to expect many marginal ones to fall by the wayside, with the field left only to the more able firms with better management and greater resources. Yet, during the shakeout period, virtually all firms may find themselves losing money because of the severe price competition and the

[13] "Trouble in Computer Land," p. 74.

dumping of excessive inventories. A stayer must be prepared to weather some rough times before the industry stabilizes.

In such a new industry, we often find the transience of uniqueness. Osborne certainly had a unique product offering in its early months. But the firm vastly underestimated how quickly the uniqueness would be matched, and even surpassed, by competitors. Research and development efforts must not be delayed simply because a firm now has a successful product. Strategy and product countering can be expected in the turmoil of such new industries. This necessitates very careful monitoring of production and inventories so that these do not expand faster than current sales warrant.

Finally, we see in the Osborne example the dangers of cannibalization carried to the extreme. Cannibalization, of course, refers to one product of the firm taking away sales from one or more of its other products. Generally, a new product's success will to some extent be at the expense of other products in the line, but hopefully there will be enough new business to increase total sales. In Osborne's case, the foolish announcement of the new Executive computer—before it was even ready to go to market—practically killed sales for the older Osborne 1. Encountering a month and more of virtually no sales is more than most firms could endure. Competition made the new product necessary, but its market impact could have been far better anticipated. The threat of cannibalization should not preclude new product introductions, but it should be anticipated and prepared for.

For Thought And Discussion

1. What factors account for the surge of competitors in the portable computer field? Should this have been anticipated by a prudent executive?
2. What kind of controls would you advise Osborne to have set up to prevent the debacle that befell it.?
3. Did Osborne Computer have any unique strengths that could have enabled it to survive in this hotly competitive industry?

Invitation To Role Play

1. Place yourself in the role of Adam Osborne in late 1982. Sales are exceeding the wildest expectations. Yet, you sense that IBM will soon be a factor in this market, as well as many smaller firms. Plan your strategy for 1983 to protect the viability of your enterprise and pave the way for further growth.
2. As a management consultant you have been called in by Robert Jaunich in late spring of 1983. Company losses are mounting. You have been charged to develop recommendations to save the company.

CHAPTER

16

Boise Cascade—
Decentralization Carried
To The Extreme

In the 1960s, growth by merger and acquisition, fostered by astute financial manipulations, focused attention on certain business wizards. They captured the public fancy and the adulation of investors and bankers as corporate growth in sales and profits—and the prospects of more of the same—seemed unbounded. Not the least of these "geniuses" was Robert V. Hansberger, who transformed a $35 million lumber operation into a $1.8 billion conglomerate in 13 years.

The management style of Hansberger in his overseeing of diverse operations was to let each division or minicompany have wide scope, thus creating a highly decentralized organization. Boise Cascade had been cited as "a spectacular example of 'free form' management . . . relatively free from job descriptions, organization charts, and other inhibiting restrictions."[1] Such a situation was particularly attractive to bright young MBAs who flocked to the company that was growing rapidly and that could offer them wide latitude to use their knowledge and talents in dozens of near-autonomous operating groups.

Unfortunately, Boise Cascade, in its quest for rapid growth, built on a precarious base. Like a structure of cards, its diverse ventures began collapsing in the early 1970s as management mistakes, combined with

[1] "Boise Cascade Shifts Toward Tighter Control," *Business Week*, May 15, 1971, p. 86.

critical environmental scrutiny, brought its fastest-growing division to the block, caused severe retrenchment and divestment of many of the acquisitions, and led the corporation itself to the brink of bankruptcy.

HANSBERGER AND THE METEORIC GROWTH OF BOISE CASCADE

Robert Hansberger was born in 1920 on a farm near Worthington, Minnesota. He studied engineering at the University of Minnesota and later received a master's degree in business administration (with great distinction) from Harvard Business School. He joined Container Corporation of America in 1947 as assistant to the executive vice–president and had risen to corporate director of the budget by 1953. He left in 1954 to become vice–president of Western Kraft Company, where he played a major role in the design and construction of the industry's first economical pulp and paper mill with a relatively small capacity of 120 tons/day. This mill completely changed existing ideas of economies of scale, which had assumed that only mills of much larger size were economically practical. This led directly to Hansberger's appointment as president of the Boise Payette Lumber Company in 1956. He was 36 years old.

At the time Hansberger became president of Boise Payette (founded in 1913), it owned three sawmills, all located in the state of Idaho. The company produced slightly more than 100 million board feet of lumber in 1956. By 1959, it had 10 sawmills scattered across the states of Washington, Idaho, and Oregon, and produced 504 million board feet (thus becoming one of the three largest softwood lumber producers in the United States). Between 1956 and 1959, the company also entered into a number of new operations, including a millwork plant, a paper bag factory, and concrete plants. One of the first mergers of Hansberger was with the Cascade Lumber Company, at which time the name was changed to Boise Cascade. In the first 3 years of Hansberger's presidency, sales rose 250 percent to $126,000,000, and earnings were up 370 percent to $5,600,000. This was only an inkling of what was to come.

By 1970, Hansberger had made some 35 acquisitions, and Boise Cascade had equaled or passed in sales its major competitors, Georgia-Pacific, Weyerhaeuser, International Paper, U.S. Plywood-Champion, and Johns Manville, with revenues of $1.7 billion and earnings of $76 million. Unlike these giant competitors, Boise did not dominate any single market, such as plywood, lumber, paper, pulp, or building materials. Rather, the company represented an integration from raw material to end product, as Hansberger sought to develop a broad-based, forest-products company. He shrewdly borrowed against timber lands acquired by merger to get into paper and packaging, lumber, and other things.

In the 1960s, diversification was fashionable and often viewed as the way to keep a company growing vigorously in earnings per share. So Hansberger turned his sights beyond the basic forest-products business of Boise. He went into what seemed at the time to be great growth areas. A batch of acquisitions was made between 1966 and 1969 in real estate, especially recreational land and housing. Divco-Wayne, the largest producer in the fast-growing mobile homes industry, was bought. Boise went into urban renewal and modular housing. More unrelated diversifications were Princess Cruises, a charter pleasure cruise operation, and CRM, which published *Psychology Today* magazine. Hansberger defended his hodgepodge:

> From the outside we may look like a conglomeration. But the process is certainly not. Today, we are an idea company, with the only limitation being that we engage in things that have a definite relation to something in which the company has experience.[2]

Such expansion was costly, and a high ratio of debt to equity (for example, in 1966–67, there was $1.25 of debt for every $1 of equity) suggested that the company was becoming overextended. However, through several mergers and accounting manipulations, the figure was brought down to $0.50 of debt per equity dollar by 1970.

In 1966, after Boise entered the recreational land development field, there was a more urgent need for cash than ever before, because expenditures are incurred for things like roads, sewers, golf courses, and other facilities before installment sales can generate much cash flow. In 1969, the answer to the need for an immediate source of money appeared to be found. Boise acquired Ebasco (formerly Electric Bond & Share), primarily a holding company engaged in the construction and design of heavy industrial facilities and office buildings in the United States. Ebasco had $237 million of Latin American bonds payable in U.S. dollars from the sale of some utility holdings to foreign governments, and these could be borrowed against. The Ebasco merger also brought substantial tax credits so that Boise's taxes could be reduced.

With the substantial and successful growth of the past decade, an aggressive and enthusiastic young management, a strong position in some of the seemingly most rapidly growing areas of business for the coming years, and now, with the chronic liquidity problem apparently corrected, the future looked very good for Hansberger and his company as they entered the decade of the 1970s.

---

[2] "Cinderella," *Forbes*, November 15, 1972, p. 72.

THE RECREATIONAL LAND COMMITMENT

Boise entered the land development business in a 50 percent joint venture with R. A. Watt, a land developer and home builder in the greater Los Angeles area. Watt had built 17,500 homes during the preceding 20 years, as well as many industrial, commercial, and apartments buildings. Further acquisitions in this area continued in 1967 with the acquiring of a San Franciso area contractor, Perma-Bilt Enterprises, which had projects underway at a total value of $45 million.

The U.S. Land Company of Indianapolis was acquired shortly after. This was a major developer of lake-oriented resort properties. Five major developments were in operation: a 1700-acre project near Gary, Indiana; a 1500-acre one near Chicago; 1300 acres near Cleveland; 2500 acres near Washington, D.C.; and a 3200-acre project in the foothills of the Sierra Nevada Mountains, not far from San Francisco. The lots ranged in price form $2000 to $20,000, and each development surrounded a 200– or 500–acre man-made lake.

Lake Arrowhead Development Company was also acquired in 1967. This was a year-round and second-home developer in the San Bernardino-Los Angeles area.

Two new developments were also started in the fall of 1967: a lakeland homesite development called Lake Los Angeles, a 4000–acre project about 75 minutes from Los Angeles; and a $38 million development on the Palos Verdes Peninsula of California.

By 1968, sales of recreational land were $90 million; in 1969, this had spurted to $165 million. Profits also began building rapidly: in real estate accounting, sales and profits are booked in the year a property is sold, even though the money may not be collected for some years. How are profits determined? Future development costs are estimated, and then prorated to the various parcels of land. Although not a very conservative method of accounting, this is the standard procedure. To bring a bit more conservatism into its accounting, Boise set up larger reserves for possible defaults on land sales than in 1966 and 1967.

As the real estate expansion continued, Boise acquired a total of 126,000 acres, in tracts of 700 to 31,000 acres. This land consisted of 29 projects scattered over a dozen states from the East Coast to Hawaii. The net investment in realty was $142 million by the end of 1970, about 70 percent being in recreational communities. Between 1967 and 1972, Boise sold over $360 million of recreational land.

The growth potential for such developments seemed unmistakable. In a nation with more leisure time, good and relatively cheap transportation, and more affluence, a second home became the dream of many families. Planned recreational communities, with choice amenities available such as lakes, country clubs with golf courses and "Olympic size" swimming pools, other facilities such as skiing at certain sites, and offering security against vandalism and theft, seemed the answer. The growth of land sales and profits since 1966 seemed proof that this was a premier growth industry.

No Boise executive in the late 1960s would have believed that anything could destroy the golden future of the company, spearheaded now by its land development operations. In 1969, its stock climbed to $75 a share.

But, in just a few short years, the stock was to fall to $9 a share, and there was concern that Boise might follow Penn Central into the corporate graveyard. The land development operation led the company into its debacle.

The Downfall

Two things conspired to destroy the recreational land commitment. Neither would have been a factor a decade earlier. But Boise and other land developers were facing an environment of far more social criticism of business methods and stronger ecological concern than had ever been experienced before.

In the rush to acquire firms active in recreational land development, Boise also obtained some of their executives and salespeople. At first, Boise, with its management policies of loose control and maximum decentralization, was content to let the land companies run themselves. But these land developers tended to be of the old school, unconcerned with consumer satisfaction as long as a sale could be made quickly. Their attitude toward land was also selfish: ". . . cut it up, develop it, sell it, and get out. If the buyer was unhappy later, the developer and salesmen were long gone."[3] These acquisitions were paced by fast-talking salespeople who promised far more than Boise could deliver in the way of access roads and highways, recreational facilities, and investment potential. To create a feeling of urgency and the belief that lots were selling fast, high-pressure sales personnel used two-way radios by which they could radio the central "communications" office to ask tensely whether such and such a lot was still "available."

However, public attitudes and policies were rapidly changing nation-wide, particularly in California, where Boise's recreational developments predominated. Reflecting environmentalists' and consumerists' inputs, practices that would have been uncontested a decade before now became subject to virulent criticism and legal and governmental regulation.

[3] "Boise Cascade Shifts," p. 86.

INFORMATION SIDELIGHT

THE IDEA OF "STRATEGIC FIT"

For a firm bent on diversification, the desirability of strategic fit is generally acknowledged—although not always adhered to. Strategic fit refers to the mutually reinforcing effects that different business activities can have on the organization's overall effectiveness. Sometimes this idea is graphically referred to as $2 + 2 = 5$, that is, the sum of the benefits of the combined operations is more than if they had remained separate.

Several forms of fit can be recognized. *Product-market fit* is obtained when the different products can use the same distribution channels, sales promotion techniques, and can be sold to the same customers with the same sales force. *Operating fit* results from economies of purchasing, warehousing, overlapping of technology and engineering, production compatibility, and the like. *Management fit* occurs when existing management know-how and experience can be effectively transferred to the newly acquired activities. The common thread of fit then can provide a unifying focus and build on joint managerial, financial, and technological strengths.

On the other hand, the popularity of conglomerate mergers, both in the late 1960s and early 1970s, and later in the 1980s, when there was little or no fit or similarity, has cast doubt on the necessity of fit. Some of these conglomerates have been notably successful with an extreme of diverse business activities. For example, International Telephone and Telegraph (ITT) products and subsidiary companies range from Sheraton hotels, Wonder Bread, Avis Rent-a-Car, to finance companies, chemicals, lawn care, and even business schools.

But other conglomerates have found that trying to manage many unrelated product markets and technologies has either brought severe problems—as we have seen with General Foods and the Burger Chef operation and now Boise Cascade—or else have resulted in $2 + 2 = 3$ (for example, Mobil Oil and its Marcor acquisition). Many conglomerates, after the initial acquisition spree, have been forced to sell off some of their subsidiaries in order to get the organization on the profit track again.

In general, we can conclude that a common thread or strategic fit is not absolutely essential for all of a firm's business activities, but that it increases the probability of successful assimilation and synergy.

The marketing tactics of Boise led to lawsuits against the company and its subsidiaries, with charges of misrepresentation in the sales of recreation land in 19 California subdivisions and 1 in Nevada. Civil actions were filed by the California Attorney General's office and the Contra Costa County District Attorney, and class action lawsuits were filed in state and Federal courts. In Maryland, the state's Real Estate Board halted sales for 90 days on Boise's 3500-acre Ocean Pines project, charging that the company was using unlicensed salespeople. Boise eventually had to spend $60 million to settle the lawsuits.

Other problems were also confronting some of the projects. Ecologists were mobilizing public opinion against communities planned for a Puget Sound shoreline, a Hawaiian beach, and other locations. The bad publicity was front page news.

Amid increasing public pressure, Boise was forced to reevaluate its land operations. Moving toward a heavier investment in recreational facilities, the company also attempted to meet local demands for more open spaces, underground utilities, and full sewage-treatment facilities. None of these came cheap: on a 3000–acre project, a sewage system might cost $4 million.[4] Such higher costs lowered the profit margin, unless lot prices could be raised substantially. But sometimes this was not possible. For example, demand tended to dry up as lot prices were raised from $8000 to $12,000.

Despite efforts by Boise to improve acceptability of its selling methods and its ecological impact, the bad image gained as the most visible land developer ripping off consumers and raping the environment was difficult to overcome. Sluggish sales were resulting, and its customer default ratio was one of the worst in the industry (a situation not helped by an estimated 5 percent of sales to its own salespeople speculating on quick investment profits).

In 1970, after almost a decade and a half of climbing steeply, sales for Boise Cascade fell 1 percent below the 1969 level. Worse, profits plummeted 55 percent. Then, in 1971, the ax fell. The company reported a staggering $85.1 million loss, of which $74 million was accounted for by the beleaguered land development operation.

Plagued by deficits and lawsuits, Boise began to work its way out of the land business. Getting out did not come easily or cheaply. Real estate is a difficult business to pull out of: if contractual obligations on the numerous projects are not fulfilled, customer receivables disappear; and if a customer sees no neighbors in his recreational community, he is likely to stop

4 Ibid., p. 90.

payment. The company swallowed write-offs and losses of $100 million in 1971 and $200 million in 1972. Some projects were sold to other firms. For example, projects in New Jersey were sold to Kaufman & Broad, a housing producer; Larwin, a land developer-builder subsidiary of CNA, bought a Boise project in the Pennsylvania Pocono Mountains and land sites in Chicago—all these at "fire sale prices."

Now the huge debt of Boise—$916 million—was becoming a serious factor. Bankers and insurance companies who had lent the money were in a position to dictate. They forced Boise to begin selling off assets to reduce the heavy debt load. And, in October of 1972, Robert Hansberger, the "genius" who built the huge conglomerate from three small lumber mills in 1957, was forced out of management of the company.

THE STRUGGLE BACK

Boise's troubles did not end with its land development business. The Ebasco merger of 1969, made to generate badly needed current assets, turned sour. The $237 million worth of Latin American bonds acquired with the merger turned out to be illiquid. These bonds had been obtained by Ebasco from the sale of utility operations in Argentina, Brazil, Chile, Colombia, and Costa Rica. Changes in governments in these countries jeopardized the investments. In 1972, for political reasons, Boise sold two Latin American utilities at prices below book value.

Other acquisitions were also faltering. The Divco-Wayne acquisition of the largest producer of mobile homes was suffering as the two top people left within months, and Divco began making mistakes in production planning. The Princess Cruises Boise had bought in 1968 lost $2.5 million in 1970, and was sold.

The debt-ridden conglomerate continued to retrench and sell off diversifications in an attempt to return to its business of the 1950s, forest products. However, to raise cash to pay down on its long-term and realty debt, even some of the basic forest products operations went to the block. In 1973, the Union Lumber operation was sold to Georgia Pacific Corporation for $120 million. Union had earned a respectable $8 million on sales of $29 million in 1972. However, this and other divestments reduced Boise's debt to close to 33 percent of equity by the end of 1973. Virtually all of its construction and engineering group, which generated sales of $378 million in 1970, was now gone. Of the land sales projects, only two remained in 1973, and the company hoped to be rid of these in a few years.

Except for the Union divestment, the mainstay of Boise—its timber, building materials, and paper-packing groups—remained intact. The company still had some 7 million acres of timberlands. In 1971, however, 44 percent of its $1.8 billion sales had come from nonforest products; by 1973, almost zero revenue came from this.

John B. Fery presided over this rapid divestment of Boise's farflung operations. After Hansberger was ousted, Fery, one of his proteges and an executive vice–president, was chosen to revive the company. Fery was the first major executive to identify the serious nature of Boise's real estate woes, and he pressed for the company to rid itself of this operation despite the cost. He was Boise's chief spokesman with creditors during the dark days of 1972, and he engineered the retrenchment that put Boise on a much sounder footing, albeit hundreds of million of dollars smaller in sales.

The basic soundness of the company was manifested in 1973, when Fery moved Boise back into the black. Although sales dropped to $1.3 billion, it registered a profit of $90 million as opposed to a $171 million deficit in 1972, and an $85 million deficit in 1971. With a tighter, more centralized control, and a planned diversification strictly within Boise's basic line of business, the future again became promising for Boise Cascade.

ANALYSIS

In an interview in 1974, after time to view the Boise situation from a more objective and distant vantage point, Hansberger said that the major problem was to be able to switch quickly enough to a changing social clime in California: ". . . we were the biggest land developer in California . . . but tremendous changes were taking place there, and California has the tendency to be one of the first states to effect changes, especially social changes . . . environmental issue was hot there, and came suddenly upon the company . . . we could not change quickly enough."[5]

When queried about the questionable practices of Boise salespeople of making promises that could not be kept and ultimately causing dozens of lawsuits, Hansberger noted that, in acquiring companies in the land business, Boise had kept their personnel and their sales practices, ". . . while their loose ways of doing business were very rapidly becoming obsolete, it was difficult to find the expertise that would be viable in the future." He admitted that, at first, these subsidiaries were perhaps too autonomous, were given too much latitude, but ". . . it takes a while to change a massive sales force, replace it, retrain it, or reorient it."[6] He noted that he did try to impose stiff controls by sending out company people to represent themselves as customers, with salespeople knowing this was taking place.

[5] "Interview with Robert Vail Hansberger," *Dun's*, September 1974, pp. 12–14.
[6] Ibid.

INFORMATION SIDELIGHT

MANAGEMENT BY EXCEPTION

In controlling diverse and far-flung operations, the task of closely monitoring all phases of the operation becomes difficult. Successful managers are content to direct their attention to performances that deviate from the expected. In this aspect of control, then, the manager is apprised only of significant deviations from expected performance. Other less significant deviations can be handled by subordinates. With this approach to control, the manager is not overburdened by a host of details so that other important parts of the job, such as planning, are neglected.

Major advantages of management by exception are, first, that management efficiency can be improved by freeing time and attention for the most important problems and, second, that subordinates are permitted more self-management.

In the Boise example, we would not expect that all the details of the recreational land subsidiary performance would be closely monitored. However, the other extreme of "hands off" controls, of which Boise was guilty for a crucial time, was hardly prudent and, of course, resulted in major problems. Attention given to deviations from expected performance at important points of the operation should have represented the minimum acceptable control standards. Some exceptions that should have received attention were: default ratio, lawsuits instituted, letters of complaint, government investigations, declines in number of queries and in consumer visits to properties, ratio of building to sales, and threatened restrictions of local governances.

One of our problems was our visibility—we were a prime target because of our size, so we restricted our salespeople . . . strict controls with tougher terms of sale, down payment requirements, what they could represent to customers in terms of products . . . this made it tougher to sell against competition which wasn't so visible . . . a lot of our salesmen just went down the street and got a job with someone else who didn't impose these rigid controls on them. When you begin to lose your sales force, you begin to lose your sales volume. And that's when the viability of the land projects began to evaporate.[7]

Hansberger placed the blame for the problems that confronted Boise

[7] Ibid.

primarily on outside factors, such as the changing milieu of California. But any firm has to operate and adjust to an ever-changing environment. Today, governmental regulations and public policies are changing rapidly, reflecting public pressures arising from consumerism and ecological concerns. These are social constraints to be contended with for a long time to come. The successful firm is responsive to such changes and anticipates and/or quickly adjusts to them. Boise fell down here on two counts. Unconcerned at first about the questionable business practices taking place in its name, the company was slow to recognize the seriousness of customer complaints and ecological pressures. When the critical nature of the problem was finally recognized, drastic action was taken, but too late.

Boise's solution at that point was to repudiate and get rid of the part of the business that was coming up against environmental problems, despite the cost. Although perhaps the best solution, given the late awareness of the problem, there was another alternative. The company could have moved more slowly in land development projects, guided by a firm commitment to honesty in dealings and an ecological compatibility—in other words, more responsive management practices. Instead of disavowing the situation, Boise might have adjusted.

Certainly, a large part of the internal problems of Boise was the consequence of the rapidity of expansion through highly diversified acquisitions in the late 1960s. In those days, such a strategy was heralded and was characteristic of other wildy growing conglomerates. Most of these also found themselves overextended financially and managerially and had to cut back drastically and even fatally, and the value of their stocks tumbled. A highly decentralized or "free form" management such as Hansberger had at one time thought to be the key to corporate success was really a consequence of acquiring such widely divergent companies that no one in the parent organization had the expertise to manage and control them closely. Consequently, the running of such acquisitions was left to the original executives. If they were capable, things usually turned out well; if they were less than scrupulous, unresponsive to social and ecological demands (as most of the land development subsidiary executives of Boise turned out to be), or not very competent, serious damage had often been done before this was detected. Then the parent company had the formidable task of replacing them, usually without the management resources to do so quickly and effectively. Therefore, the plight of Boise with its land development operations was not unique; it reflected the fallacy of heedless and reckless growth, growth beyond the assimilation abilities of a parent firm.

Even today, investors remain skeptical of highly diversified companies, the conglomerates. Some such companies are doing an excellent job,

Table 16.1   Boise Cascade Sales and Profits, 1971–1980

Year	Sales (billions)	Net Profits (millions)
1971	$1.8	deficit $85
1972	1.15	deficit 171
1973	1.3	90
1974	1.45	103.6
1976	1.9	97
1978	2.6	136
1980	3.0	136

Source: Company published data.

although their stock market prices scarcely reflect this; others are still trying to cope with unwise and poorly structured diversifications. The retrenchment of Boise in repudiating almost all the acquisitions made in the 1960s left a solid base from which to build more carefully and more compatibly in the future.

Update

To see how a company can bounce back from adversity should be inspiring. And Boise Cascade did that, streamlining its operation, cutting almost to the bone, but emerging a stronger and more profitable company. Table 16.1 shows the revenues and profits for the bad years and for the recovery years.

By 1984, sales had reached $3.82 billion. And, interestingly, John Fery was still chief executive.

For Thought And Discussion

1. Why do you think high-pressure tactics were considered necessary for selling recreational land? What pros and cons do you see of such business methods?
2. What potential do you see at present for recreational land development? Is this likely to change by 1990? Why or why not?
3. Do you think Boise was wise to have divested itself so completely of the land operation?
4. Boise, in acquiring the various land developers, bought itself into an industry where there was little real strategic fit. How would you defend this venture, and what safeguards would you recommend to minimize the chances of such problems as actually occurred?

Invitation To Role Play

1. Place yourself in the role of Robert Hansberger in the late 1960s. What are some specific ways in which you would have built more controls for the land operation?
2. As the vice-president for the recreational land division, how would you have developed and controlled a sales force so that it would be both effective in generating sales and high in integrity and fair dealing? What problems, if any, would you expect to encounter in achieving this?

Five

ETHICAL AND SOCIAL RESPONSIBILITY PROBLEMS

CHAPTER 17

STP—No Ethical Controls

This is the story of a notable success that came from developing an image of those who used the product that many car owners thought worthy of emulating—all this brought about and supported by heavy advertising. Almost a classic success story. Except for one thing. The product really offered users no benefits—the experts who knew spoke of it in derogatory fashion as "mouse milk," and what could be more impotent than that? Eventually, bad publicity surfaced about the product, and the Federal Trade Commission took action against the company for misleading advertising.

THE PRODUCT

The principal product of the STP Corporation in the 1960s was STP, a brand of lubricating oil additive supposed to improve car performance (in addition, the firm marketed STP Gasoline Treatment and STP Diesel Fuel Treatment). The name STP means "Scientifically Treated Petroleum." It was sold in 15-oz cans at around $1.50 a can, and was poured into the crankcase of a car, preferably with every oil change, as a supplement to the motor oil itself.

Although the ingredients of STP remain a closely guarded secret, the major component of all additives is a polyisobutylene polymer dissolved in petroleum oil. Such a polymer-oil solution is called a viscosity-index (VI) improver. This helps motor oil retain its normal thickness despite the large temperature changes that result from hard driving. In other words, with a VI improver, hot oil thins less than it normally would, thus helping lubrication over a wide temperature range.

So far so good. STP promotional messages stressed that the additive would help reduce oil consumption, free sticking valves, make engines run more smoothly, and prevent many other repairs. There was even the strong intimation that the use of a can of STP with every oil change would forestall the expense of a valve and ring job. So intriguingly simple it all seemed: just pour this elixir in the crankcase of a car and make its ailing engine healthy and powerful again.

Unfortunately, there were those who disputed such claims—among them, most petroleum engineers, who had labeled these additives "mouse milk." These experts were in general agreement that there was rarely any benefit for a normal engine. The auto firms likewise were critical of STP and similar additives: "No one has ever presented any scientific data to prove that additives do anything good," noted Ray Potter, supervisor of fuels and lubricant research at Ford.[1] The automakers had even found that regular use of polyisobutylene compounds could sometimes clog small oil passages and cause engine damage, and they refused to recommend the use of additives in their owners' manuals.

So, what do we have here? A product of dubious benefit, and one with experts in almost complete agreement on its worthlessness, at least under normal driving conditions. How can such a product wrest a niche in the marketplace? But it did, and with gusto.

ANDY GRANATELLI

The success of STP is really the story of Andy Granatelli, who became president of STP Corporation in 1963. How he moved STP from a smallish $9 million in sales in 1963 to sales of $85 million and profits of almost $12 million by 1970 has to make him one of the most astute executives to come around—or one of the best promoters.

Granatelli had gained a public reputation as a race driver and a person closely connected with racing. When he was only in his early 30s he made his first million with a company called Grancor, which developed and sold parts and supplies for racing cars. In 1958, he sold Grancor and became owner of Paxton Products, which made superchargers and similar items. In 1961, he sold Paxton to the Studebaker Company (later to become Studebaker-Worthington in a 1967 merger). He stayed on to run the subsidiary, but then,

---

[1] Quoted from "Big Profits in Little Cans," *Time*, August 8, 1969, pp. 70–71.

in 1963, was persuaded to take over as president of the STP Division of Studebaker.

Until then, additives had been sold as something to keep "clunkers" operating a little longer. And this was a limited customer segment, one with little growth potential in an era of prosperity. Granatelli changed this image for STP. He surmised that if speed could sell cars and tires, it should be able to sell additives as well. "One of the first things Andy realized," said a company executive, "is that to expand sales he had to expand the market . . . Andy changed the image of STP from an additive to a performance product by promoting it through racing, on the theory that if race drivers used it on $50,000 cars to keep engines cool and maintain lubrication, the general public would buy it for the same reason."[2]

Granatelli offered extra money to race drivers who would paste STP decals conspicuously on their cars or even on their jackets and coveralls. He subsidized cars at major races—of course, well-publicized as STP cars. A major coup came when an STP–sponsored car driven by Mario Andretti won the Indianapolis 500 on May 30, 1969. The implication was that STP was the vital ingredient enabling Andretti to achieve the extra performance. Publicity gained for STP from the decal-decorated car and pictures of Granatelli alongside Andretti was worth millions to the company.

Something more subtle than simply a performance product was operative under Granatelli's management: the mystique of fast cars and of the machos who drove them—a reference group that a certain segment of the car-driving public looked up to and psychologically wished to emulate. Hence, these customers could easily be persuaded to buy a product indelibly identified with this group.

Granatelli poured on the advertising to promote the race-driver image, the "Racer's Edge," as STP publicity called it. The 1969 advertising budget was $10 million. This was an amount equal to 20 percent of the previous year's sales, an advertising-to-sales ratio matched by only a handful of firms, and these chiefly in the drug and cosmetics industry, such as Colgate-Palmolive, J. B. Williams, and Alberto Culver. The advertising hit 3 radio networks, 2 TV networks, and some 30 auto buff magazines, with ads featuring the STP motto—the "racer's edge"—and pictures of Granatelli and race cars and drivers. Even Dolly Granatelli, his wife, participated in very successful radio and TV commercials. By 1969, STP was spending $0.18 more per can for advertising than it spent on the can and the contents.

---

[2] As quoted in "The Wheeler Who Deals in STP," *Business Week*, May 31, 1969, p. 57.

Table 17.1 Sales and Profit Growth of STP Corporation, 1963–1970

Year	Sales (000)	Percentage Change	Net Income (000)	Percentage Change
1963	$ 9,340		$ 1,733	
1964	12,781	36.8%	2,439	40.7%
1965	18,475	44.6	3,537	45.0
1966	20,828	12.7	4,037	14.1
1967	30,886	48.3	4,807	19.1
1968	44,000	42.5	6,000	24.8
1969	65,335	48.5	9,052	50.9
1970	85,936	31.5	11,601	28.2

Source: STP annual reports.

The great sleeper in all of this was the STP logo. It helped to fuel the burgeoning popularity of the product. In its ads starting in 1966, STP offered the little decals free with the coupon. And kids by the thousands began swamping the company for this, the newest status symbol. The appeal spread to adults, with stickers being plastered on trucks, passenger cars, tractors, and even limousines. By the end of 1967, STP had to hire six secretaries solely to answer 4000 requests a day for the free stickers. By 1969, the company was giving away 50 million a year. Requests were pouring in from toy makers, confectioners, electronics firms, clothiers, and others to use the STP logo on products. Granatelli readily gave his permission to use the logo without charge, seeing this as a powerful way to broaden recognition of the product and brand. Eventually, the opportunity to tap some of the demand for the logo was realized, and the company established a mail-order marketing organization to handle a full line of STP jackets, caps, coveralls, T-shirts, and such products.

Sales sprinted ahead. See Table 17.1 for the sales and profit performance from 1963, when Granatelli first took over, to 1970, when the zenith was reached. Note the almost 50 percent spurt in sales in one year, 1969, and the over 50 percent gain in profits, a phenomenal achievement.

The identification of STP with speed resulted in an unwanted byproduct that developed in California early in 1968. A particularly potent hallucinogenic drug widely used by hippies was dubbed STP.

As the decade of the 1960s drew to a close, Granatelli could not help but be optimistic about the future. He could see great potential in expanding the product line, first with a cooling system additive, and then spreading into other markets, particularly the industrial and marine markets. Furthermore, Granatelli saw tremendous opportunities abroad, and overseas sales indeed had tripled in a single year. In Japan, sales of STP exceeded the sales of any single state of the Union, while selling at more than twice the price in this country. Granatelli could happily observe: "There's only one other symbol used more than STP and that's Coke. But they've been around longer than we have."[3]

COMPETITION

Were there any competitors of STP? There were, but they had all been left far behind. Wynn and Bardahl were the two oldest firms in the field. Bardahl advertised its product as a preventative of repairs, although compared to STP it did little advertising. The Bardahl product image was that of a steady, dependable product, but without glamour. Wynn's Friction Proofing was similar to Bardahl in image and market position. Wynn was founded by a lawyer in 1939; he had mixed a home brew "friction proofing" in a 55-gallon drum and sold bottles of it to local garages. Both Wynn and Bardahl had broad product lines, with Wynn having 26 related products and Bardahl 18.

PHA Hi-Performance Oil Treatment was the least well known of the four major oil additives, although the company tried to project a top quality performance image. Stud, a Union Carbide product, was the latest entry into the oil additive field. It had rapidly climbed to the No. 2 market position behind STP, primarily on the strength of an aggressive advertising campaign "guaranteeing to equal or exceed the performance of any oil treatment or your money back." Although formula for each additive was a closely guarded secret, the major ingredient, polyisobutylene, was the same; and the results were similar.

WHY THE STP SUCCESS?

How can we account for the phenomenal success of STP? Was it primarily due to the willingness to spend heavily on mass-media advertising? Was it primarily due to race drivers publicly promoting it? What role, if any, did the popularity of STP decals have on the success of the product?

To test certain hypotheses regarding the image and appeal of STP, one researcher asked students and other car owners to write down the two or three associations that most readily came to mind upon seeing the letters "STP." The following responses predominated.[4]

[3] Ibid., p. 57.
[4] Research conducted by Sidney C. Wooten, Jr., "Self-Concept Theory, the Symbolic Value of Products, and Consumer Behavior: A Study in Interrelationships." Unpublished MBA thesis, George Washington University, January 1971, pp. 84–86.

Granatelli	Racing
Racer's edge	Indianapolis 500
Speed	High performance
Sports cars	Names of various high-performance
Andretti (who won the 1969	and sports cars, such as Charger,
Indianapolis 500)	Corvette, etc.

Clearly, STP had succeeded in developing an association of its product with the professional racing community and with higher-performance cars— in other words, with a reference group that a significant segment of younger car-owning consumers admired or wished to emulate. The overwhelming and unexpected popularity of the STP logo became a highly visible indication of an individual's wish to be identified with this reference group.

That the product itself, offered at a premium price many times higher than the cost of production, was of dubious benefit remained disregarded in the glamour associated with the aura of professional racing.

CLOUDS ON THE HORIZON

By the late 1960s, despite a rate of sales and profit growth that seemed to be not only continuing, but even intensifying, some communications began appearing that revealed the general uselessness of STP and other oil additives for most passenger car engines. For example, *Time* and *Business Week* had articles about this in 1969.[5] Although these publications were directed to people not typical customers of STP, still they presaged more adverse publicity to come.

Then, in July 1971, *Consumer Reports,* the respected consumer advocate magazine, made a harsh indictment against STP.[6] Not only did it charge that STP oil additive was a useless concoction, but it also warned that the product could be harmful to engines and might even void a new car warranty.

Although *Consumer Reports* agreed that STP helped engine oil retain its normal thickness despite large temperature changes, it noted that major oil refiners had already taken care of this with their multi-viscosity oils (labeled 5W-20, 10W-30, and so on), and that adding STP tended to make the oil thicker than desirable. For example, a 20W motor oil was found by testing

---

[5] "Big Profits in Little Cans," pp. 70–71; and "The Wheeler Who Deals in STP,"pp. 31–32.

[6] "STP, Does Your Car Really Need It?" *Consumer Reports,* July 1971, p. 422.

to have been changed to a 40 with the addition of the recommended amount of STP. Although it admitted that this would help with an old, oil-burning clunker of an engine by making loose mechanical joints and fittings quieter and seemingly tighter, perhaps even cutting down on oil consumption, *Consumer Reports* stated that any 40 or 50 oil would do this and would be far cheaper. With a normal engine, such a thick oil mixture would cause hard starting and noticeable drag in cold weather, and the engine would not be properly lubricated. Furthermore, *Consumer Reports* noted that, because STP can change the viscosity of a new car's oil to a much thicker grade than auto manufacturers recommended, a new car warranty could be voided. General Motors (GM) and Ford officials were quoted specifically as to how the use of additives would affect a new car warranty:

> GM: If in the analysis of a warranty repair there is evidence that the use of additives is responsible for, or has contributed to the vehicle malfunction or part failure, this fact would be taken into consideration in determining General Motors' responsibility.

> Ford: If supplementary additives . . . modify the properties of the lubricants so that they no longer meet Ford specifications, then warranty terms may be affected.[7]

Granatelli quickly responded. He called the *Consumer Reports* article "an attempt to sabotage the successful business of our company with a twisted set of alleged facts assembled by incompetents."[8]

STP On The Ropes

Despite Granatelli's counterattack, both earnings and stock prices of STP plunged. The stock, which had peaked at almost $60 early in 1971, was down to $3 in 1973. Profits by 1973 had fallen to barely $1 million from the $11.6 million of 1970. Figure 17.1 shows the rise and then the collapse of income during the Granatelli years of 1963 through 1973.

To add to Granatelli's troubles, the Federal Trade Commission (FTC) began looking into a 22-page petition filed early in 1973 against STP by the Center for Automotive Safety, a Ralph Nader-inspired consumer group. The petition asked the FTC specifically to order the company to:

---

[7] Ibid.
[8] As quoted in "FTC Tries to Dull the Racer's Edge—STP," *Iron Age*, June 21, 1973, p. 17.

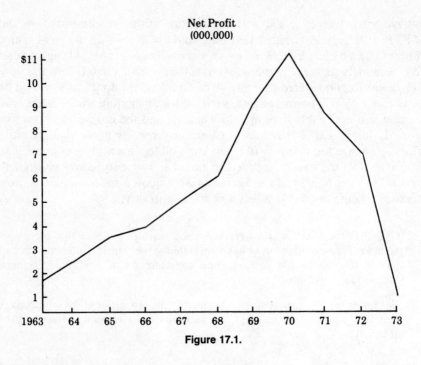

Figure 17.1.

1. Stop asserting unfair and deceptive claims for STP oil treatment.
2. Substantiate all future advertising claims relating to STP oil treatment.
3. Refund to buyers the product funds obtained through unfair and deceptive advertising.

Grantelli stated: "We believe this unknown group (the Center) is simply seeking publicity by the device of bringing totally unfounded and irresponsible charges against us."[9] When asked whether the STP Corporation planned to issue scientific data to support its advertising claims, Granatelli responded: "I take offense at having to defend myself against an unknown group of two or three guys out to get publicity."[10]

In 1973, the FTC finally charged the company with deceptive advertising. And, in 1973, Granatelli left STP.

[9] Ibid.
[10] Ibid.

INFORMATION SIDELIGHT

ROLE OF BOARD OF DIRECTORS IN A FIRM

The board of directors is the ultimate authority (with a few exceptions, when matters require the approval of share-holders) for direction and control of corporate activities. Realistically, however, the board—which most often is composed of both insiders (management) and outsiders (non-management), with individual board members having varying interests, loyalties, and knowledge about the company and its problems—meets only periodically and has to rely on the full-time executives for most planning and operating decisions. A generally accepted role for a broad of directors is to:

1. Confirm management decisions on major changes in policies and organization.
2. Counsel the executives on matters in which particular board members have needed expertise and objectivity.
3. Be involved in the selection and confirmation of major executive appointments.
4. Regularly review results of current operations.

Cutting across these responsibilities is the need to consider the overall impact of the activities of the firm on society as well as compliance with laws.[11]

Boards show a wide range in their discharge of these responsibilities. Some are mere rubber stamps of the chief executive officer (CEO) of the company. This is especially true when most of the board is composed of insiders who will be subordinate to the CEO, the chairman of the board. At the other extreme, some boards are the dominant decision-making group in the organization.

In the case of STP in the days of Granatelli, we would have to conclude that the board exercised no ethical controls and apparently saw no problems with legal compliance.

Coming Back

Although the reign of Granatelli was over, and the glory days gone, the company doggedly began making a comeback from the lows of 1973. The

---

[11] George A. Steiner and John F. Steiner, *Business, Government, & Society*, 3rd Ed. (New York: Random House, 1980), pp. 546–548.

comeback, however, was not without more charges of deceptive advertising and false and unsupported claims. Sales and profits rose somewhat in 1974 and began climbing steadily after that, although they were still well below the peaks attained in 1970.

The complaint initiated by the FTC in 1973 was settled in September of 1976, with the company agreeing with the consent order not to use false and misleading advertising and to support any claims for the oil additive with competent and reliable scientific tests or other objective data. Two of the FTC commissioners, including the chairman, dissented from accepting the consent order. Chairman Engman criticized the acceptance by the FTC:

> I dissent because this order is too weak. Though the consent order prohibits claims that are not substantiated, I have the statutory "reason to believe" that STP Oil Treatment is of no significant value to the majority of cars which regularly use the proper grade of oil. I accordingly have difficulty in accepting an order which does not explicitly require STP to qualify its future claims.[12]

However weak the consent order was seen to be, STP still did not abide by it. The FTC was forced to sue the company in 1978 for violation of the 2-year-old cease and desist order. The new complaint charged as false STP's advertisements that its oil treatment reduced oil consumption by 20 percent in certain road tests. An agreement concerning this was negotiated by the FTC and the STP Corporation and made public in February 1978, with STP agreeing to a $500,000 record-setting fine plus another $200,000 to be spent for a corrective advertising campaign. Under the terms of the settlement, a notice was to be placed in 14 publications, most of them with heavy business readership, such as *The Wall Street Journal, Business Week, Forbes,* and *Harvard Business Review;* the only more consumer-oriented magazines on the schedule were *Esquire, Guns & Ammo, National Geographic, Newsweek,* and *People.* The ads were to be mostly full-page reading as follows:

> FTC Notice. As a result of an investigation by the Federal Trade Commission into certain allegedly inaccurate past advertisements for STP's Oil Additive, STP Corporation has agreed to a $700,000 settlement.

The notice also included a statement by STP that:

---

[12] "Legal Developments," *Journal of Marketing,* October 1976, p. 119.

Agreement to this settlement does not constitute an admission by STP that the law has been violated.[13]

The new STP chairman, Craig A. Nalen, said that he doubted the corrective ads would have any impact at all on STP sales. "Nowhere is there any challenge to the efficacy of the product," he said. "It's merely a question of some defective tests done years ago."[14] Despite the critical limelight, the FTC did not probe into whether or not the products worked, but was only concerned with the lack of documentation for STP's advertising claims. The products of STP were not reformulated, and *Consumer Reports* did not change its negative position.

Nevertheless, Nalen brought STP back to increasing profits. Nalen himself was a former marketing executive with General Mills. He at first shunned an offer to run STP: "I was skeptical about the products as much as anybody else. It took a lot of head scratching for me to decide to go to STP."[15] However, he was finally persuaded to take the job as a result of studies made by an independent laboratory and several "lubrication experts" about whom Nalen said: "Their analysis showed that STP oil treatments result in a reduction of oil consumption and wear rate."[16] The next steps were to sign the consent agreement with the FTC and begin the slow job of rebuilding the company's battered image.

Costs were substantially reduced by trimming the sales force from 180 to 100, and by eliminating a policy of giving discounts to dealers for shelf space. A number of new products were tested and then introduced, including a multigrade diesel oil claimed to be good for at least 50,000 miles, a passenger-car oil good for 12,000, and a synthetic compression oil for machinery. Retail outlets were shifted from service stations and garages to supermarkets, with 65 percent of STP products sold in supermarkets by 1977, compared with only 30 percent 5 years before. Extensive advertising was continued—for example, a $200,000 four-page ad in *Reader's Digest*—using test results to document the claims made for the additive. Actor Robert Blake, who played the role of a supercop on the TV show "Baretta," replaced flamboyant Granatelli as the company's television pitchman. Table 17.2 shows the gain in sales and profits during this rebuilding period.

[13] As reported in "Legal Developments in Marketing," *Journal of Marketing*, October 1978, p. 91.

[14] "Corrective Ads for STP Publicize Settlement Costs to Business Execs," *Advertising Age*, February 13, 1978, p. 1.

[15] As quoted in "What Craig Nalen Did to Turn STP Around," *Business Week*, January 10, 1977, p. 38.

[16] Ibid.

Table 17.2   STP Corp. Sales and Profits, 1973–1976

Year	Sales	Net Profit
1973	$54,605,000	$1,033,436
1974	62,377,000	3,453,000
1975	65,269,000	3,882,000
1976	69,737,000	6,627,000

Source: Published company reports.

In 1978, giant Esmark, Inc., offered to acquire STP from parent Studebaker-Worthington, which owned 60 percent of the stock, for about $117,000,000, paying $22.50 for each share of STP stock. Studebaker-Worthington agreed to vote its holdings for the merger. Philip Thomas, vice–president—corporate communications, for Esmark, called STP "a fantastic company and a perfect fit" for Esmark. He said Esmark had conducted intensive tests on STP oil treatment before it began serious negotiations on the acquisition and, as a result, was convinced "the product works."[17]

About the time the merger was finalized, STP began national advertising for a new product, "Son of a Gun," a pump spray that it claimed would restore and beautify vinyl, rubber, leather, and wood. Carrying a suggested $2.95 price, Son of a Gun was promoted via 30- and 60-second network commercials, and promoted to both male and female audiences—a first time for the company that a product was promoted other than to men. STP Oil Treatment, which had not been advertised for about a year, also began to be backed by new TV ads, with Robert Blake in his continuing role as STP's spokeman. The company had fully recovered from the dark days at the turn of the decade.

WHAT CAN BE LEARNED?

We can consider the STP case from two perspectives: as customers, and as company executives. From both viewpoints we see rather awesome implications, as well as cautions.

The effectiveness of advertising and proper image building is manifested beyond doubt. That the product itself may be of little, if any, good, and may even be harmful, makes the power of the advertising all the more significant.

---

[17] "STP Presents Its New Parent with a New 'Son'," *Advertising Age*, March 27, 1978, p. 50.

We know that advertising can induce people to try a product for the first time. But unless it is satisfactory and meets their expectations, they will not buy it again—this is practically a truism. Surely it is valid. Yet, the STP example seems to disprove it. The answer lies in the user's inability to assess the effectiveness of STP. Who could say that one's car was helped or hindered by it? Certainly, any judgment could only be made over a long period of use. But many products are like this: their performance and quality cannot be easily and quickly assessed because of their complexity or hidden ingredients.

About the FTC and the general stance against deceptive practices, where do we draw the line? Is the action of the FTC against STP too harsh? Are the regulators too zealous? Does every advertising claim have to be supported with unimpeachable test results? Are hard sell and image building to be completely ruled out so that the helpless consumer can be protected, even from a careless purchase of a $1.50 can of oil additive? Or, to take the other side, does the action of the FTC in permitting a rather innocuous consent agreement—soon to be violated—and a less than $1 million settlement for doing so, represent a cop-out? Do these actions have any deterrent value? As you can see, the issues are hard to resolve, and cannot be to everyone's satisfaction.

A firm in today's critical environment must be particularly careful not to arouse the watchdogs of public opinion—the press—to any witch hunts that could translate into public relations problems through inflammatory headlines. And government regulatory actions are ever alert to presentiments of misdeeds. This suggests that a firm should be more scrupulously honest today than ever before. Ah, but the temptations are to shade the truth or to perform the deceptive or morally questionable act. Firms today need to be more cognizant of controlling their conduct, of avoiding practices that can be viewed as unethical or even illegal. The larger the firm, the greater should be the concern for this, because of the visibility that large size imparts.

This suggests that controls should be established within the organization to monitor questionable conduct. Some firms are establishing such controls through a public relations department or a legal staff. Ultimately, the board of directors must increasingly concern themselves with these controls. The board has the power to change practices within the firm. They should have the objectivity and the broad perspective to view the total impact of certain actions that may not be so readily apparent to a management more concerned with day-to-day operating concerns. A number of proposals have been made for reforming the board of directors so as to exercise more ethical controls. Some of them involve bringing in more outside directors, some special-interest directors as representatives of the general public, environmentalists, or minority groups, as well as other reforms.[18] To go into more detail about such proposals is beyond the scope of this book. But let us note again that the environment for doing business today is far more stringent than it was several decades ago. A firm must be more concerned about its ethical practices, because the consequences of not doing so can result in loss of public support and of eventual government intervention.

A final thing to learn from the STP example is that a firm can come back. It can be on the ropes, yet bounce off and still be viable and even successful. Criticism can be short-lived. Adversity is not forever.

Update

The company has by no means repudiated the theme of associating its products with the racing community. At the close of fiscal year 1980, it announced a long-term agreement to sponsor Richard Petty, seven-time world stock car champion, and his son, Kyle Petty. Furthermore, it was also sponsoring top driver Gordon Johncock. Record revenues and earnings were being posted. Son of a Gun, the vinyl protector, was successful and experiencing good sales growth. A new product, STP Foaming Engine Degreaser, was introduced in 1980 and was meeting sales goals.

For Thought And Discussion

1. How would you, as an STP executive, answer the charge that STP was only "mouse milk"?
2. Do you think another oil additive firm could have successfully pursued a different image for its brand from STP's?
3. Was the success of STP in the 1960s attributable primarily to its willingness to spend much more on advertising than its competitors? Why or why not?
4. What specific recommendations would you make for the board of directors to exercise ethical controls?

Invitation To Role Play

As an STP company spokesperson, how would you answer the charge before the Federal Trade Commission of deceptive advertising? Defend your position as persuasively as possible.

How might you rationalize your position before your board of directors?

---

[18] For a summary of the many proposals made for reforming the board of directors, see George A. Steiner & John F. Steiner, *Business, Government, & Society*, 3rd Ed., pp. 551–558.

18

Nestle—The Consequences Of Ignoring Social Issues

When a firm is a huge international conglomerate, with diversifications into many product lines, bad publicity and negative public reactions about a single product seemingly should be no particular cause for alarm. The inclination is to ignore such a "minor" problem, and it should go away.

But the expectations of Nestle went awry. The attitudes of the general public toward the firm continued to worsen, exacerbated certainly by a negative press and vocal protestors. Far from diminishing over a few weeks and a few months, the situation worsened over years. And far from affecting only the particular product involved—infant formula marketed to underdeveloped countries—other products and other divisions of the company became the object of virulent protests. Nestle had for too long ignored assaults on its public image, and now the road back to public acceptance was slow and rocky.

BACKGROUND

The Trouble Begins

By the early 1970s, suspicions were arising that powdered infant formula manufacturers were contributing to the high rates of infant mortality in less developed Third World countries by their aggressive marketing efforts directed to people unable to read the instructions or use the product properly because of their living conditions. The possible link between infant formulas and mortality through product misuse began to be discussed by medical professionals, industry representatives, and government officials at a number of international conferences. But public awareness of the problem had not surfaced as yet.

Then, in 1974, a British charity organization, War on Want, published a 28-page pamphlet, *The Baby Killer*. In it, two multinationals, Nestle of Switzerland and Unigate of Britain, were criticized as engaging in ill-advised marketing efforts in Africa. With the printing of this short publication, the general public became not only aware of the problem, but increasingly concerned.

This concern was to intensify less than a year later. A German-based Third World Working Group reissued a German translation of *The Baby Killer,* but with a few changes. Although the British version criticized the entire infant formula industry, the German activists singled out Nestle for "unethical and immoral behavior" and retitled their version *Nestle Kills Babies*.

The accusation enraged executives at Nestle headquarters, and they sued the activists for defamation. The trial lasted 2 years and focused worldwide attention on the issue. Though Nestle won the lawsuit, the court advised the firm to review its current marketing practices. "We won the legal case, but it was a public relations disaster," one Nestle official admitted. "The baby-killing accusation was a natural for antiwar groups and others looking for a cause. The company was dealing with the situation on a scientific and nutritional level, but the protestors were dealing on an emotional and political level."[1]

The Nestle Company

The Nestle Company, formally known as Nestle Alimentana, S.A., is headquartered in Vevey, Switzerland. It is a giant worldwide corporation, with sales of $12.5 billion in 1983. It owns or controls extensive interests in numerous companies of the food and cosmetics industries in various parts of the world. Products include instant drinks (coffee and tea), dairy products, cosmetics, frozen foods, chocolate, and pharmaceutical products. In addition, it holds interests in catering services, as well as restaurant and hotel operations such as the Stouffer Corporation, which was acquired in 1973. By 1980, Nestle was marketing its products in Europe, Africa, North America,

---

[1] "Infant Formula Protest Teaches Nestle a Tactical Lesson," *Marketing News,* June 10, 1983, p. 1.

Latin America, the Caribbean, Asia, and Oceania. Its three top product groups were dairy products, instant drinks, and culinary/sundry products. Infant foods, including the controversial infant formula, and dietetic products accounted for considerably less than 10 percent of total conglomerate sales.

Nestle's appetite for acquisitions has continued unabated in recent years. In 1975, it purchased food processor Libby, McNeill & Libby. In 1979, it acquired Beech-Nut, the baby-food producer. Other purchases of note include CooperVision, a contact lens maker, such well-known candy brands as Chunky, Bit-O-Honey, Raisinettes, Oh Henry, Goobers, and Sno Caps, and most recently, Hills Bros. Coffee Company, and Carnation.

The Infant Formula Industry

Nestle first developed and marketed a milk food used to nourish premature infants in 1867. This was in response to the urgent need of premature infants who were unable to take any food. Borden also introduced a similar sweetened and condensed milk.

Infant formula foods are somewhat more recent, developed in the early 1920s as an alternative to breast feeding. Infant formula is a specially prepared food for infants (under 6 months) and is based on cow's milk. It is scientifically formulated to approximate the most perfect of all infant foods, human breast milk. Today, a number of different artificial milk products are available for infants, and these range in nutritional value from very high (humanized infant formula) to very low (various powdered, evaporated, and sweetened condensed milks).

Sales of infant formula had increased sharply after World War II and hit a peak in 1957, with 4.3 million births in developed countries. From this point on, births started a decline that continued into the 1970s. The result was a steep downturn in baby formula sales and profits. Therefore, the industry began searching for new business. This was found in the Third World countries where the population was still increasing: the less developed countries of Africa, South America, and the Far East.

Total industry sales for infant formula alone, excluding all other commercial milk products, is about $1.5 billion. Of this, an estimated $600 million comes from the less developed countries. Hence, this market segment comprises a significant total potential.

Nestle maintained a strong market share—some 40–50%—of the Third World market for baby formula. Competitors included three U. S. firms, American Home Products, Bristol Myers, and Abbott Labs, which shared 20 percent of the market. Foreign firms accounted for the remainder. In 1981, the market was estimated to be growing at 15-20 percent per year.[2]

THE ISSUE: MISUSE OF THE PRODUCT, AND MARKETING PRACTICES

> If your lives were embittered as mine is, by seeing day after day this massacre of the innocents by unsuitable feeding, then I believe you would feel as I do that misguided propaganda on infant feeding should be punished as the most criminal form of sedition, and that these deaths should be regarded as murder.[3]

This lone indictment from a doctor in 1939 evolved from a single cry into a crescendo of protest against the infant formula industry.

Incapability of the Market to Use the Product Correctly

A large number of Third World consumers live in poverty, have poor sanitation, receive inadequate health care, and are illiterate. Therefore, misuse of infant formula would seem inevitable. Water is obtained from polluted rivers or a common well and is brought back in contaminated containers. A refrigerator is considered a luxury item, and fuel is very expensive.

Consequently, powdered formula may be mixed with contaminated water and put into unsterilized bottles and nipples. In addition, mothers are tempted to dilute the formula with excess water so that it will last longer. An example was cited by one physician at a Jamaican hospital of malnutrition in two exclusively bottle-fed siblings, 4 months and 18 months old, respectively. A can of formula would adequately feed a 4-month–old baby just under 3 days. However, their mother so diluted the formula as to feed the two infants for 14 days. The mother was poor and illiterate, had no running water or electricity, and had 12 other children.[4]

Studies have given three reasons for the trend to less nursing and more bottle feeding in the less developed countries:[5]

---

[2] Kurt Anderson, "The Battle of the Bottle," *Time*, June 1, 1981, p. 26.

[3] As quoted in Cicely D. Williams, "The Marketing of Malnutrition," *Business and Society Review*, Spring 1980–81, p. 66.

[4] U. S. Congress, Senate, Committee on Human Resources, Subcommittee on Health and Scientific Research, *Marketing and Promotion of Infant Formula in the Developing Nations*, Hearing, 95th Congress, 2nd Session, May 23, 1978 (Washington, D. C.: Government Printing Office, 1978), p. 6.

[5] Prakash Sethi and James E. Post, "Public Consequences of Private Action: The

First, a changing sociocultural environment. This consists of urbanization, changing social mores, and increased mobility in employment. Infant formula was seen as representing social mobility and a symbol of highly regarded modern products and medical expertise. The smiling white babies pictured on the fronts of formula tins suggested that rich, white mothers feed their babies this product and that, therefore, it must be better. High income consumers in these less developed countries were the first to use infant formula in imitation of Western practices. Bottle feeding was looked upon as a high status practice, and lower income groups readily followed.

Second, the health care professional. Many hospitals and clinics endorsed the use of infant formula. A mother's first experience with a hospital may be to deliver a baby. Therefore, any products or gifts received there carry medical endorsement. Also, hospital practices are perceived as better and deserving of emulation. Babies are routinely separated from their mothers for 12 to 48 hours and are bottle fed whether or not the mothers plan to breast feed.

Third, the marketing and promotional practices of infant formula manufacturers, which we will discuss shortly.

In 1951, approximately 80 percent of all 3-month–old babies in Singapore were being breast fed; by 1971, only 5 percent were. In 1966, 40 percent fewer mothers in Mexico nursed 6-month–old babies than had done so 6 years earlier. In Chile in 1973, there were three times as many deaths among infants who were bottle fed before 3 months of age than among wholly breast-fed infants. Other statistics of increased illnesses and higher death rates of bottle-fed infants were plentiful.[6]

Quality Control Problems

Nestle had some serious quality control problems in its production of the formula in its far-flung plants:

In April 1977, the Colombian General Hospital encountered an increase in mortality at the premature ward. Bacteria was traced to a Nestle factory. But 25 deaths occurred before the cause was found.

Also in 1977, the Australian Department of Health reported that 134 infants had fallen seriously ill as a result of being fed contaminated infant milk formulas produced by Nestle. Government officials estimated 20 million lb of contaminated milk had been exported to Southeast Asian countries.

Marketing of Infant Formula in Less Developed Countries," *California Management Review*, Summer 1979, pp. 35–48.

[6] For more such statistics, see Leah Margulies, "Bottle Babies: Death and Business Get Their Market," *Business and Society Review*, Spring 1978, pp. 43–49.

The Australian story started in 1976. The Nestle Tongala plant noticed an increase in bacterial counts in samples of infant milk powder. Inspection revealed cracks in the spray drier used to turn liquid milk into powder form. The bacterium was found to be a variant of salmonella that causes severe gastroenteritis. The State Health Department was not informed, and Nestle attempted sterilizing the equipment without halting production; but the bacterium continued to be discovered. The drier was kept in operation for a full 8 months after the contaminants were found.[7]

Perspective of Criticisms of Misuse

In fairness to Nestle, the critics who condemned the company and other infant food manufacturers for even attempting to market in underdeveloped countries disregarded any benefits of such products over the alternatives. The problem of water contamination also affects the alternatives to commercial infant foods. Such alternatives are various "native" cereal gruels of millet/rice used as weaning foods. The nutritional quality of these gruels tends to be low, and this deficiency is in addition to contamination of the water and containers used to cook the material. Furthermore, the millet/rice often has microbiological contamination. Although it is true that infant formula mixed with contaminated water and containers presents dangers, commercial formulas are more nutritious than local foods and are closer to breast milk than native weaning foods; they are therefore easier to digest. A further rebuttal to the critics is that not all people in less developed countries face water contamination. Millions can safely mix powdered formula with local water without water contamination.[8]

Criticisms of Nestle's Marketing Practices

Nestle has undoubtedly been an aggressive marketer in many Third World countries. Its promotional efforts have been directed to physicians and other medical personnel as well as consumers. Direct consumer promotion of infant formula has taken many forms. Media have included radio, newspapers, magazines, and billboards—even vans with loudspeakers have been used. It has widely distributed free samples, bottles, nipples, and measuring spoons. In some countries, direct customer contacts have been made through "milk nurses," and these have been the subject of particular criticism.

---

[7] Reported in Douglas Clement, "Nestle's Latest Killing in Bottle Baby Market," *Business and Society Review*, Summer 1978, pp. 60–64.

[8] John Sparks, "The Nestle Controversy—Anatomy of a Boycott," Public Policy Education Fund, Inc., June 1981.

INFORMATION SIDELIGHT

THE USE OF MISSIONARY SALESPEOPLE (DETAIL PEOPLE)

Missionary salespeople—these are called detail people in the drug industry—are commonly used by many firms to provide specialized services and cultivate customer goodwill. They generally do not try to secure orders.

Missionary salespeople are employed by manufacturers to work with their dealers. They may put up point-of-purchase displays, train dealer salespeople, provide better communication between distributor and manufacturer, and, in general, try to have their brand more aggressively promoted by the dealer. In the drug industry, the detail people leave samples and explain research information about new products to the medical professionals to encourage prescriptions and recommendations for their brands.

Nestle employed about 200 women who were registered nurses, nutritionists, or midwives. These professionals were often nicknamed, "milk nurses." Critics maintained that these milk nurses were actually sales personnel in disguise who visited mothers and gave product samples in an attempt to persuade mothers to stop breast feeding. With their uniforms giving them great credibility, this practice was condemned as being too persuasive for naive consumers.

Promotion to physicians and other medical personnel has also been controversial. This type of promotion has generally involved the use of detail people who discuss product quality and characteristics with pediatricians, pediatric nurses, and other related medical personnel. (The use of detail people, who are a type of missionary sales representative, is common practice, as described in the above "Information Sidelight.") Materials such as posters, charts, and samples were made available to physicians, hospitals, and clinics without charge. Physicians and other hospital personnel have also received company-sponsored travel to medical meetings.

Critics felt that the promotion of infant formula had been too aggressive and had contributed to the decline in breast feeding. Despite increased criticisms, however, sales of infant formula in poor countries continued to escalate. It had become the third most advertised product in the Third World, after tobacco and soap. And it was generally recognized that new mothers in such countries were most susceptible to advertising. A 1969 study of 120 mothers in Barbados found that 82 percent of the ones given free samples later purchased the same brand, whether the samples were received from the hospital or at home.[9]

In summary, the criticisms of promotional practices were:

Bottle feeding contributes to infant mortality in less developed countries.

Baby booklets ignore or deemphasize breast feeding.

Media promotions are misleading in encouraging poor and illiterate mothers to bottle feed rather than breast feed their infants.

Advertising portrays breast feeding as primitive and inconvenient.

Free gifts and samples are direct inducement to bottle feed infants.

Posters and pamphlets in hospitals, and milk nurses are viewed as "endorsement by association," or "manipulation by assistance."

Prices of formulas at the milk banks are still too high for many consumers, who are then tempted to dilute the formula.

THE SITUATION WORSENS FOR NESTLE

With the publication of the two articles, *The Baby Killer* and *Nestle Kills Babies,* and the subsequent lawsuit by Nestle, which received worldwide publicity, two groups were formed and solidified the opposition that was to lead to boycotting Nestle products and services: the Interfaith Center on Corporate Responsibility and the Infant Formula Action Coalition (INFACT).

Since the early 1970s, various agencies had been trying to reduce the promotion and advertising practices of infant formula companies. These agencies included the Protein Advisory Group in 1970 and 1973, the World Health Assembly in 1974, and the World Health Organization (WHO) in 1978.

As a byproduct of the growing condemnation of the industry, Nestle and other firms began to make some changes in their promotional practices, at least on paper. The changes were brought about under the auspices of the International Council of Infant Food Industries (ICIFI), which was formed in 1975 by nine infant–food manufacturers, including Nestle. The changes included: product information would always recognize breast milk as best;

---

[9] Reported in "A Boycott Over Infant Formula," *Business Week,* April 23, 1979, pp. 137–140.

infant formulas would be advertised as supplementary, and that professional advice should be sought; nurse uniforms would be worn only by professional nurses.

But the self–regulation apparently was not sufficient to allay the criticisms. Documentation by the International Baby Food Action Network confirmed over 1000 violations of the "code" since 1977. Some critics compared "asking for self–regulation was like asking Colonel Sanders to babysit your chickens."[10]

With continued reported violations, a boycott was organized in the United States in July 1977, and soon spread to nine other countries. It was to last until January 26, 1984, in the United States and Canada, with other countries following suit.

Nestle was singled out as the sole object of the boycott because of its 50–percent worldwide market share and the adverse publicity that had centered on it more than other firms who were engaged in the same business practices.

The demands of INFACT and the boycotters were:

1. Stop the use of milk nurses altogether.
2. Stop distributing all free samples.
3. Stop promoting infant formula to the health–care industry.
4. Stop consumer promotion and advertising of infant formula.

The public image of Nestle was now heading for the "pits" and could no longer be ignored by management. Indeed, as the following "Information Sidelight" suggests, a firm's public image ought to be zealously safeguarded and never permitted to erode as Nestle's did.

The boycott soon had the support of over 450 local and religious groups across America, and proponents claimed it was the largest non-union boycott in U. S. history. Boycott activity was strongest in Boston, Baltimore, and Chicago, where INFACT established an office with five full-time staffers. Thousands of signatures were gathered on various petitions urging removal of Nestle products from supermarket shelves. Some grocers acquiesced, agreeing to remove such products as Taster's Choice from their shelves. The boycott also hit college campuses. With the slogan, "Crunch Nestle," boycotts were encouraged on products ranging from milk chocolate to tea, coffee, and hot chocolate. The college boycott reportedly began at

[10] "Killer in a Bottle," *The Economist*, May 9, 1981, p. 50; and Douglas Clement, pp. 60–64.

INFORMATION SIDELIGHT

THE PUBLIC IMAGE SHOULD BE A MANAGEMENT CONCERN

A firm's public image— how it is generally viewed by its various publics—plays a vital role in the attractiveness of the firm and its products to employees, customers, and stockholders, as well as to such outsiders as creditors, suppliers, government officials, and other diverse groups. With some things it is impossible to satisfy all the various publics: for example, a new highly-automated plant may meet the approval of creditors and stock-holders, but it will undoubtedly find resistance from employees who see jobs threatened. On the other hand, high-quality products, strict service standards, and a commitment to being a "good neighbor" should bring almost complete approval and pride of association, whereas shoddy products and false claims—or a reputation, deserved or undeserved, of a bad corporate citizen—would be widely decried.

A firm's public image, if it is good, should be cherished and protected. It is a valuable asset that usually is built up over a long and satisfying relationship of a firm with its various publics. If a firm has developed a quality image for its products, this is not easily countered or imitated by competitors. Such an image may enable a firm to charge higher prices, to woo the best distributors and dealers, to attract the best employees, to expect the most favorable creditor relationships and lowest borrowing costs. It should also allow the firm's stock to command a higher price-earnings ratio than other firms in the same industry without such a good reputation and public image.

Wellesley College and soon spread to others, such as Colgate, Yale, and the University of Minnesota.

This boycott was undoubtedly effective, not only directly in causing lost business and profits for the company, but in crystallizing public opinion against the company and in invoking governmental response. For example:

The government of New Guinea enacted stringent laws to curb the artificial feeding of babies in the summer of 1978. Bottles and nipples now could only be obtained by prescription. Other countries also began introducing legislation to reduce the promotion of breast-milk substitutes.

In May 1981, WHO adopted a restrictive ad code that applied only to the infant food industry. A portion of Article 5 of the Code states, "There shall be no advertising or other forms of promotion to the general public of products within the scope of this code."[11] The products covered were infant food formulas and other weaning foods.

The European Parliament in France voted overwhelmingly for strict enforcement of the WHO Code throughout the 10-nation Common Market. The European Parliament also placed responsibility on Common Market firms for the actions of their subsidiaries abroad in observing the WHO Code.

NESTLE FIGHTS BACK

Nestle's first efforts to combat vituperative accusations resulted in more harm than good, as we have seen. As its public image continued to worsen, the worldwide boycott finally surfaced in 1977. Now Nestle could no longer ignore the protests and hope they would go away. Obviously, they were not going to go away. Initial strategy at this point was to treat the boycott and widespread protests as a public relations problem. The public relations department of the firm was upgraded into the Office of Corporate Responsibility. The world's largest public relations firm, Hill & Knowlton, was hired to assist. Over 300,000 packets of information were mailed by Nestle to U. S. clergymen, informing them that they were wrong in their denunciations of Nestle. Finally, Daniel J. Edelmon, a renowed public relations specialist, was hired. He advised the company to keep a low profile and to try to get third party endorsements of its actions.

Finally, in 1981, after failing to improve its image and mute the critical cries against it, Nestle dismissed its two public relations firms and took on the task of reestablishing its reputation itself. Ignoring the situation had not helped; public outcries, rather than lessening, had increased. And efforts to denounce the critics angrily had only exacerbated the situation. Now the firm was ready to try a new tack in efforts to establish its credibility as a humane and responsible corporate citizen.

One of the first steps was to endorse WHO's Code of Marketing for Breast Milk Substitutes—a step three other U. S. manufacturers did not make until 2 years later. The code, which imposed only voluntary compliance, banned advertising to the general public, as well as distribution of samples to mothers.

Next, Nestle sought an ethical group to work with in vouching for its compliance with the code, and found it in the Methodist Task Force on Infant Formula.

[11] "World Health Organization Drafts Restrictive Ad Code," *Editor & Publisher*, April 11, 1981, p. 8.

Nestle's relations with the press had been abysmal. For example, in the first 6 months of 1981, the *Washington Post* published 91 articles critical of Nestle. In the company's multi-faceted attempt to rebuild its image, the policy for dealing with the media was changed to an "open-door, candid approach."[12]

The most effective restorative strategy finally adopted was the establishment of a 10-member panel of medical experts, clergymen, civic leaders, and experts in international policy to monitor Nestle's compliance with the WHO code publicly and to investigate complaints against its marketing practices. This Nestle Infant Formula Audit Commission (NIFAC) gained credibility with the acceptance of the chairmanship by Edmund S. Muskie, former Secretary of State, Vice Presidential candidate, and Democratic Senator from Maine. The Commission was established in May 1982.

This so-called Muskie Commission worked with representatives of WHO, International Nestle Boycott Committee (INBC), and UNICEF to resolve conflicts in four areas of the WHO code. Points of contention were educational materials, labels, gifts to medical and health professionals, and free or subsidized supplies to hospitals. These were resolved, and Nestle agreed that, on educational material distributed, social and health aspects of formula vs. breast feeding would be addressed. Its infant formula labels would clearly state the dangers of using contaminated water and the superiority of mother's milk. Personal gifts to health officials (which smacked of bribery and seeking of preferential treatment) were banned. Finally, free samples of formula distributed to hospitals were to be limited to supplies going to mothers incapable of breast-feeding their children.

At last, after years of an adversarial posture, which had only resulted in a growing crescendo of criticisms and boycotting, with bitter accusations that the company was causing the deaths of millions of Third World babies because of its marketing practices, the situation was improving. "We have all learned a lesson . . . ," said Rafael D. Pagan Jr., president of the Nestle Coordination Center for Nutrition. "Companies should be sensitive and listen carefully to what consumers and members of the general public are saying. When problems surface, they should seek a dialogue with responsible leaders and try to work out the problems together."[13]

Early in 1984, after a decade of confrontation with protestors and 7 years of boycotting, most groups agreed to a suspension of their boycott. Although some diehards refused to accept the conciliatory efforts of Nestle, several large groups—the American Federation of Teachers, the American

---

[12] "Fighting a Boycott," *Industry Week*, January 23, 1984, p. 54.

[13] "Nestle Gains Formula Accord: Product Boycott is Suspended," *Marketing News*, February 17, 1984, p. 5.

Table 18.1   Nestle Sales and Profits, 1974–1983 (In thousands of Swiss Francs)

Years	Sales	Profits
1974	16,624,000	742,000
1975	18,286,000	799,000
1976	19,063,000	872,000
1977	20,095,000	830,000
1978	20,266,000	739,000
1979	21,639,000	816,000
1980	24,479,000	638,000
1981	27,734,000	964,000
1982	27,664,000	1,098,000
1983	27,943,000	1,261,000

Sources: Company annual reports.

Federation of Churches, the Federation of Nurses & Health Professionals, the United Methodist Church, and the Church of the Brethren—had either withdrawn from the boycott or decided not to join it.

The company admitted, however, that perhaps 20 obdurate boycott leaders and 50,000 followers in the U. S. may never stop ostracizing the company no matter what Nestle does.[14]

The results in lost business for Nestle because of the infant food controversy are impossible to pinpoint. Estimates ranged up to $40,000,000 in lost profits as direct results of the boycott. However, lost business could have been far greater than this, with some coming in the years before the boycott began, as consumers turned to alternative brands from firms with better reputations. Even during the years of the boycotts, not all consumers were militant protestors; but they could certainly take their business elsewhere as sort of a silent protest. Admittedly, infant food accounted for only 3 percent of total Nestle sales worldwide. But other Nestle products were blackened to an unknown degree by the embattled public image of this one minor part of the total business. One of the more obvious negative consequences of the boycotts was the loss of meetings and convention business at Stouffer facilities, with some planners opting to schedule at other locations to avoid any association with negative publicity.

Table 18.1 shows the sales and profits for the Nestle conglomerate during some of these years. As you can see, by the late 1970s, profits were declining from the years before the protests had become so pronounced. By 1981, however, sales and profits were rising substantially, partly as the result

---

[14] "Fighting a Boycott," p. 55.

of acquisitions. Looking at total sales and profits figures, we cannot measure how much is the direct effect of the confrontation; more important, we can only guess at the extent of unrealized potential.

WHAT CAN BE LEARNED?

The Nestle debacle should be sobering for many firms. It should raise some real concerns about the possibility of damage to the public image, damage that can be difficult to rebuild. Specifically, these are major points to be learned from this experience.

The Vulnerability of the Public Image. A reputable image, or at least one that is neutral and not negative, can be quickly besmirched. A firm should not underestimate the power of social awareness and activist groups. Furthermore, the large firm is the most vulnerable—even if other firms in the industry are engaged in the same practices—and is the most desirable target for activist groups. Size brings with it greater visibility and public recognition than is the case with smaller competitors. This makes it the target of choice: to bring down the giant. And public sentiment—on the athletic field, in business, or wherever—is not on the side of the big and powerful.

The Power of a Hostile Press. A bad press can both arouse and intensify negative public opinion. It can fan the flames. A firm cannot plan on the press being objective and unbiased in such reporting. The press tends to be eager to find a "fault object," and when this is a large and rather impersonal firm, the likelihood is all the greater that bad actions or the negatives of a particular situation will be emphasized far more than the positive and helpful side of the issue. Although infant formulas had many benefits and were a very positive health influence in many situations, publicity focused almost exclusively on alleged marketing abuses and customer misuses.

The Longevity of a Besmirched Reputation. Nestle's expectations that the controversy would die out were certainly squashed by the duration and increasing virulence of the protest movement. Without constructive efforts by Nestle in the early 1980s, the gathering strength of the protest movement probably would have resulted in ever-greater boycotting, and most likely in restrictive legislation by many countries. Thus, a tarnished reputation is not suddenly going to become bright and shiny just because of the passage of time. Some sort of strong positive efforts must be made by the firm to try to restore its image—or it will not be improved.

Public Relations Deficiencies. Public relations is not the answer when certain aspects of a firm's operation are the focal points of criticism. The act must be cleared up first. The public relations efforts of Nestle were notoriously impotent, despite hiring two of the largest and most expensive public relations firms in the world. Without improving the operations under question, no amount of public relation statements—even mailing some 300,000 pamphlets to clergy propagandizing Nestle's position—could produce positive and lasting results.

The Potential of Marketing to Impact on the Public Image. Many of Nestle's problems emanated from its marketing efforts in Third World countries. Normally, such marketing efforts would be viewed as effective; under different circumstances they could even have been lauded as models for introducing a new and improved product. But here they were seen as far too effective in swaying a naive population in not wholly desirable directions. A firm's marketing efforts are the most visible aspects of its operation. This visibility can sometimes be a curse, as it was with Nestle.

Suggested Reactions with a Darkening Public Image

The Nestle example gives us helpful insights on how best to react to smears and protests. Ignoring the problem seems ill-advised, if the protests are severe enough and if the issue is inflammatory enough. And certainly, alleged culpable loss of life—whether from chemical dumps or spills, or from the ill-advised use of infant formula—is usually inflammatory enough.

Direct confrontation and an adversarial stand is seldom effective either. As Nestle found out the hard way, its court case, even though won by Nestle, only increased the negative publicity and fueled the protests. Even if the weight of evidence is on the firm's side, propaganda and one-sided criticisms from the opposition will likely win over the general public.

So it seems more prudent for the firm that unwittingly falls into the snare of public image problems regarding its social role to approach the situation with a spirit of cooperation and constructive participation with opposing groups—despite some diehard activists who may refuse all efforts at conciliation. We cannot fault the efforts of Nestle from 1981–1983 in working with the more reasonable critics. But we can severely fault the company for waiting so long to take such constructive actions.

Many firms need a greater sensitivity to potential problem areas involving corporate social performance. They need to try to anticipate potential problems and nip them quickly. Failing this, an organization should strive to resolve as many of the objections as it can—even if this means assuming the burden of an inequitable compromise position. Otherwise, the consequence may be a gradually deteriorating image problem, even if negative public perceptions are not fully based on facts.

A firm doing business in sensitive areas needs to prove that it is a responsible corporate citizen and not an insensitive giant organization. More attention to the public image may well prevent the type of image problems that bedeviled Nestle for years.

For Thought And Discussion

1. Faced with activist protestors, do you think a firm has any recourse but to yield to their complete demands? Is there any room for an aggressive stance?
2. Could the public relations efforts of Nestle have been used more effectively?
3. Do you think Nestle was unfairly picked on? Why or why not?

Invitation To Role Play

1. As the staff assistant to the CEO of Nestle, you have been asked to develop a position paper as to the desirability of withdrawing infant formula from the market in Third World countries. Discuss the pros and cons of such a move, and then make your recommendations and support them as persuasively as you can.
2. You are the manager of a Stouffer hotel. A delegation of clergy and lay people has approached you with the threat of boycotting your premises. Be as persuasive as you can in trying to dissuade them from doing so.

CHAPTER 19

Conclusions—What Can Be Learned?

In considering mistakes, two things are worth noting: 1) even the most successful organizations make mistakes, but can and do survive as long as they can maintain a good batting average; and 2) making mistakes can be an effective teaching tool. The difference in overall success or failure is what is learned from these errors to avoid the repetition of similar mistakes.

A number of generalizations can be drawn from the mistakes described. Of course, we need to recognize that management, like all the social sciences, is a discipline that does not lend itself to laws or axioms. Examples of successful exceptions to every principle or generalization can be found. But the executive does well to heed these generalizations.

SUCCESS DOES NOT GUARANTEE CONTINUED SUCCESS

That success does not guarantee continued success or freedom from adversity is a sobering realization that must come from examining these cases. Almost all the organizations described—except for the World Football League and, to some extent, Burger Chef—were notably successful. Most of them had exhibited enviable growth records; some had grown to such a large size that they dominated their industry. Yet they succumbed to grievous mistakes, some at the very pinnacle of their growth and success. How could this possibly have happened to these firms, firms with such experience, such momentum, and such resources, both financial and managerial, behind them?

We are forced to conclude that, far from ensuring continued success and mastery, success may actually promote vulnerability, may leave a firm more easy prey to hungry competitors. The reason for this? Complacency. It is difficult for a successful firm not to become smug about its position and disdainful of lesser competitors. Such an organization is usually resistant to drastic changes—because they can be traumatic and disruptive to what has heretofore been successful. Success encourages the viewpoint that the future is a mirror of the past. With such attitudes permeating an organization—even though they may not be overtly communicated—a changing environment can go undetected for far too long.

The environment is dynamic. It is changing, sometimes subtly, other times more drastically and recognizably. This fact needs to be realized by all organizations. To rest on laurels is perilous. In view of a changing environment, which opens up opportunities as well as problems, a firm can be an innovator, a leader. Not all firms are willing to accept the rewards and risks of this fact. But a firm must at least be adaptive if it is not to be wounded by the changing environment. We have examined several firms that were too long oblivious to the changes around them: Penney, Coors, A. C. Gilbert, and Boise Cascade. In Gillette's case, it was aware of change—the popularizing of the stainless steel blade—but was reluctant to cannibalize its highly profitable Super Blue, and so procrastinated for an unduly long time.

The two terms—*adaptive* and *innovative*—are somewhat different, although related. For our discussion we will consider them different degrees of responsive behavior on the same dimension. *Innovative* may be defined as originating significant changes, implying improvement. *Adaptive* implies a better coping with changing circumstances, but a response somewhat less significant than an innovative reaction.

A useful perspective can be gained by considering a continuum of behavior, such as:

Degrees of Responsiveness to Environmental Change

Inflexible, unchanging	Adaptive	Innovative

Thus, a firm can be judged as occupying a certain point along this continuum: the more conservative and rigid firm toward the left, and the more progressive one that is constantly developing new ideas toward the right. Even the historical trend of a firm can be viewed on such a scale. For example, the Ford Motor Company in its early years was extremely innovative, as it was one of the pioneers in the effective use of the assembly line; however, the long adherence to a single unchanging product, the Model

T, in the face of changing consumer wants and more aggressive competition would have placed the firm eventually at the other extreme on the scale.

NEED FOR GROWTH ORIENTATION—BUT NOT RECKLESS GROWTH

The opposite of a growth commitment is a status quo philosophy, not interested in expansion or the problems and work involved. We saw three cases where a growth orientation was lacking. With Montgomery Ward, growth plans were shelved under the mistaken belief that expansion would be less costly some time in the future. With Penney, there was an unwillingness to change traditional ways of doing things that were stifling growth. For Gilbert, contentment with status quo seemed to have reached an extreme until a drastically worsening sales and profit picture and a takeover by new management hastened the company on its path of ill-conceived expansion efforts.

In general, how tenable is a low-or-no-growth philosophy? Although at first glance it seems workable, upon closer inspection such a philosophy can be seen as sowing the seeds of its own destruction, unless reversed before too late. More than 2 decades ago it was pointed out:

> Vitality is required even for survival; but vitality is difficult to maintain without growth, at least in the American business climate. The vitality of a firm depends on the vigor and ambition of its members. The prospect of growth is one of the principal means by which a firm can attract able and vigorous recruits.[1]

Consequently, if a firm is obviously not growth-minded, its ability to attract able people diminishes so that it is vulnerable to competition. Customers see a growing firm as reliable, eager to please, and getting better all the time. Suppliers and creditors tend to give preferential treatment to a growth-oriented firm, because they hope to retain it as a customer and client when it reaches a large size.

On the other hand, as we have seen with Grant, Korvette, Boise Cascade, and Burger Chef, growth can be too extreme, can exceed the abilities of the organization to assimilate, control, and provide sufficient managerial and financial resources. Consequently, we may conclude that a firm's objectives might best be directed neither to reckless headlong growth, nor to simply maintaining the status quo. Both extremes are dangerous.

IMPORTANCE OF ORGANIZATIONAL COMPATIBILITY

Organization is often taken for granted by an established firm. The role of the organization in the success or failure of the enterprise or of a particular

---

[1] Wroe Alderson, *Marketing Behavior and Executive Action* (Homewood, Illinois: Irwin, 1957), p. 59.

venture or division tends to be downgraded in favor of the supposedly more important strategic planning and decision-making functions. But we have seen three concrete examples in which organizational problems dominated the mistake.

With Korvette, the mistake was in not recognizing that an organization must change as a firm grows to relatively large size. One person can no longer oversee all the important aspects of the operation. Now authority must be delegated, new executive levels and responsibilities created, the use of staff improved. Not to have recognized such requirements strikes us as unsophisticated and naive; yet it is a rather common phenomenon that the person who exhibits great ability and innovation in founding a firm may be seriously flawed in coping with large size.

Although Edsel's mistakes were varied, the crucial one may well have been its establishing a separate organization to sell and service Edsels, thereby greatly increasing the breakdown point, managerial problems, and the need to find and maintain an adequate dealer force. Had such an organizational mistake not been made—who knows?—we might still have Edsels on the market today.

The last organizational mistake we examined was that of W. T. Grant. Here the organization was well established and was suitable for a large-size operation. But the violent growth demands placed upon it with little prior warning proved beyond its ability to cope. Consequently, it could provide neither sufficient trained personnel for the great growth nor enough research and store planning staff people to adequately handle the demands for increasing selling space by millions of square feet a year. The fault was not so much the organization as the severe growth demands suddenly thrust upon an otherwise adequate one.

The organization must be considered in major decisions. It must be compatible with any new role in which it is to be placed. It is a resource that can be constraining if demands are not to exceed its capability of meeting them. Otherwise, change and growth may have to be slowed until the organization can be built up to achieve the desired compatibility with expectations. On the other hand, an organization bulging with capable and ambitious people may almost demand serious growth efforts, lest its strength be dissipated as the able abandon it for better opportunities.

DESIRABILITY OF SYSTEMATIC EVALUATIONS AND CONTROLS

Organizations need feedback to determine how well something is being done, whether improvement is possible, where it should occur, how much is needed, and how quickly it must be accomplished. Without feedback or performance evaluation, a worsening situation can go unrecognized until too late for corrective action. That was apparently the situation with Gilbert. For some reason, sales declines and loss of competitive position up to 1961 did not arouse any particular concern; certainly, no serious attempt was made to find the causes and take action accordingly. With Boise Cascade, serious emerging problems of overall performance were hidden in sales and profit figures. Operations apparently were not carefully monitored for the recreation land division until a plethora of customer and environmentalist complaints brought the company to the realization that drastic action was needed; this came too late to save both the division and the president of the company.

As firms become larger, the need for better controls or feedback increases, because top management can no longer personally monitor all aspects of the operation. This was where Eugene Ferkauf found the Korvette operation too much for him, but he was unable to install adequate controls and reorganization in time to prevent overwhelming problems. The trend toward diversification and mergers, which often results in loosely controlled decentralized operations, also makes timely feedback on performance critical.

The need for careful financial and expense controls seems irrefutable. After all, if costs and inventories get severely out of line—and what can be worse, when this is not recognized until too late—then the viability of the firm can be jeopardized. Yet, when firms are new and rapidly growing, as Osborne Computer was in its brief flirtation with stardom, such controls may be overlooked. Even older firms, when they embark on a vigorous expansion program, may be complacent to worsening financial and inventory problems; and they can be just as vulnerable as newer firms, as the W. T. Grant Company found to its horror.

Performance standards are another means of control crucial to large and far-flung operations. Unless operating standards and procedures are imposed—and enforced—the results are likely to be lack of uniformity of performance, great unevenness of quality and service, and a lack of coordination and continuity among the different units—instead of a tight ship, a very loose and undisciplined one will be the natural consequence. The lack of standards regarding facilities, personnel, managerial and franchisee selection, food preparation, and service and maintenance was a major contributor to Burger Chef's problems, especially when competing with McDonald's, whose insistence on tight and rigorously enforced standards was the strongest of all business firms.

NEED FOR MANAGERIAL ALERTNESS TO CHANGING CONDITIONS

Company executives, through observation and through feedback from customers, salespeople, and other sources such as creditors and suppliers, can usually obtain a rather good feel for basic changes occurring in competition, in customer preferences, in governmental restrictions, and the like. But a firm needs to be alert to such changes, to encourage good communications and feedback, and to be willing to react or respond to these emerging changes. Yet, we have seen a number of examples of firms unheeding of changes that should have been obvious. The Gilbert Company failed dismally in this area; the Penney Company for a lengthy period was myopic; Boise Cascade had its fatal period of faulty alertness, as did Coors, Adidas, and the STP Corporation. Such a common failing, the lack of alertness! But it goes with the success syndrome described earlier.

If a firm is to practice managerial alertness, it must keep abreast not only of competitive changes, but also of emerging social and environmental pressures. For example, if Boise Cascade had been better attuned to the growing consumer resentment of high pressure and deceptive selling practices, as well as the environmentalist fear of careless land use that was beginning to affect all recreational land development, it might not only have escaped consumer and government censure and lawsuits, but also have been able to muster a strong positive approach to these matters and become a bellwether of the recreational land industry. Similarly, with STP, the clues to a harsher public and governmental stance against unsupported advertising claims should have been obvious. But the feeling, "they won't pick on us," was unrealistic and poor judgment.

IMPORTANCE OF IMAGE

The image that people have of a firm or a brand is of major importance. Several of the cases were affected by image problems. Korvette lost its positive image as a reliable discounter offering greater values when its food and furniture operations became questionable. When it tried to upgrade, the low-price discount image remained and diluted efforts to trade up successfully to a higher-quality store. Grant's lack of a specific image—whether as a discounter, a five–and–10–cent store, or a department store—impeded its aggressive efforts to expand. Burger Chef's lack of a distinctive image placed it at a major disadvantage vis-à-vis McDonald's and other successful fast-food franchise operations. But a good image, a quality image, such as Gilbert had attained from decades of reputable toys, can be cut down rather quickly. In Gilbert's case, 2 or 3 years of an image-destructive operational strategy destroyed a positive image. The Coors image or mystique also proved to be vulnerable. And then there was Nestle. For some crucial years, it tried to ignore growing worldwide criticisms of its practices in underdeveloped countries, only to enrage protestors to the point of boycotting its far–flung operations that were not even involved with the controversial product and practices.

Consequently, a positive image is precious and should be preserved at all costs. To change or upgrade an image is usually a long process unless a firm has great patience and strong resources. Penney was able to change its image of a small-town, soft-line retailer, but it took a decade or longer; and a positive fashion image is taking even longer. For most firms, the best course of action may be to go with what the firm has, rather than try to make a radical change. An alternative is to introduce a different brand, a different division, anything to escape a negative or fuzzy image.

NECESSITY OF PRUDENT CRISIS MANAGEMENT

Crises are unexpected happenings that pose threats, ranging from moderate to catastrophic, to the organization's well-being. We saw one example where poor responses to a crisis—lack of good crisis management—led to ruination. In the Gilbert Company, frenetic efforts to correct a suddenly realized crisis vastly exacerbated the problem.

Most crises can be avoided, if precautions are taken and if the organization is alert to changing conditions, has contingency plans for dealing with them, and practices risk avoidance. For example, it is only prudent to stipulate that all the key executives of a division or of the firm do not travel on the same air flight; it is prudent to insure key executives so that their incapacity will not endanger the organization; it is prudent to set up contingency plans for a strike, an equipment failure or plant destruction, unexpected economic conditions, or a serious lawsuit. Some risks can be covered by insurance; others need good planning done in a calm atmosphere. The mettle of any organization may be severely tested by an unexpected crisis. But such crises need not cause the demise of the company if alternatives are weighed and actions taken only after due deliberation. Above all, however, crises usually necessitate some changes in the organization and the way of doing business. Such changes can be hasty, disruptive, and ill-advised, as with Gilbert. At the other extreme, they may be too few and too late. The middle ground is usually best. And with advance planning, the trauma can be minimized and effective solutions more likely to be forthcoming.

DESIRABILITY OF JUDICIOUS IMITATION

Some firms are reluctant to adopt successful practices of their competitors; they want to be leaders, not followers. In the example of Gillette, even when a highly successul new product was practically forced upon it, there was resistance. This was partly because of fear that existing products would be adversely affected. But there was also a psychological basis: top management's reluctance to admit that the industry leader was in this instance only a follower.

There are good arguments for systematically observing the operations of successful competitors (and even similar, but noncompetitive, organizations), evaluating them and identifying those aspects that contribute most to the success, and then adopting them if compatible with the resources of the imitator. Let someone else do the experimenting and take the risks of innovating. Although there can be some risk if an imitator waits too long, this is usually far less than the risk of an untested product or operation failing:

> No single company, regardless of its determination, energy, imagination, and resources, is big enough or solvent enough to do all the productive first things that will ever occur in its industry and to always beat its competitors to all the innovations emanating from the industry . . . each organization (should) look to imitation as one of its survival and growth strategies.[2]

In few firms was the need for judicious imitation more pronounced than with Burger Chef. Confronted with the outstandingly succcessful and highly publicized operation of McDonald's, it did not attempt to improve its own faltering operation by imitating the success that had been analyzed in trade journals and even in the public press for years.

By imitation, we do not mean a slavish effort to be identical. Burger Chef still needed to develop its own identity. But the standards of performance, the training and selection of franchisees, and the imposition of strict controls to ensure that performance was up to prescribed standards—these could certainly have been closely duplicated.

On the other hand, Nike, the successful competitor of Adidas, rode to its success by using the same strategy originated by the older firm, only doing so more aggressively and with more pizzazz than the old master.

NECESSITY OF LONG–TERM STRATEGY OBJECTIVES FOR MANAGEMENT OF THE 1980s

The desperate situation of Chrysler, and to a lesser extent the rest of the U. S. auto industry and a number of other major industries, brought to light a disturbing realization. The prevalent management thinking with its emphasis on short-term profit objectives was vulnerable to aggressive foreign firms that were willing to sacrifice for the short term in building for the future. As we saw in the Chrysler case, the diminishing relative productivity of large

---

[2] Theodore Levitt, "Innovative Imitation," *Harvard Business Review*, September-October 1966.

parts of U. S. industry could be attributed to numerous factors, some of which management had little or no direct control over, such as government regulations and tax policies. Still, substantial blame must lie with a management unwilling to commit enough resources to research and development, use the newest technologies for modern plant and equipment, and work more closely with labor, encouraging a teamwork approach. Management in certain industries, especially the auto industry, must also be faulted for complacency about quality control and customer complaints and dissatisfaction. A columnist in an editorial in a major newspaper commented about the U. S. auto maker's plight as follows:

> Perhaps the public's apathy toward the current plight of the American auto companies . . . suggests . . . that the industry today is paying for yesterday's arrogance and dishonesty in dealing with its customers. Did your new car in 1965 turn out to be a lemon? Tough luck, but you were on your own. And did your 1971 automobile turn from shiny beauty into a rusty monstrosity inside of two or three years, only to have the manufacturer and his dealer shrug off the tragedy?[3]

Perhaps we can learn from these past sins of omission. Not only should long-term strategy objectives involve investment goals and labor incentives aimed at increasing productivity, but customer satisfaction should also be given priority attention:

> The rules for the auto industry are the same as the rules for people. You've got to be basically nice and lead a reasonably decent life if you want others to love you and if you want to make claims to their loyalty in times of trouble.[4]

ROLE OF SOCIAL AND ENVIRONMENTAL INFLUENCES

Several cases illustrate the new milieu facing business: the role that the general public and their agents—the various governmental bodies that respond to their demands—can play in curbing what critics claim are undesirable practices. In the STP example, the undesirable practice was what some saw as misleading, deceptive, or, at the least, unsupported advertising claims. With Boise Cascade, the concern was both environmental degradation and unacceptable selling techniques. In the Nestle case, the

---

[3] George E, Condon, "No Tears Are Wept at Auto-Makers' Plight," *The Cleveland Plain Dealer,* May 18, 1982, p. 3–B.
[4] Ibid.

controversy concerned human life itself according to the allegations of critics worldwide.

An important lesson can be gained from these three cases. No longer can social and environmental issues be disregarded. No longer can a bad press and a deteriorating public image be ignored. Like it or not, business faces more restraints than in the past, and critics are rarely on the side of the big and powerful.

GENERAL CONCLUSIONS

We learn from mistakes. Yet every management problem seems cast in a somewhat different setting, requiring a different strategy. One author has likened business strategy to military strategy:

> . . . strategies which are flexible rather than static enhance optimum use and offer the greatest number of alternative objectives. A good commander knows that he cannot control his environment to suit a prescribed strategy. Natural phenomena pose their own restraints to strategic planning, whether physical, geographic, regional, or psychological and sociological.

And:

> Planning leadership recognizes the unpleasant fact that, despite every effort, the war may be lost. Therefore, the aim is to retain the maximum number of facilities and the basic organization. Indicators of a deteriorating and unsalvage-able total situation are, therefore, mandatory . . . No possible combination of strategies and tactics, no mobilization of resources . . . can supply a magic formula which guarantees victory; it is possible only to increase the probability of victory.[5]

Thus we can pull two concepts from the military to help guide business strategy: the desirability of flexibility in view of an unknown or changing environment, and the idea of a basic core that should be maintained under all circumstances. The first suggests that the firm should be prepared for adjustments in strategy as conditions warrant. As we have seen, most of the cases ultimately reached such adjustments, although not always promptly. The second suggests that the basic core of a firm's business should not be tampered with; it should be the final bastion to fall back to for regrouping if necessary. Boise Cascade was able to do this, to fall back to its basic

    [5] Myron S. Heidingsfield, *Changing Patterns in Marketing* (Boston: Allyn and Bacon, 1968), p. 11.

business of forest products and again begin expansion from that point; Gilbert and Korvette abandoned their basic strengths, one drastically and with finality, the other to a degree.

In regard to the basic core of a firm, every viable firm can be seen as having some distinctive function or "ecological niche" in the environment of doing business:

> Every business firm occupies a position which is in some respects unique. Its location, the product it sells, its operating methods, or the customers it serves tend to set it off in some degree from every other firm. Each firm competes by making the most of its individuality and its special character.[6]

Woe to the firm that loses its ecological niche.

For Thought And Discussion

1. Design a program aimed at mistake avoidance. Be as specific, as creative, and as complete as possible.
2. How would you build into an organization the controls to ensure that similar mistakes will not happen in the future?
3. Which would you advise a firm to be: an imitator or an innovator? Why?

Invitation To Role Play

You have been assigned the responsibility of ensuring that your firm has adequate alertness to changing conditions. How would you go about developing such alertness? Be as specific as you can.

---

[6] Alderson, p. 101.